DATE DUE

Officially Withdrawn

This is the first book to address the full range of performance issues for the violoncello from the Baroque to the early Romantic period. The development of playing techniques and stylistic transitions is traced regionally through a comparison of Italian, French, German, English, and East European performance traits. Through a close study of contemporary violoncello methods, music, early instruments, periodicals, diaries, letters, and pictures Dr. Walden provides a cohesive overview which examines construction methods for instruments and bows, fingering and bowing techniques, special effects and ornamentation, accompanying skills, and the stylistic preferences of the most famous soloists. Richly illustrated with over 300 music examples, plates, and figures, this book allows the reader to apply the information to his or her own manner of playing period music.

CAMBRIDGE MUSICAL TEXTS AND MONOGRAPHS

One Hundred Years of Violoncello

CAMBRIDGE MUSICAL TEXTS AND MONOGRAPHS

General Editors: John Butt and Laurence Dreyfus

The series Cambridge Musical Texts and Monographs has as its centers of interest the history of performance and the history of instruments. It includes annotated translations of important historical documents, authentic historical texts on music, and monographs on various aspects of historical performance.

One Hundred Years of Violoncello

A History of Technique and Performance Practice, 1740–1840

VALERIE WALDEN

CAMBRIDGE
UNIVERSITY PRESS

PUBLISHED BY THE PRESS SYNDICATE OF THE UNIVERSITY OF CAMBRIDGE
The Pitt Building, Trumpington Street, Cambridge CB2 1RP

CAMBRIDGE UNIVERSITY PRESS
The Edinburgh Building, Cambridge CB2 2RU, United Kingdom
40 West 20th Street, New York, NY 10011-4211, USA
10 Stamford Road, Oakleigh, Melbourne 3166, Australia

© Cambridge University Press 1998

This book is in copyright. Subject to statutory exception and to the provisions of relevant
collective licensing agreements, no reproduction of any part may take place without the
written permission of Cambridge University Press.

First published 1998

Printed in the United Kingdom at the University Press, Cambridge

Typeset in Baskerville 11/13pt   [AH]

A catalogue record for this book is available from the British Library

Library of Congress cataloguing in publication data

Walden, Valerie.
One Hundred Years of Violoncello: A History of Technique and Performance Practice,
1740–1840 / Valerie Walden
   p.   cm. – (Cambridge Musical Texts and Monographs)
Includes bibliographical references and index.
ISBN 0 521 55449 7 (hardback)
1. Violoncello – Performance. 2. Violoncello music – 18th century – Interpretation (Phrasing, dynamics, etc.) 3. Violoncello music – 19th century – Interpretation (Phrasing, dynamics, etc.) 4. Violoncello music – 18th century – History and criticism. 5. Violoncello music
– 19th century – History and criticism. 6. Performance practice (Music) – 18th century.
7. Performance practice (Music) – 19th century. 8. Embellishment (Music) 9. Musical
accompaniment. I. Series.
ML915.W25   1997
787.4'143'09033–dc21   96–47436   CIP MN

ISBN 0 521 55449 7 hardback

This book is dedicated with deepest appreciation
to the faculty and staff of
the School of Music, University of Auckland
and to the memory of Tony Jennings,
who furnished at least one conundrum.

Contents

Illustrations

Preface

It has always remained a source of wonderment to me that one can walk into the Auckland Public Library, an archive not exactly central to the European artistic community, and find first editions of the tutors of J. L. Duport and Bernhard Romberg sitting cozily next to each other on the 'cello shelf. This state of affairs is certainly a tribute to the enduring love of 'cellists for their instrument, for these two large volumes were brought to New Zealand by nineteenth-century pioneers, who undoubtedly would have had many more practical items that needed to be included in their luggage other than a 'cello and an instruction book. Nevertheless, I am extremely grateful that this was the case, because those two methods, sitting next to each other as did their authors so many years previous, were the provocateurs of my research.

Past that initial point of discovery, I have received a great deal of help and encouragement from many people. My editor, Penny Souster, and my copy-editor, Lucy Carolan, patiently guided these present efforts. Dr. Gerald Seaman and Coral Bognuda supervised my initial study, and I remain indebted to Dr. Seaman for his expertise with Russian materials and to Professor Bognuda for her analysis of violoncello technique. Many thanks are again extended to Jane Young de Monteverde for her interview with Edmund Kurtz and to Dr. Sylvette Milliot for her assistance with French iconographic sources. Her introduction to Dimitry Markevitch has been invaluable, as has been the generosity of Mr. Markevitch.

I would like to especially thank Chapman University librarians Patty Dillon and Gina Wilkinson for their assistance with source materials. John Moran, Peter Trevelyan, Dr. Tilden Russell, and Anthony Elmsly also made available the efforts of their research and Gary Sturm and Lisette Voyatzis, of the Smithsonian Institute, and John Koster and Dr. Margaret Downie Banks, of The Shrine to Music Museum, very graciously added to my knowledge about bows and instruments. Assistance with German and French translations was extended to me by Professor Danielle Jamieson, Miriam O'Connor, and Marlene Hochstein; however, any errors are certainly my own. And lastly, this book would not have been possible without the help of my husband, Max, whose love and support, as well as technological competence, kept me functioning in the twentieth century.

I wish to make one final point about the musical notation used in this book. To the best of my ability with modern technology, I have avoided "sanitizing" the musical examples by putting them into modern notation. The varied and often frustrating notation used in the eighteenth and nineteenth centuries for violoncello music conveys a part of the instrument's history and I did not wish to cheat anyone of the intellectual exercise of reading five clefs or six different thumb signs.

Abbreviations

AMZ	*Allgemeine Musikalische Zeitung*
BMZ	*Berlinische Musikalische Zeitung*
JAMIS	*Journal of the American Musical Instrument Society*
MGG	*Die Musik in Geschichte und Gegenwart*
NG	*The New Grove Dictionary of Music and Musicians*
QMMR	*The Quarterly Musical Magazine and Review*
tc1	treble clef notated one octave higher than played

Introduction

Commentaries on violoncello playing from the first part of the nineteenth century often make the observation that "the violoncello has been rising gradually since the beginning of the last century into estimation, and may now be said to enjoy an almost equal reputation with the violin as a concerto instrument."[1] Apart from such newly recognized popularity as a solo instrument, appreciation for the violoncello's "strong, rich, beautiful, and manly tone" accounted for its becoming indispensable to vocal, orchestral, and chamber music accompaniments. While this perception differs little from present evaluations, such remarks by nineteenth-century writers speak to the variety of changes through which the violoncello and the art of performance were transformed in the years previous to their statements.

To describe these multifaceted changes is to recount the history of the violoncello, but history is, after all, about people. An accurate and meaningful account of eighteenth- and early nineteenth-century violoncello history therefore becomes the story of a singular group of violoncellists, a description of their lives and the manner in which they made music. The parameters of this story are the years 1740 to 1840. There are several reasons why this period forms a convenient unit for study, but before discussing performance history in detail, a few general comments help to place specific aspects of the violoncello in context. During those years, two threads responsible for an ensuing social reformation became intertwined, those of innovation and nationalism. Both were significant to the development of violoncello performance.

From the beginning of the eighteenth century, minds were electrified by new methods of scientific inquiry and innovation. Each decade witnessed changing ideas – induced by an evolving view of how man and his world fit together – in mathematics, science, industrial technology, philosophy, economics, and political thought. The "enlightened" thinking which emerged became an especially pronounced social force among the French, who, in

---

1 "On the Rise and Progress of the Violoncello," *QMMR*, 6, no. 23 (1824), 351.

1

the last decade of the eighteenth century, took the concept of political change to revolutionary extremes. Nationalism as a cultural phenomenon was generated as a regional answer to French domination.

Innovation and developing nationalism are reflected to some degree in all of the social and cultural institutions of eighteenth- and nineteenth-century Europe, including music. The coalescence of innovation and nationalism is particularly discernible in stringed instrument performance. Technological innovations resulted in remarkable instruments coming from the workshops of Stradivari, Bergonzi, Montagnana, Guarneri, and Grancino, to name just a few. Bow making evolved in the families Tourte, Dodd, and Tubbs, and through the work of numerous men who remain forever anonymous. Fomented by violinists' ever-present desire for increased performance capabilities, alterations to the dimensions and the fittings of instruments and bows continued throughout this entire period. Simultaneously, regional schools of performance evolved in Italy, France, England, Germany, Austria, and the many provinces of Eastern Europe.

Appreciation for the violoncello as a defined entity is discernible from the beginning of the eighteenth century, as playing techniques were gradually liberated from earlier restrictions. Social regard was achieved with much self-satisfaction, the luminaries of each generation convinced that they were the architects of a new age of perfection. The premise that violoncellists were modernist performers was, in part, a self-perpetuating idea traceable to the publication and replication of several articles on violoncello history. The most widely quoted of these was that appearing in J. B. de La Borde's *Essai sur la musique ancienne et moderne.* This account asserts that the violoncello is the

instrument which succeeded the viol for accompanying in concerts. It is made like the violin, except that it is much larger and is held between the legs.

Father Tardieu, of Tarascon, brother of the celebrated *maître de chapelle* of Provence, conceived it about the beginning of this century; it was equipped by him with five strings...

He made a prodigious fortune with this instrument, which he played very well. Fifteen or twenty years after, he reduced the violoncello to four strings, dispensing with the upper D string.[2]

Musicologists now consider the violoncello to have evolved, together with other members of the violin family, in the first half of the sixteenth century. Initially, there was little uniformity as to the nomenclature of violoncello-type instruments. In seventeenth-century Italy, alone, there were at least twenty-four differing terms to denote stringed instruments which played in the bass clef, examples being *basso da brazzo, basso di viola, violone, violoncino,*

---

2 J. B. de La Borde, *Essai sur la musique ancienne et moderne* , 4 vols. (Paris: Ph. D. Pierres, 1780), vol. I, p. 309.

and *violonzello*.[3] Labeling discrepancies are accountable, in part, to variations in the number of strings and tunings utilized. Instruments of the sixteenth century were strung with three to six strings and the tunings
generally varied in a combination of fifths and major thirds. Use of four or
five strings became the norm in the early seventeeth century, but diverse
tunings persisted. Those that were common included $B\flat_1$–F–c–g, C–G–d–
g, or as mentioned by La Borde, C–G–d–a–d^1.[4] C–G–d–a was also favored
after 1600 and became standard for four-stringed solo instruments, especially after the introduction of metal-wound strings in the 1660s.

Violoncellists of the eighteenth and nineteenth centuries knew little
about the early use of their instrument and were uniformly convinced that
La Borde's information was correct. From a musical point of view, the development of idiomatic performance repertoire for the violoncello affirmed their premise. Impelled by the advent of metal-wound strings,
which then led to the smaller instrument dimensions devised by the
luthiers Guarneri and Stradivari, solo works specified for *violoncello* are
found from 1689 onwards. Although almost all such compositions were
written for a specific audience and remained in manuscript, the complexity of the music of such composers as Vivaldi and Bach attests to the virtuosity of the performers whom they knew.

Notwithstanding the sophisticated Italian string school of the early eighteenth century, until the fourth decade of the century violoncello technique
was dominated by that of the violin and viola da gamba, the latter instrument being much preferred to the violoncello by performers and audiences until this point. However, the influence of Italian string players and
the growing demands placed upon the tenor/bass instrumental voice in
opera orchestras and in chamber ensembles compelled change. Need for
precision of pitch, volume of sound, and matching sonority with other
members of the violin family rendered the viola da gamba inevitably unsuitable for much eighteenth-century repertoire. The Italians were the first
to recognize this stylistic transition, while musicians in the rest of Europe
gradually replaced use of the viola da gamba with that of the violoncello,
acceptance of the latter by Parisians being the final death-knell for the viol
family.

As musicians became increasingly interested in the capabilities of the
violoncello, playing techniques developed to meet performance challenges. Eagerness by players to demonstrate the possibilities of the violoncello resulted in sonatas and concertos for the instrument readily

---

3 Stephen Bonta, "Terminology for the Bass Violin in Seventeenth-Century Italy," *JAMIS*, 4 (1978), 6.
4 Klaus Marx, *Die Entwicklung des Violoncells und seiner Spieltechnik bis J. L. Duport (1520–1820)*,
   vol. XIII of Forschungsbeiträge zur Musikwissenschaft (Regensburg: Gustav Bosse Verlag, 1963),
   pp. 24–25.

multiplying during the 1730s. However, in 1741 the final testimony to the increasing popularity of the violoncello appeared. Discerning that there was now a lucrative interest in the instrument from both professional and amateur musicians, Michel Corrette published his *Méthode théorique et pratique pour apprendre en peu de temps le violoncelle dans sa perfection*. This French method book signals the advent of the violoncello as a recognized and appreciated performance medium.

The hundred years following the publication of Corrette's method are replete with a fascinating array of personalities, men whose life's work was to play the violoncello. The Duport brothers, Boccherini, Bréval, Romberg, Dotzauer, and Merk are all names well known to modern violoncellists. There were many others. Their story unfolds, gleaned from a variety of resources, including contemporary biographies, performance reviews, private diaries, violoncello articles and study methods, and, of course, their music. Study of these sources makes it clear that many violoncellists knew each other, either in person or by reputation. The same sources also make it clear that during this era, individuality in performers was highly regarded and few violoncellists completely agreed with each other as to how the instrument should be played.

They were an enterprising group. Those whose careers encompassed the years before 1789 experimented with the new ideas about bows and instrument fittings and, region by region, worked out how to play the instrument in a way suitable to the changing musical tastes of their audiences. The violoncellists whose careers spanned the years of revolution and war faced greater obstacles. The instability of the times left few of them with any secure employment. Building on the performance techniques devised by their teachers, many of these players were forced to exploit the public concert hall, embracing and embellishing the concept of virtuosity, as approbation by the public superseded that of the nobility as the avenue to success.

The apex of this era of change and growing nationalism is the twenty-five-year period from 1790 to 1815. By 1790, Paris had become the center of a vital school of both violin and violoncello performance. The members of these schools – violinists Viotti, Rode, Baillot, and Kreutzer and violoncellists J. P. and J. L. Duport, Janson, and Lamare – left Paris and spread their doctrines of performance throughout the rest of Europe. They were met in their travels by Germans, the violinist Spohr and the violoncellist Romberg. All of these performers knew the prominent composers Boccherini, Cherubini, Mozart, Haydn, Beethoven, and Spontini. Dodging the marching armies that dominated the countryside, these players worked and performed with and for each other in Madrid, Milan, Paris, London, Hamburg, Berlin, Leipzig, Mannheim, Dresden, Vienna, Munich, Prague, Riga, Moscow, and St. Petersburg. They shared their preferences for in-

strument and bow designs and argued about stylistic concepts and technical methodology. Through this process, the performance techniques which
form the basis of modern Italian, English, Spanish, French, German, Bohemian, and Russian string pedagogy came into being.

The years following the Napoleonic Wars witnessed the codification of
violoncello performance techniques, as players regained a stable social
environment. Aided by a wealth of publications, newly instituted conservatories of music, and easier methods of travel for touring virtuosos,
uniformity of both playing techniques and instrument and bow construction becomes increasingly perceptible toward the middle of the nineteenth
century. The end of the era is conveniently marked by the death of two of
the period's most influential and publicly acclaimed personalities,
Bernhard Romberg and Pierre Baillot, who passed away within a year of
each other in 1841 and 1842.

The following pages examine the one hundred years of violoncello performance that falls between the publication of Corrette's *Méthode* and
Romberg's death. It is hoped that this account presents an informative and
helpful guide to the technique and performance practices of the period. It
is also hoped that the individuality and humanness of the men who made
the music has likewise been conveyed. In a present world that grows increasingly international, and thereby more homogeneous as to the manner
in which music is studied and performed, distinctive performance styles
are gradually vanishing. The degree of diversity present in the playing
styles of eighteenth- and nineteenth-century violoncellists may come as an
interesting surprise and perhaps a reminder that, while each considered his
method to be superior to any other, musicians of this era neither expected
nor valued absolute uniformity.

1

Violoncellists and schools of performance

Familiarity with violoncellists of bygone eras comes to most of us through those learning exercises and favorite pieces taught from generation to generation. These compositions in their re-edited forms usually convey little about the playing characteristics of their authors and nothing about the human qualities of the life which gave them creation. After the close of their careers, most violoncellists simply disappear from view, their playing forgotten and their contributions to violoncello performance obscured by time and changing values. Reacquaintance gives modern players an opportunity to appreciate our custodial legacy. It is also illuminating to compare those career elements which have changed much in musicians' lives over the course of several centuries with other facets which remain amazingly consistent.

Examining our predecessors' lives not only teaches us about individuals, but additionally pieces together the puzzle of how national schools formed. These schools constituted the underlying foundation of nineteenth-century performance and, to varying degrees, that of the twentieth century as well. However, their development was not simultaneous nor, before the advent of national conservatories, can schools be identified exclusively by a uniformity of technical mannerisms, for individuality was an accepted and appreciated component of eighteenth- and early nineteenth-century violoncello performance. Notwithstanding these factors, playing techniques and approaches to musical style were gradually systematized to suit local conventions, with definable regional methods of performance a result. Often instigated by an individual, favorable political or economic factors were most expeditious to the process, but sometimes there were also arbitrary reasons for an especially gifted or innovative teacher establishing himself in a specific locale. Conversely, if an area ceased to provide an agreeable performance environment, violoncellists took their expertise to more inviting residences.

ITALY

As with other members of the violin family, the roots of violoncello performance are found in Italy. However, the violoncello did not receive its
appellation until the 1660s and semantic vagaries make it difficult to distinguish musicians who specialized in playing violoncello-type instruments
before this time. After the term "violoncello" came to be used with some
consistency, it is clear that it was performers associated with Bologna who
first played a key role in furthering the use of their instrument.[1]

Seventeenth-century Bologna was a vibrant cosmopolitan city, supporting one of the most eminent universities in Europe. Two institutions in particular sustained the presence of enterprising violoncellists, the Accademia
Filarmonica and the Basilica of San Petronio. Prominent names from the
early generations of Bolognese violoncellists include Giovanni Battista
Vitali (1632–92), Petronio Franchesini (*c.* 1650–80), Domenico Gabrielli
(*c.* 1651–90), Giovanni Bononcini (1670–1747), Giuseppe Jacchini (*c.* 1663–
1727), and P. G. Boni (*fl.* first half of the eighteenth century). Gabrielli's
sonatas date from 1689–90 and are the earliest extant works for solo violoncello.[2]

Chronology of publications demonstrates that violoncello expertise
spread outward from Bologna, first to Modena and Ferrara, and then to
other Italian musical centers.[3] Significant in the distribution of Bolognese
musicians was the dissolution of the orchestra at San Petronio between
1696 and 1701. The migration of Italian musicians became commonplace
in the eighteenth century, as the rest of Europe became enamored of Italian singing and string playing. This was a circumstance aggravated by the
disjointed political structure of Italy. Unlike other schools of performance,
the eighteenth-century Italian school of violoncello was not centered
around a single location or player, but encompassed performers who
played with a technical and stylistic manner recognized as "Italian" by
their contemporaries. Attributes of this style, greatly influenced by opera,
included superior technical expertise, attention to melodiousness, and a
preference for distinctive compositional forms.[4]

Italian violoncellists were continual instigators in the quest for ever
more complex, yet idiomatic playing techniques. However, little of this
information is recorded in teaching manuals. The only familiar Italian violoncello methods are Francesco Scipriani's *Principij da imparare a suonare il
Violoncello e con 12 Toccate a solo* (before 1753), Salvatore Lanzetti's *Principes*

---

1 Stephen Bonta, "From Violone to Violoncello: A Question of Strings?" *JAMIS*, 3 (1977) and "Terminology for the Bass Violin in Seventeenth-Century Italy".
2 Elizabeth Cowling, *The Cello* (London: B. T. Batsford Ltd., 1975), pp. 77–78.
3 Bonta, "From Violone to Violoncello," 90.
4 Sylvette Milliot, *Le violoncelle en France au XVIIIe siècle* (Paris: Champion-Slatkin, 1985), pp. 82–91.

ou l'application de violoncelle (*c.* 1756–67), and Pietro Rachelle's *Breve metodo di violoncello* (Ricordi, 1837). Instead, the Italian style of playing was dispersed throughout Europe through personal contact and the publication of a large body of performance material. Unfortunately, little is known about the lives of many well-regarded Italian violoncellists, for not only are documented teaching techniques scarce, but the peripatetic nature of most Italian careers meant that – apart from compositions – little but a few anecdotes and recorded fragments survives.

The financial rewards obtainable through eighteenth-century London's extensive musical life made that city a highly desirable destination for many performers, including numerous Italian violoncellists. Those who left their mark include Giorgio Antoniotti (Antoniotto). Born in Milan in 1692, Antoniotti left Italy at some point for Holland. One of the last Italian composers to write for the viola da gamba, his first opus designates five sonatas for violoncello, with the following seven being for either violoncello or viola da gamba. This set was published in Amsterdam in 1736.[5] He then went to London, but historians vary in their assessment of how long he remained there. Hawkins states that he stayed for only one year, while Fétis asserts that he lived in London for twenty years.[6] In any case, Antoniotti published a treatise on harmony and counterpoint while in London in 1761. The work, first written in Italian and then translated into English, "was subscribed to by all of the principal musicians of the era."[7] Antoniotti returned to Milan about 1770, where he continued his work on theoretical harmony with Giovanni Sacchi. He died in Milan in 1776.

Giacobbe Basevi Cervetto, born in Italy *c.* 1682, became one of London's most prominent performers. He arrived in London between 1728 and 1738, probably making several trips as an instrument dealer before actually settling in the city. Legend states that he bought instruments from Stradivari.[8] Cervetto appeared in many subscription concerts and was a longtime member of the Drury Lane theater orchestra. Although Charles Burney described his tone quality as being rough, numerous anecdotes attest to his personal popularity in London.[9] Cervetto was a well-known acquaintance of the Burney family, playing frequently at soirees held at Burney's home. Further description by the historian states that the violon-

5 F. J. Fétis, *Biographie universelle des musiciens et bibliographie générale de la musique,* 8 vols. and supplement (second edition, Paris: Librarie de Firmin-Didot et Cie, 1887–88), vol. I, p. 120.
6 *A Dictionary of Musicians from the Earliest Times,* ed. John Sainsbury, 2 vols. (London: Salisbury and Co., 1825/R 1966), vol. I, p. 24.
7 Ibid.
8 William W. Hill, Arthur Hill, and Alfred Hill, *Antonio Stradivari: His Life and Work* (R/New York: Dover Publications, 1963), p. 246.
9 Edmund S. J. Van der Straeten, *History of the Violoncello, the Viola da Gamba, their Precursors and Collateral Instruments* (London: William Reeves, 1914), pp. 151–152.

cellist was "an honest Hebrew, had the largest nose, and wore the finest diamond ring on the forefinger of his bow hand."[10]

Consisting of works for use on the violin or violoncello, Cervetto's first opus received publication in 1741, while his final "6 Lessons or Divertiments" for two violoncellos appeared in 1761. He was especially successful as a businessman; he died in London on January 14, 1783, bequeathing £20,000 to his son.

Giovanni Battista Cirri was born in Forlì on October 1, 1724 and received his musical training from local organists. He was ordained into the church in 1739, but continued a musical career. Leaving Forlì, Cirri went first to Bologna, where he was attached to the Basilica of San Petronio and, in 1759, became a member of the Accademia Filarmonica. Having met the Duke of York in Forlì, he then left Bologna, traveling first to Paris and then settling in London in 1764.[11]

Cirri remained in London for the next fifteen years, becoming a favorite of the nobility. He was appointed chamber musician to the Duke of York and director of music to the Duke of Gloucester. He was also frequently heard as a soloist in public, taking part in the young Mozart's concerts in 1764 and 1765, the Bach–Abel concerts, and playing concertos in the intermission at the opera. Being a popular addition to London's musical scene, he also participated in concerts at Hickford's Room and provided music for the Catch-Club.[12] Cirri published numerous works for chamber ensembles during this period. His older brother fell ill in 1780 and Cirri returned to Forlì, eventually receiving the position of *maestro di cappella* at Forlì Cathedral. He died on June 11, 1808.

Salvatore Lanzetti was born in Naples *c.* 1710. He studied in Naples and then worked in Lucca and Turin, taking a position in 1727 with Vittorio Amedeo II. By the latter part of the 1730s, Lanzetti was in Paris and then London, where he lived until at least 1754. He also made a tour of Germany, giving concerts in Frankfurt am Main in May 1751. He returned to Italy about 1760 and rejoined the royal chapel in Turin. Lanzetti composed numerous sonatas and chamber compositions for his instrument, as well as his pedagogical work. He died in Turin *c.* 1780.[13]

Several Italian violoncellists established themselves in France. Jean-Baptiste Canavas (Canavasso) was born in Turin on March 25, 1713. Leaving Italy, he resided in Chambéry, Savoy in the early 1730s, where he was employed as a land-surveyor for Vittorio Amedeo. Jean-Jacques Rousseau, also employed in the same capacity, organized chamber recitals in which

10 Percy A. Scholes, *The Great Doctor Burney*, 2 vols. (Oxford University Press, 1948), vol. I, p. 98.
11 Owain Edwards, "Cirri," *NG*, vol. IV, pp. 410–411.
12 C. F. Pohl, *Mozart und Haydn in London*, 2 vols. (Vienna: Carl Gerold's Sohn, 1867), vol. I, p. 55; *The Morning Chronicle, and London Advertiser*, March 3, 1774; March 5, 1774; May 7, 1774; May 10, 1774; May 14, 1774.
13 Guido Salvetti, "Lanzetti," *NG*, vol. X, p. 459.

Canavas participated over a period of several years. Rousseau mentions that the violoncellist later married and settled in Paris.[14]

In moving to Paris, Canavas followed his brother and sister. His younger brother, Joseph, was a respected violinist and his sister sang with the Paris opera. Jean-Baptiste became a member of the King's chapel and, in 1746, was appointed as head of the "Vingte-quatre violons de la Chambre," the renowned group instituted by Lully. He maintained this position until 1779, when he was pensioned off. He and his brother also played for the opera orchestra until at least 1776. Indicative of the prominence both enjoyed among other Parisian musicians was their membership in the Société Académique des Enfants d'Apollon. Canavas published two sets of sonatas, the op. 1 appearing in 1767 and the op. 2 in 1773. He died in Paris on June 8, 1784.[15]

Carlo Graziani became part of the musical establishment in both France and Germany. He was born in Asti during the first half of the eighteenth century. Nothing is known of Graziani's life in Italy. The first recorded incident occurs in Paris, where he participated in the Concert Spirituel in 1747. He obtained a position with the distinguished orchestra of La Pouplinière, employment that lasted until the nobleman's death in 1762. Granted a ten-year privilege to publish instrumental music in 1758, he brought out his first two sets of violoncello sonatas in Paris.[16]

Following the dissolution of La Pouplinière's orchestra, Graziani traveled to England, where he appeared in London with the eight-year-old Mozart at Hickford's Rooms on May 17, 1764. Another concert given within the same week was with violinist Felice de Giardini.[17] Graziani is next found in Germany, where he and his wife, a singer, gave concerts in Frankfurt am Main on September 16 and 23, 1770. He and his wife were then invited to Berlin. Graziani succeeded the gambist Ludwig Christian Hesse as violoncello teacher and chamber musician to Prince Friedrich Wilhelm II, while his wife joined the court opera. Graziani, himself, was replaced by J. P. Duport in 1773. Retiring to Potsdam, Graziani died in 1787. His compositions included concertos, sonatas, and incidental works for violoncello, a duo for viola and violoncello, and an aria for soprano with violoncello obbligato.[18]

The most renowned Italian violoncellist of the eighteenth century was Luigi Boccherini. Born in Lucca on February 19, 1743, Boccherini was a

14 *The Confessions of Jean Jacques Rousseau* (New York: Random House, n.d.), pp. 190–191.
15 Georges Cucuel, *La Pouplinière et la musique de chambre au XVIIIe siècle* (Paris: Librairie Fischbacher, 1918), pp. 341–346.
16 Ibid., pp. 348–349.
17 Pohl, *Mozart und Haydn in London*, vol. I, pp. 55, 100.
18 Robert Eitner, *Biographisch-bibliographisches Quellen-Lexikon der Musiker und Musikgelehrten*, 10 vols. (New York: Musurgia, 1898), vol. IV, pp. 354–355.

member of an artistic family. His father was a violoncellist or contrabass player, his sister a dancer, and his brother a dancer, violinist, and well-regarded librettist. Boccherini first studied violoncello with Francesco Vanucci, the local *maestro di cappella*. He left for Rome in 1757, spending several months there to study with the *maestro di cappella* at St. Peter's basilica, G. B. Costanzi. At the end of that year, Boccherini and his father were invited to Vienna to take positions in the court theater; his brother and sister arrived shortly thereafter. Boccherini's early continuo sonatas were composed to demonstrate his proficiency; he performed them in Vienna with accompaniment by his father.[19]

During the following years, Boccherini alternated residences between Vienna and Lucca, taking final leave of Vienna in April 1764 for a permanent position in Lucca. He remained employed by his native city for the next three years, but traveled during this time. It is known that he spent time in Milan during 1765, where he performed both his own and Haydn's string quartets with Manfredi, Nardini, and Cambini. Manfredi was also from Lucca and by that point in his career, Boccherini and the violinist had developed a close friendship. The death of his father led to Boccherini's decision to give concerts outside of Italy and the two friends left Lucca at the end of 1766, with Paris being their final destination.[20]

In the pre-Revolutionary years of the eighteenth century, acceptance by Parisian musical connoisseurs was the gateway to an artist's fame and fortune. The first step in this process was to be invited into the musical salon of Baron de Bagge, the Prussian chamberlain. If a performer achieved success at the Baron's soirees, performances then followed at the prestigious Concert Spirituel, where Boccherini and Manfredi performed on March 20, 1768.[21]. Boccherini evidently pleased the Baron, for the latter housed him in his own lodgings during Boccherini's two-year stay.[22] Through this relationship, the Italian came to know J. B. Janson and the Duport brothers, and it also led to his first publications with Vénier.[23]

Manfredi and Boccherini left Paris in the latter part of 1768, embarking for Madrid at the behest of the Spanish ambassador. Boccherini joined the establishment of Don Luis, the younger brother of King Charles III, remaining in his employ until 1785. Already a fluent composer of sonatas, concertos, string trios and quartets, Boccherini now began composing string quintets using two violoncellos. This combination of instruments

19 Germain de Rothschild, *Luigi Boccherini: His Life and Work*, trans. Norbert Dufourcq (Oxford University Press, 1965), pp. 1–14.
20 Ibid., pp. 18–23.
21 Constant Pierre, *Histoire du Concert Spirituel 1725–1790* (Paris: Société Française de Musicologie, 1975), p. 293.
22 C. Sanford Terry, "Baron Bach," *Music and Letters*, 12, no. 2 (April 1931), 135.
23 Fétis, *Biographie universelle*, vol. I, p. 452.

was suitable for the small number of musicians employed by the Infante while isolated at Las Arenas and Boccherini performed his works with the Font family string quartet.[24] These quintets became especially popular in Paris owing to the influence of Baillot, who featured them in virtually all of his chamber music concerts until he ceased performing in 1840.[25] Baillot also included excepts from Boccherini's works in the study methods published by the Paris Conservatoire.

Although he remained in Spain, Boccherini recommenced associations with Austrian and German musicians during the early 1780s. He exchanged letters with Haydn through the publisher Artaria, a fact that was reported by contemporary biographers.[26] Friedrich Wilhelm II of Prussia also became a patron of Boccherini's. Although this relationship was instigated by the Prussian ambassador in 1783, it was likely encouraged by J. P. Duport. Boccherini became Chamber Composer to the Berlin court in 1786 and received an annual stipend until the King's death in 1798. In total, Boccherini composed fifty-six works for the Prussian court.[27]

Although nothing is known of Boccherini's activities between 1787 and 1796, it is apparent that until 1802, he continued to fulfill commissions and to publish. Afflicted with tuberculosis, Boccherini had ceased performing by this time, but numerous young musicians made pilgrimages to meet with him. These visitors included Rode and Romberg, who, like Baillot, greatly admired the older composer.[28]

The final twenty years of Boccherini's life saw the deaths of his patron, two wives, and his daughters. Additional difficulties resulted from the devaluation of his royal pension after the French invasion and monetary disagreements with the publisher Pleyel.[29] Reduced to living with his family in a single-room apartment, he was severely depressed when the pianist Sophie Gail met him in 1803.[30] Boccherini lived with his remaining sons for two more years, until his death on May 28, 1805.[31]

FRANCE

Acceptance of the violoncello as a solo instrument came slowly to French musicians and audiences, because of both the excellence of French

---

24 Rothschild, *Boccherini*, p. 44. The Infante had established his residue at Las Arenas, having been prohibited by his brother, Charles III, from taking his place at the court in Madrid. The Infante's transgression was to have married a woman of inferior social rank.
25 Joël-Marie Fauquet, *Les sociétés de musique de chambre à Paris de la restauration à 1870* (Paris: Aux Amateurs de Livres, 1986), pp. 293–331.
26 *Dictionary*, ed. Sainsbury, vol. I, p. 240.
27 Rothschild, *Boccherini*, pp. 52–53.
28 "Rode," *Revue Musicale*, (December 18, 1830), 174; Rothschild, *Boccherini*, p. 74.
29 Rothschild, *Boccherini*, pp. 49, 80–82.
30 Fétis, *Biographie universelle*, vol. I, p. 454.
31 Rothschild, *Boccherini*, p. 82.

gambists and French antipathy for Italian culture. However, by the 1730s, Italian string players were performing in Paris, with resulting effects on French style. Numerous Italian violoncellists contributed to the dissemination of knowledge about the violoncello, while several French viol players became enamored of the violoncello and traveled to Italy for study. The most prominent of these Italian-trained French violoncellists was Jean Barrière (*c.* 1705–47), the earliest French composer to publish idiomatic works for the violoncello. His compositions, like those of the 1720s and 1730s by Boismortier and Corrette, were formative in the development of violoncello playing in France.

In addition to the influence of specific personalities, several concert organizations indirectly furthered the development of the French violoncello school by promoting the performances of solo works. These included the Concert Spirituel and the Société Académique des Enfants d'Apollon. The Concert Spirituel was organized in 1725 to provide public concerts of sacred music during the penitential seasons of the church year, when opera was prohibited; it was in existence until 1790 and was then reinstituted during the Restoration. The Société Académique des Enfants d'Apollon was a private group sponsoring a yearly concert, whose members included amateur and professional musicians. Initiated in 1741, it was disbanded in 1790 and then reorganized in 1806.[32] Members included Canavas, the Duport brothers, Bréval, Hus-Desforges, Baudiot, Norblin, and the lawyer and avid dilettante Raoul.

French performance techniques are recorded in numerous treatises and tutors. The methods of Corrette (1741) and Azais (*c.* 1778) were written by non-violoncellists, while that published by the Conservatoire (1805) is a composite of ideas, heavily influenced by Baillot. Those of Tillière (1764), Cupis (1772), Raoul (*c.* 1802), Aubert (1802), Bideau (1802), Bréval (1804), Müntzberger (*c.* 1804), Duport (1806), P. Vaillant (*c.* 1815), Baudiot (1826, 1828), Hus-Desforges (1829) and Vaslin (1884) were written as personal testaments to individual performance methodology.

The advent of the French violoncello school is the legacy of Martin Berteau. He was born in Valenciennes *c.* 1708. As with many of his French contemporaries, Berteau is reputed to have begun his musical training on the viola da gamba, perhaps studying in Germany with a Bohemian named Kozais (Kozecz).[33] The early years of his career are replete with unproven anecdotes. Among them are an association with the Italian violoncellist Francesco Alborea (Franciscello), stories regarding numerous performances at the Concert Spirituel, and gossip testifying to a love of wine.

32 Maurice Decourcelle, *La Société Académique des Enfants d'Apollon 1741–1880* (Paris, 1881).
33 Wilhelm Joseph von Wasielewski, *The Violoncello and Its History*, trans. Isobella S. E. Stigend (London: Novello, Ewer, & Co., 1894/R 1968), p. 87.

Documentable facts about his life in Paris indicate that he was living in the French capital in the mid-part of the eighteenth century and was active as a violoncello performer, composer, and teacher.[34] Although there are few recorded instances of his performances, contemporaries considered his playing to be exceptional; Rousseau, for instance, praised his innovative use of natural harmonics.[35] His many students attributed their own success to their study with Berteau, lauding him in published works well after his death. At some unknown point in Berteau's career he left Paris to take a position with King Stanislas of Poland. He apparently remained with this household until his death on January 22, 1771.[36]

François Cupis was born in Paris on November 10, 1732. Cupis was the youngest son of a minor noble. Several of his siblings were also artistic: Charles was a horn player, Jean-Baptiste a violinist and dancer, and Marie-Anne a dancer with the opera. François is purported to have been a reckless youth, given to thievery and drunkenness. However, he studied with Berteau in 1751 at the Collège des Quatre Nations, apparently becoming a creditable violoncellist.[37] He was a member of the Concert Spirituel orchestra in the years 1764 to 1771 and 1774 to 1777 and of the Académie Royale de Musique orchestra between 1767 and 1770.[38] Fétis also stated that he was a member of the Opéra orchestra, playing with the small group (*petit chœur*) which accompanied recitatives.

François inherited substantial wealth upon his sister's death in 1770. Shortly afterwards, he married, renounced his professional obligations and retired to an estate outside Paris. Living a quiet family life, he taught, composed, and wrote his violoncello method.

The last three decades of Cupis' life were far less tranquil. Records demonstrate that he lost two wives and three children. His fortune was destroyed in the course of the Revolution and its aftermath, and his estate was liquidated in 1799. Moving back to Paris, he continued to compose and to publish works for violoncello. Cupis also published a method for viola in 1803. The last years of his life were spent in a room in the same building as his sister-in-law, where he died on October 13, 1808. The only items of value left at his death were three violoncellos, made respectively by Le Pileur, Ranault et Chatelain, and de Pierray.[39]

Jean-Pierre Duport was born in Paris on November 27, 1741. The Duport family was an important part of the Parisian artistic establishment, Duport *père* being director of the *bals de l'Opéra* and a fine amateur violoncellist.

34 Jane Adas, "Le célèbre Berteau," *Early Music,* 17, no. 3 (August 1989).
35 Jean-Jacques Rousseau, *Dictionnaire de musique* (Paris: Duchesne, 1768/R 1969), p. 449.
36 Milliot, *Le violoncelle en France,* p. 590.
37 Ibid., p. 379.
38 Julie Anne Vertrees, "Cupis," *NG,* vol. III, p. 98.
39 Milliot, *Le violoncelle en France,* pp. 384–386.

Little is known about Jean-Pierre's childhood except for the fact that he studied violoncello with Berteau.[40] An unsubstantiated but oft-repeated story from a contemporary journal reports that as a young man, Duport journeyed from Marseilles to Genoa to spend two hours with the renowned Italian violoncellist Franciscello.[41]

Duport made his performance debut at the Concert Spirituel on February 2, 1761. Joining the household of the Prince de Conti (Louis-François de Bourbon) in 1763, Duport became the most eminent violoncellist in Paris. He remained in the employ of the Prince for six years, performing at both private and public venues and playing frequently at the Concert Spirituel.[42] It is there and at Baron de Bagge's that he would have met Boccherini during the Italian's visit to Paris in the years 1766–68.[43]

Duport left Paris in 1769, traveling first to England. Charming his hosts, he stayed there for two years before leaving for Spain, where he possibly visited Boccherini.[44] Duport returned to Paris in the spring of 1773, again performing in numerous concerts at the Concert Spirituel.[45] He stayed in Paris for only one year and then left to join the Kapelle of Frederick the Great in Berlin. In addition to his duties as first violoncello in the opera orchestra and performing chamber music, Duport became violoncello instructor to Prince Friedrich Wilhelm II. Upon the Prince's elevation in 1786, Duport left the opera and became superintendent of the court's chamber music.[46] As both the King and the Crown Prince were ardent music lovers, the Prussian court hired the finest performers and attracted visits from virtuoso soloists, including the violinists Pugnani and Viotti. The court also became a center for violoncello performance, with Duport premiering works by Carl Stamitz, Peter Ritter, Mozart, Beethoven, and Boccherini.[47]

This rich musical life lasted until Friedrich Wilhelm's death in 1797. Although Friedrich Wilhelm III also appreciated music, his own preference was for opera. Composers therefore ceased sending chamber music which featured the violoncello to Berlin. However, Duport retained his position until 1806. In this year, the Prussians suffered a major defeat against Napoleon at Jena and the court consequently left Berlin. The Kapelle was dissolved, to be restructured only intermittently during the remainder of the

40 Lillian Moore, "The Duport Mystery," *Dance Perspectives*, 7 (1960), 12–13.
41 *AMZ*, 14 (July 1812), col. 470.
42 Pierre, *Histoire du Concert Spirituel*, pp. 279–293.
43 "Les Frères Duport," *Revue Musicale*, 3, no. 8 (March 1828), 174.
44 *AMZ* (February 1819), col. 108.
45 Pierre, *Histoire du Concert Spirituel*, p. 301.
46 *AMZ* (February 1819), cols. 108–109.
47 Fritz Kohlmorgen, "Die Brüder Duport und die Entwicklung der Violoncelltechnik von ihren Anfängen bis zur Zeit Bernhard Rombergs" (Ph.D. thesis, Friedrich-Wilhelms Universität, 1922), pp. 17–21.

war. Duport was given his pension in 1811 and retired to Potsdam, where he died on December 31, 1818.

Jean-Louis Duport was born in Paris on October 4, 1749. A student of Jean-Pierre, he made his debut at the Concert Spirituel, accompanied by his brother, on February 2, 1768.[48] From there, Jean-Louis quickly worked his way into the Parisian musical establishment, working with the most respected Parisian performers and such visiting artists as Crosdill and Boccherini. An additional element in his relationship with Boccherini and Baron de Bagge was the tie of freemasonry: the Baron favored artists who had this association.[49]

Duport eventually took a permanent position with the household of the Prince de Guéménée. The foremost violoncellist in Paris after his brother's departure, Jean-Louis performed continually, both privately and publicly, and also taught and composed. In 1782, another important association was forged through the patronage of Baron de Bagge, that with the violinist G. B. Viotti. Viotti came to Paris in that year and became the immediate darling of the concert-going public. Duport and Viotti became close friends, playing frequent concerts together. Duport was a member of Viotti's orchestra for the Concert de la Loge Olympique and the violinist later composed three *divertissemens* for him.

Duport also made notable acquaintances outside of Paris. Vidal tells of a visit to Voltaire in Ferney; on hearing Duport play, Voltaire is reputed to have said, "Mr. Duport, you make me believe in miracles: you know how to turn an ox into a nightingale."[50] Duport visited England in early 1783 and stayed there about six months.[51] During this period he participated in benefit concerts and the Hanover Square series, performing his own concertos, two-violoncello works with James Cervetto, and in various chamber ensembles.[52]

The French Revolution ended Duport's successful Parisian life. Fleeing France in 1790, Jean-Louis joined his brother in Berlin and remained there until the Kapelle was disbanded in 1806. In Berlin and Potsdam, Duport was occupied with the opera orchestra, with chamber music, and with teaching. He held the position of first violoncello in the opera orchestra until 1805. At that time, Romberg joined the Kapelle and the two shared the position.[53] Romberg had visited Paris in 1785 and was already on famil-

48 Pierre, *Histoire du Concert Spirituel*, p. 148.
49 Roger Cotte, "Baron Bagge," *NG*, vol. II, p. 173.
50 Antoine Vidal, *Les instruments à archet, les faiseurs, les joueurs d'instruments, leur histoire*, 3 vols. (Paris: J. Claye, 1877/R 1961), vol. II, p. 353.
51 Duport's activities in London are traced through announcements and reviews in the *The Public Advertiser*. Duport is mentioned in concerts beginning with that of February 19, 1783 and ending with a performance held on May 19, 1783.
52 *The Public Advertiser*, March 27, 1783; April 10, 1783.
53 Herbert Schäfer, *Bernhard Romberg: sein Leben und Wirken* (Münster: Aschendorffsche Verlagsbuchhandlung, 1931), p. 48.

iar terms with Duport. He held the latter in great esteem and dedicated his op. 10 *Fantaisie pour le Violoncelle* (1805) to him.

According to Duport, Berlin's requirements left him more free time than had been the case in Paris and he used this time to organize his teaching methodology into a violoncello method, the *Essai sur le doigté du violoncelle, et sur la conduite de l'archet*, which he published in 1806. It is considered the founding work on the principles of modern violoncello fingering. The comprehensiveness and care with which this treatise was crafted was recognized as soon as it was published: as J. F. Reichardt remarked, "the friends of the violoncello, this beautiful, noble instrument, must be very grateful for his diligence with which he has composed his work."[54]

Duport left Berlin after the Battle of Jena, returning to Paris. Although he was granted the status of *Professeur honoraire* at the Paris Conservatoire, his past political associations made it impossible to find a permanent position in Paris at this time and he joined the household of King Charles IV of Spain, who was residing in Marseilles. This employment lasted until 1812, when Duport again returned to Paris. He was then named first violoncello, *récitant droit*, in the Imperial Chapel and obtained a full professorship at the Conservatoire in 1814, teaching through the following year.[55] Unlike younger performers such as Baudiot, who held the same positions, Duport was forced into retirement by the events of the Restoration. However, he continued to compose, and to perform for private concerts and at the revitalized Concert Spirituel until his death on September 7, 1819.[56]

Another student of Berteau was Jean-Baptiste-Aimé-Joseph Janson, born in Valenciennes on March 9, 1742. Like his teacher, whose home town was also Valenciennes, he played the viola da gamba as well as the violoncello.[57] Traveling to Paris in 1755, the thirteen-year-old made a successful debut at the Concert Spirituel on March 3.

Janson joined the household of the Prince de Conti in 1764, a year after J. P. Duport. At this time, he was a frequent soloist at the Concert Spirituel, often alternating performances with Duport. Rivalry between the two performers may have been behind Janson's departure in 1766. He joined the household of the hereditary Prince of Brunswick on his travels to Italy, but returned to Paris the following year, remaining until 1769.[58] As before, he was a frequent performer at Parisian musical events.

Janson spent much of the following decade traveling through Europe,

54 *BMZ*, no. 8 (1806), 29.
55 T. Lassabathie, *Histoire du Conservatoire Impérial de Musique et de Déclamation* (Paris: Michel Lévy Frères, 1860), p. 442.
56 For a review of Duport's performance at the Concert Spirituel in 1816, see *AMZ* (February 1817), cols. 149–150.
57 Ernst Ludwig Gerber, *Historisch-Biographisches Lexikon der Tonkünstler und Neues Historisch-Biographisches Lexikon der Tonkünstler*, 4 vols. (Graz: Akademische Druck- u. Verlagsanstalt, 1977), vol. I, col. 686.
58 Pierre, *Histoire du Concert Spirituel*, pp. 149, 285–288, 289.

visiting Denmark, Sweden, Poland, and Germany. His violoncello concertos gained wide acceptance, being published in both Paris and Germany.[59] Spending the majority of the 1780s in Paris, Janson achieved continuing success as a composer; his symphonies became popular works at the Concert Spirituel.[60] Janson weathered the Parisian political events of 1789–90 and was appointed to a position with the Opéra orchestra. He was also honored with the appointment *Professeur de Première Classe* at the Conservatoire upon its founding in 1795.

While Janson was able to survive the political upheavals of the Revolution, he was not so lucky in the intrigues that plagued the Conservatoire in its formative years. Publishing a letter in the *Journal du Commerce* in support of J. F. Lesueur against the director of the Conservatoire, Bernard Sarrette, Janson was removed from his position in 1802.[61] Publicly vilified for this indiscretion, Janson rapidly became ill. He died in Paris on September 2, 1803, just as the government was preparing to reinstate him. His obituary reads:

Janson the elder, the celebrated violoncellist, ex-professor at the Conservatory of music, artist renowned for his talents and his integrity, has just, at the age of 59 years, succumbed to distress and illness, at a time when an honorable appointment, to which he was appointed by the government, could have restored his fortune, repaired his losses, and given him back happiness and health.[62]

Jean Tricklir was born in Dijon in 1750. He was pledged to the church at an early age and studied violin and violoncello as part of his ecclesiastical training. At fifteen, he received permission to travel to Mannheim for further study.[63] Fétis reports that he remained there for three years.

Tricklir obtained his release from the church and spent the next period of his life traveling to and from Italy, making three trips in all. In 1776 he visited Paris, where he performed at the Concert Spirituel in May.[64] Returning to Germany in 1782, Tricklir first took a position with the Elector of Mainz, but soon left to join the household of the Elector of Saxony. He stayed in Dresden until his death on November 19, 1813.

Tricklir was known by his contemporaries as a musical theoretician and an accomplished composer. He published two treatises, the first of which describes a device of his invention which attempted to prevent the effects of atmospheric change on the tuning of stringed instruments. His composi-

59 For Janson's German publications, see *The Breitkopf Thematic Catalogue: the Six Parts and Sixteen Supplements, 1762–1787*, ed. Barry S. Brook (New York: Dover Publications, 1966), col. 855.
60 Pierre, *Histoire du Concert Spirituel*, pp. 310–328.
61 C. P. Ducancel, *Mémoire pour J. F. Lesueur* (Paris: Goujon Fils, 1802), p. 157.
62 *Correspondance des Amateurs Musiciens*, no. 45 (October 1, 1803), 3.
63 Gerber, *Lexikon*, vol. I, cols. 682–683.
64 Pierre, *Histoire du Concert Spirituel*, p. 305.

tions were primarily concertos and sonatas for violoncello. These works were popular with contemporaries and, in fact, his fourth concerto was given the unusual accolade of being performed at the Concert Spirituel by J. L. Duport, who then republished it in an edited version.

Jean-Baptiste Bréval was born in Paris on November 6, 1753. The family trade was wig-making, but he and his brother, the violinist Stanislas-Laurent, broke with family tradition and studied music: Bréval is believed to have studied with Berteau and Cupis.[65] Making his debut at the Concert Spirituel on August 15, 1778, Bréval worked in close proximity to J. L. Duport and acted as his accompanist on at least one occasion in March 1780.[66]

Bréval gained early fame as a composer, publishing numerous works during the 1770s and 1780s. These include compositions for violoncello, violin, chamber music, and symphonies concertantes. Although many of his works require great virtuosity, he was highly regarded for his ability to produce pleasing music for amateur performance and for teaching.[67] As a performer, Bréval introduced his own solo works at the Concert Spirituel, but was employed primarily as an orchestral player. He was principal violoncellist of the orchestra of the Société de la Concert de la Loge Olympique and an orchestra member of the Concert Spirituel until 1790 and of the Opéra-comique from 1790 to 1800. Bréval likewise took a chair in the Opéra orchestra, working there from 1781 to 1806 and again from 1809 to 1814.[68]

The Revolution appears to have had little effect on Bréval's career and it is probable that he continued to make his living from orchestral work and teaching. There are varying reports as to whether he obtained a position at the Paris Conservatoire upon its opening. There is no mention of him in Conservatoire documents, but an *AMZ* report on the Conservatoire, written from Paris, lists him as a professor of violoncello.[69] Certainly Bréval's compositions were used as teaching material at the Conservatoire, as they are listed as performance pieces in 1797 and 1800 at concerts for the annual distribution of prizes.[70]

Bréval also participated in other Parisian musical organizations. He was on the administration committee for the Concerts de la rue de Cléry at their inception in 1800 and remained a member of the Société Académique des Enfants d'Apollon after that organization's reinception in 1806. However, although he continued to play in the Opéra orchestra until 1814,

65 Fétis, *Biographie universelle*, vol. II, p. 70.
66 Pierre, *Histoire du Concert Spirituel*, pp. 309–313.
67 See *Correspondance des Amateurs Musiciens*, no. 52 (November 19, 1803), 1.
68 Milliot, *Le violoncelle en France*, p. 304.
69 *AMZ* (March 1801), col. 412.
70 Constant Pierre, *Conservatoire National de Musique et de Déclamation* (Paris: Imprimerie Nationale, 1900), pp. 967–968.

he became less active in the years following 1802. Bréval's final compositions were published in 1804–05 and his last major work, the *Traité du
violoncelle*, was published in January 1804. This method was not well received, earning an unfavorable review in the *Correspondance des Amateurs
Musiciens*.[71] This poor reception and the fact that the tutor was almost immediately superseded by Duport's *Essai* may account for Bréval's eclipse
from Paris's musical scene after 1806. Having purchased a house in l'Aisne
in 1794, he returned there after his retirement in 1814.[72] He died in Colligis,
Aisne on March 19, 1823.

Jean-Henri Levasseur was born in Paris on May 29, 1764. His father was
the inspector general from 1755 to 1757, and a vocal instructor at the Paris
Opéra.[73] Levasseur began his studies under Cupis and later took lessons
from J. L. Duport. He made his solo debut at the Concert Spirituel on December 8, 1786, performing a concerto by Duport.[74] He was appointed
principal violoncello of the Opéra orchestra in 1789 and retained this position until 1823.

Levasseur, together with Janson, was named as *Professeur de Première
Classe* of violoncello at the Conservatoire upon its formation. Avoiding the
political difficulties of the era, Levasseur was a major force in establishing
the continuity of teaching methodology for the violoncello class of that
institution. He was a contributor to the *Méthode de violoncelle* written for the
Conservatoire and his students, Baudiot and Norblin, continued his
teaching traditions as each was appointed in turn to a position at the
Conservatoire.

As a performer, in addition to his duties at the Opéra, Levasseur was
attached to the Chapelle of the Emperor Napoleon and, later, to that of
the King. He published few works for his instrument. Fétis noted ten
opus numbers, which include a set of exercises for the violoncello, and
sonatas and duos. Although he died in 1823, his position was not filled
until 1826.[75]

Jacques-Michel Hurel de Lamare was born in Paris on May 1, 1772. As
the seventh child of poor parents, Lamare was entered into the Institute of
Pages in the Music of the King at age seven. His initial study of the violoncello may have been with Levasseur.[76] He was granted lessons with J. L.
Duport in 1787, but these were discontinued when Duport left Paris after
the Revolution. Lamare obtained a position in the orchestra of the Opéra-

71 *Correspondance des Amateurs Musiciens* (June 20, 1804), p. 396.
72 Milliot, *Le violoncelle en France*, p. 307.
73 Nicole Wild, *Dictionnaire des théâtres Parisiens au XIXe siècle* (Paris: Aux Amateurs de Livres, 1989),
    p. 302.
74 Pierre, *Histoire du Concert Spirituel*, p. 333.
75 Lassabathie, *Histoire du Conservatoire*, p. 439.
76 "Rise and Progress of the Violoncello," 482.

comique in 1794 and, in the years following, gained a reputation for virtuosity equal to that of J. L. Duport.

Although there is no record that Lamare ever held a position at the Conservatoire, he became closely associated with musicians who were appointed to the faculty, in particular Baillot, Rode, and Baudiot. Working with these musicians in varying combinations, and with Grasset and Auber, Lamare became a frequent performer of quartets and Boccherini quintets.[77]

Lamare left Paris at the end of 1801, traveling to London before going to Germany and Russia. He visited the Duports in Berlin and then, joined by Rode, stopped in Hamburg and Hanover before arriving in Russia.[78] In Russia, he divided his time between St. Petersburg and Moscow, where he played in a quartet, first with Rode, and then, from 1805, with Baillot. It is also likely that he associated with Romberg at this time: a *BMZ* interview disclosed that Lamare was very familiar with the German's concertos (see Chapter 9, p. 288).[79] Lamare traveled to Vienna in 1805, searching for a Stradivari violoncello and giving well-received concerts.[80] He was joined by Baillot in September, who recorded in his diary that he met with Haydn, Beethoven, and Cherubini.[81] Baillot and Lamare left Vienna on October 2, returning five weeks later to Moscow. Maintaining a rigorous performance schedule in Russia until 1808, Baillot, Rode, and Lamare then returned to Paris (they met Paris acquaintances Cherubini and Auber in Belgium en route). Lamare arrived in Paris in April of 1809.

Although Lamare had achieved great success on his tours, he found it difficult to re-establish himself as a soloist upon his return to Paris. He gave a concert in May 1809 which was poorly received, a review crediting his problems to the fact that the violoncello "is so little appreciated by the ladies, resulting in Lamare's concert appearing somewhat sad."[82] From this point on, Lamare performed only chamber music, primarily with Baillot. He is listed as Baillot's first violoncellist for the violinist's subscription chamber music series, instituted in 1814. The second violoncello part, necessary for Boccherini quintets, was taken by Norblin in 1814 and Baudiot in 1815. In addition to Boccherini quintets, programs for these concerts consisted of quartets by Haydn, Mozart, and Beethoven.[83]

Lamare retained his association with Baillot until his marriage to a

77 Brigitte François-Sappey, "Pierre Marie François de Sales Baillot (1771–1842) par lui-même," *Recherches sur la Musique Française Classique*, 18 (1978), 138 and Fauquet, *Les sociétés de musique de chambre*, p. 43.
78 François-Sappey, "Baillot par lui-même," 183.
79 "Etwas über den berühmten französischen Violoncellisten Lamare," *BMZ*, no. 26 (1806), 102.
80 Ibid., 102–103.
81 François-Sappey, "Baillot par lui-même," 183.
82 *AMZ* (June 1809), col. 605.
83 Fauquet, *Les sociétés de musique de chambre*, pp. 271–295.

woman of independent wealth on May 15, 1815, after which he left Paris for a country home in Caen. He died there on March 27, 1823. Lamare retained a high profile owing to the popularity of the three violoncello concertos composed by his friend Auber, but published under his name. These works were performed at student concerts at the Conservatoire and used as *Morceaux de Concours* as late as 1866.[84]

Pierre-Louis Hus-Desforges was born in Toulon on March 14, 1773. He was the grandson of the flamboyant violinist Giornovichi (Jarnowick). Hus-Desforges' mother was an actress who moved, with her son, from Toulon to La Rochelle. There, Hus-Desforges was placed at age eight in the cathedral school; he sang in the choir and later learned trumpet and violoncello. In September 1792, he was engaged as a trumpeter in the French cavalry, remaining in the service until he lost a finger on his right hand from a bullet wound. He then took a violoncello position in the theater orchestra at Lyons, but left after six months to enter the Paris Conservatoire, studying under Janson. Simultaneously with his studies, he joined the orchestra at the Théâtre des Troubadours.[85]

Leaving the Conservatoire in 1800, Hus-Desforges accepted the directorship of the French opera in St. Petersburg. While there, he toured Russia as a soloist and also gained recognition as a composer, publishing numerous works for violoncello.[86] Living in Russia at a time when the most eminent European musicians were there, Hus-Desforges came to know Romberg and dedicated his second concerto to the German violoncellist.

Hus-Desforges left Russia for a solo tour in 1812, but his travels during the remaining years of the war are difficult to trace. He returned to Paris in 1817 and was appointed principal violoncellist of the orchestra in the Théâtre Porte Saint Martin; he also composed music for the melodramas produced there. Leaving Paris in 1820, he established a conservatory of music in Metz, but shortly afterwards he set off on tour and eventually returned to Paris.

Hus-Desforges used the experiences gained at Metz to outline a methodology of teaching, which he published as his *Méthode de violoncelle* in 1829. The method was designed for elementary teaching and won favorable reports from reviewers.[87] Although Hus-Desforges continued to enjoy success as an artist and for his publications, he was evidently unable to find long-term employment, several times moving from one theater orchesta to

84 Pierre, *Conservatoire*, pp. 481–486, 615.
85 Fétis, *Biographie universelle*, vol. IV, p. 391.
86 Lev Ginsburg, *Istoriya violonchel'nogo iskusstva, kniga vtoraya, Russkoe violonchel'noe iskusstvo do 60'kh godov XIX veka* [History of the Art of the Cello, Bk 2, Russian Cello Art up to the 60s of the 19th Century], 3 vols. (Moscow: Muzgiz, 1957), vol.. II, pp. 109–110.
87 *Revue Musicale*, 4, no. 12 (October 1829), 287.

another. His final position was as the violoncello instructor for a music school in Pont-le-Voy. He died at Pont-le-Voy on January 10, 1838.

Charles Baudiot was born in Nancy on March 29, 1773. Information regarding his early years has yet to come to light, but it is known that he began his association with Baillot during the Reign of Terror in 1793.[88] After this time, Baudiot studied in Paris with Janson and assumed the professorship of the second class of violoncellos upon the Conservatoire's foundation in 1795.[89] Baudiot retained this position until the Conservatoire was restructured in 1802, the year Janson lost his professorship. Baudiot then took a position with the ministry of finance. However, he continued to perform chamber music with Baillot and collaborated in the Conservatoire's *Méthode de violoncelle*.

Baudiot regained his chair at the Conservatoire in 1805, after Romberg's departure. At this time, he published the first of his many works for violoncello. He resumed his association with Baillot in 1808, after the latter's return from Russia. This was a relationship that lasted until about 1820.[90] Baudiot also played with the Opéra orchestra and occupied the position of *premier violoncelle récitant gauche* in Napoleon's Imperial Chapel; unlike J. L. Duport, he retained his position after the Restoration.[91]

Although Baudiot was an active performer, he himself alluded to suffering from stage fright and contemporaries found his playing uninspiring.[92] However, he was much esteemed as a teacher and composer. Baudiot remained *Professeur de Première Classe* until 1827, arranging for the publication of his two-volume violoncello method in 1826 and 1828. His method engendered much enthusiasm; Heinrich Probst wrote to Breitkopf und Härtel that "I am in a good position to tell you what sells here. There is Baudiot's violoncello method of 396 pages which has been adopted by the Conservatoire and is receiving the acclaim of all connoisseurs."[93] Baudiot's violoncello compositions were, likewise, well regarded and were used on student programs and for the *Morceaux de Concours* until 1877.[94] Other

88 François-Sappey, "La vie musicale à Paris à travers les mémoires d'Eugène Sauzay," *Revue de Musicologie*, 60, nos. 1–2 (1974), 192.

89 Lassabathie, *Histoire du Conservatoire*, p. 192.

90 Fauquet, *Les sociétés de musique de chambre*, p. 271.

91 *Revue et Gazette Musicale de Paris*, September 30, 1849, p. 309; Milliot, *Le violoncelle en France*, p. 273.

92 Neither Fétis, Spohr, nor Chopin were complimentary of Baudiot's playing, which, although technically proficient, was reported as being dry and boring. See *Louis Spohr's Autobiography*, 2 vols. (London: Longman, Green, Longman, Roberts, and Green, 1865/R 1969), vol. II, p. 113; *Selected Correspondence of Fryderyk Chopin*, collected and annotated by Bronislaw Sydow, ed. and trans. Arthur Hedley (London: Heinemann, 1962), pp. 327–328; see also Frederick Niecks, "Recollections of Violoncellists," *Monthly Musical Record*, 49, no. 582 (June 2, 1919), 123.

93 *Breitkopf und Härtel in Paris: the Letters of their Agent Heinrich Probst between 1833 and 1840*, trans. Hans Lenneberg (Stuyvesant, New York: Pendragon Press, 1990), p. 43. The method also received a favorable review in *Revue Musicale*, 3, no. 20 (June 1828), 478–480.

94 Pierre, *Conservatoire*, p. 615.

notable compositions for violoncello were written for Baudiot by Georges Onslow.

After his retirement, Baudiot continued to compose and to write. A treatise on transposition, the first volume for piano and the second volume for violin and viola, was published in 1837 and 1838. Numerous compositions for violoncello and chamber music combinations also found a ready market. He died in Paris on September 26, 1849.

Louis-Pierre-Martin Norblin was born in Warsaw on December 2, 1781. He was the son of the French painter Norblin de la Gourdaine and spent his childhood in Poland under the patronage of Prince Radziwill.[95] In 1798, he left Warsaw for Paris and was admitted to the Conservatoire, taking his first prize in 1802. Norblin gained recognition within Paris as a soloist and, after a brief spell with the Théâtre-italien, was named solo violoncellist of the Opéra in 1811. He held this position until 1846.[96]

In addition to his successful career at the Opéra, Norblin was named first violoncello of the Chapelle Royale during the reign of Louis-Philippe and, upon Levasseur's death, was given his position at the Conservatoire.[97] Having always maintained close ties with the Conservatoire, Norblin began playing chamber music with Baillot in 1809 and, after Lamare retired in 1815, assumed the role of first violoncello for Baillot, a relationship he maintained until the violinist's death in 1842.[98]

Norblin was one of the most active and respected performers in Paris and, in addition to being Baillot's favorite accompanist, aided Habeneck in establishing the Société des Concerts du Conservatoire in 1828. This performance group was responsible for introducing Beethoven's works to Parisian audiences. Norblin was also helpful in introducing his fellow countryman Chopin to the Parisian musical establishment, for which Chopin was deeply grateful.[99] Norblin retired to his country estate in 1846. An avid numismatist, he left a noteworthy collection upon his death, which occurred in Commentry on July 14, 1854.

Olive-Charlier Vaslin was born in Montreuil-Bellay on March 10, 1794. He was considered a gifted young man and entered the Conservatoire at age fourteen. Studying under Baudiot, he took a second prize in 1809 and 1810, and his first prize in 1811.[100] Vaslin was employed in the orchestra of the Théâtre des Variétés in 1809, while he was undertaking his studies. He became a member of the Opéra orchestra in 1814.[101]

95 Vidal, *Les instruments à archet*, vol. II, p. 365.
96 Fétis, *Biographie universelle*, vol. II supplement, p. 278.
97 Lassabathie, *Histoire du Conservatoire*, p. 377.
98 Fauquet, *Les sociétés de musique de chambre*, pp. 36, 271.
99 *Correspondence of Chopin*, p. 83.
100 Pierre, *Conservatoire*, p. 616.
101 *The Musical Times*, 30, no. 559 (September 1, 1889), 548.

Vaslin is one of the most elusive figures in the history of this period. He was always obscured by Norblin and little is known about his career.[102] By his own words, he was a great admirer of Baillot and the majority of his performance opportunities resulted from his association with the violinist. Vaslin assumed the position of second violoncello with Baillot's quintet between 1820 and 1840.[103] He also occupied the first violoncello position in the concert association of the Athénée Musical, a group whose purpose was to sponsor the performances of young artists and their works. In this capacity, he gave at least one performance of the first violoncello part to the overture of Rossini's *Guillaume Tèll.*[104]

Another mark of Vaslin's standing in the community was his accession to Baudiot's position at the Conservatoire in 1827. He held this chair until 1859. Twenty-five years after his retirement, he collated his memories and observations on performance into his violoncello method, which was published in 1884. He died in Saint Julien-sur-Sarthe on August 5, 1889.

Auguste Franchomme was born in Lille on April 10, 1808. Fétis reported that Franchomme began his study of the violoncello at the age of twelve under the supervision of Mas at the Lille Conservatory. Van der Straeten added that he received his first prize at this institution in 1821 and then continued his studies there with Pierre Baumann. Franchomme then came to Paris, studying at the Conservatoire under Norblin and taking his first prize at the end of 1825.[105]

In the following three years, Franchomme held several orchestral positions. The first, commencing in 1825, was at the Théâtre de l'Ambigu-Comique. In 1827, he took a position in the Opéra orchestra, but left the following year for an appointment as solo violoncellist at the Théâtre-italien and solo violoncello of the Chapelle Royale, sharing the first desk of the latter with his teacher, Norblin.[106]

Franchomme continued his association with the Conservatoire and was a founding member in 1828, together with Habeneck and Norblin, of the Société des Concerts du Conservatoire. He retired from orchestral work in 1833 and pursued his career as a soloist and chamber musician. With his close friend the violinist Alard, he founded the Concerts du Cercle Musical in 1834, and, in 1847, the Matinées Annuelles de Quatuors. Franchomme developed close performing relationships with many of the visiting and expatriate musicians who worked in Paris during these years, including

102 Niecks reported that "Vaslin, although he did not fall out of the race until 1859, never played an important part [in Parisian musical life] not withstanding his professorship at the Conservatoire." Niecks, "Recollections of Violoncellists," no. 582, 121–123.
103 Fauquet, *Les sociétés de musique de chambre*, pp. 271–272.
104 *Revue Musicale*, 7, no. 42 (November 16, 1833), 335.
105 Pierre, *Conservatoire*, p. 970.
106 François-Sappey, "Mémoires d'Eugène Sauzay," 196.

Moscheles, Liszt, Mendelssohn, and Charles Hallé. However, he was best known for his friendship with Chopin, to whom he was introduced by Ferdinand Hiller at a dinner party, at which Liszt was also in attendance.[107] Chopin and Franchomme collaborated on the composition of the *Grand Duo Concertant pour Piano et Violoncelle sur des Thèmes de Robert le Diable* (1833) and Franchomme assisted with, and premiered, Chopin's Sonata for Violoncello and Piano op. 65.

Franchomme was given Norblin's position at the Conservatoire in 1846, remaining there until 1884. Although he rarely performed outside of Paris, Franchomme did make two trips to England, visiting the Moscheles family in 1837 and 1856.[108] He died in Paris on January 21, 1884.

GREAT BRITAIN

The development of violoncello playing in Great Britain is closely associated with the presence of many expatriate musicians. Numerous Italian violoncellists worked in London during the mid-part of the eighteenth century, while Austrian and German performers immigrated in the later years. The Duport brothers likewise exerted influence on English violoncellists, both men visiting and performing in England, and J. L. Duport enjoyed a close relationship with Crosdill. Notwithstanding the vital performance climate in Great Britain, a genuine English school did not really exist until the founding of the Royal Academy of Music in 1822, whose first professor of violoncello was Robert Lindley. The antecedents of this school can be traced to G. B. Cervetto. Although the vibrancy of London's musical institutions sustained that city as the cultural center of Great Britain, Scotland also supported a flourishing school of violoncello in the years around the turn of the nineteenth century. This was due to the intermarriage of Johann Schetky with the Reinagle family.[109] This legacy was then carried on through the work of John Gunn.

Violoncello methods published in Great Britain demonstrate the variety of influences present. French performance practices were prevalent, as evinced in the numerous acknowledged and plagiarized English editions of the Conservatoire method. The methods of Crouch (1827) and Merrick (before 1855) fall into this category. Lindley (before 1855), on the other hand, attributed his fingering system to J. L. Duport. The German style was

---

107 Frederick Niecks, "Recollections of Violoncellists," *Monthly Musical Record*, 49, no. 583 (July 1, 1919), 147.
108 Charlotte Moscheles, ed., *Recent Music and Musicians as Described in the Diaries and Correspondence of Ignatz Moscheles*, trans. A. D. Coleridge (New York: Henry Holt and Co., 1889), p. 239.
109 For a description of Edinburgh's musical life, see Michael Kelly, *Reminiscences*, ed. Roger Fiske (Oxford University Press, 1975), pp. 212–213.

transmitted through the publications of Schetky (1811), Gunn (1793), and
Reinagle (1800), while local traditions are found in the violoncello methods of Crome (1765) and John MacDonald (1811), in at least ten anonymous works, including that published by Clementi, Banger, Hyde, Collard
& Davis (1800–10), and in the method of Charles Eley (1830).

The story of the Scottish violoncello school begins with Johann Georg
Christoph Schetky, born in Darmstadt on August 19, 1737. Schetky was a
member of a musical family, the father being a secretary and singer in the
court of Hesse-Darmstadt. While he may have studied law at Jena, Schetky
was employed from the age of fifteen as first violoncello in the Darmstadt
orchestra. It is said that he was self-taught, with the exception of a month's
studies with Filtz at nearby Mannheim. Eager to compose, in addition to
playing his instrument, he studied thorough-bass with the Darmstadt vice-
Kapellmeister Endler. He began performing his own works in the same
year as he obtained a position with the orchestra, and additionally composed symphonies and chamber music.[110]

Schetky made his first tour in 1763, traveling to Hamburg with his family
for a successful series of concerts. Although the Darmstadt court refused to
sever his contract, he was allowed to continue intermittent tours until he
left the court in 1768.[111] From Darmstadt, he returned to Hamburg for two
years and then traveled to London. While there, he came under the patronage of Johann Christian Bach and began to publish chamber works.
He then accepted the appointment of first violoncello with the Edinburgh
Musical Society. Having fallen in love with Maria Theresa Reinagle, he
married and remained in Scotland for the rest of his life. Schetky, who was
blind in his left eye, retired from performing in his later years, but continued to compose.[112] He wrote varied works for violoncello, chamber music
ensembles, orchestra, wind band, voice, and two treatises for teaching. His
method for violoncello was dedicated to John Crosdill. Schetky died in
Edinburgh on November 30, 1824.

The Reinagle family, originally from Vienna, in turn produced two violoncello students for Schetky, Maria's brothers, Joseph and Hugh. Both
were born in Portsmouth, in 1762 and 1766, respectively. It was first intended that Joseph would join the Navy, but, after serving a short time as a
midshipman, he was moved to Edinburgh, where he was apprenticed to a
jeweler. The jeweler abandoned the country and it was then decided that
Joseph would join the family profession. He studied French horn and trumpet with his father, becoming sufficiently proficient to publicly perform
concertos.[113]

110 *AMZ* (October 16, 1799), col. 35.
111 David Johnson and Roger Larsson, "Schetky," *NG*, vol. XVI, p. 636.
112 Van der Straeten, *History of the Violoncello*, pp. 191–192.
113 *Dictionary*, ed. Sainsbury, vol. II, p. 348.

Probable tuberculosis made it necessary for Joseph to give up playing his wind instruments and he began working on the violoncello, studying with his brother-in-law, Schetky. Not wishing to be in competition with his younger brother, Joseph took violin lessons from Aragoni and Pinto, and became concertmaster at St. Cecilia's Hall, Edinburgh. Both Hugh and Joseph eventually made their way to London, where Hugh is said to have studied with Crosdill.[114] Concert reports do not clearly differentiate between the brothers, but Hugh's talent was extolled by Gunn, who considered him "the most *promising* performer of the instrument in Europe," as well as an excellent composer.[115] Unfortunately, Hugh apparently suffered from the same disease as his older brother; he died a premature death on March 19, 1785, while trying to recuperate in Lisbon. In London, it was remarked "what musical man of taste but must lament the loss of young Reinagle?"[116]

The Reinagle name was frequently mentioned in London concerts of 1782 and 1783, although it is not clear which brother was the performer. The most frequently cited venue was the New Rooms, Tottenham Street, where performances by a Reinagle included violoncello concertos and vocal accompaniments on the pentachord.[117] However, one of the Reinagles also performed a solo concerto on a subscription concert at the Free Masons Hall, with additional concert advertisements marking assistance with benefits for individual performers.[118] After participating in the Handel commemoration of 1784, Joseph left for Dublin under the patronage of Lord Westmorland; he stayed there for two years.[119]

Returning to London in 1786, Joseph joined the orchestra of Salomon's concerts. He frequently played principal violoncello for Haydn and in company with Viotti and Clementi. He later moved to Oxford, "in which city he was so favorably received, that he was advised by the late Lord Abingdon, and other musical amateurs, to reside there..."[120] In addition to being a respected performer, Reinagle wrote and published numerous works for violoncello, chamber music ensembles, and his method book. He died in Oxford in 1836.

John Gunn was born in Edinburgh about 1765. By his own account, he studied violoncello with Hugh Reinagle.[121] In 1790 Gunn came to London, where he stayed five years. During this time he taught both violoncello and flute, publishing tutors and chamber music for both instruments. The vio-

114 Van der Straeten, *History of the Violoncello*, p. 323.
115 John Gunn, *The Theory and Practice of Fingering the Violoncello* (first edition, London), p. 70.
116 *The Public Advertiser*, July 26, 1785.
117 *The Public Advertiser*, March 13, 1782; May 11, 1782; June 5, 1782; April 10, 1783; April 28, 1783; May 19, 1783; May 26, 1783.
118 *The Public Advertiser*, March 10, 1783; April 28, 1783; May 15, 1783.
119 *Dictionary*, ed. Sainsbury, vol. II, p. 349.
120 Ibid.
121 Gunn, *Theory and Practice*, first ed., p. 70.

loncello method was first published in 1793, and then reissued in a revised form by the author.

Upon returning to Scotland, Gunn married the pianist Anne Young, herself a later writer of a teaching method. Gunn's most important work was considered to be an historical work on the Scotch harp, which was published at the behest of the National Society of Scotland in 1807. He also wrote a treatise on harmony and the performance of thorough-bass, which was published in 1801.[122] He died in Scotland c. 1824.

The two most visible names for violoncello performance in London during the 1770s and 1780s were those of James Cervetto and John Crosdill. Cervetto was born London in 1749 and learned the instrument from his father, G. B. Cervetto. Considered by Londoners as a child prodigy, he began performing in public at age eleven, appearing at his first concert at the Little Haymarket Theatre on April 23, 1760. Also appearing in this children's concert were Gertrude Schmähling, who later became Madame Mara, and pianist Fanny Burney. James was a frequent visitor to the Burney household, often joining his father for chamber music gatherings.[123]

Between 1763 and 1770 Cervetto toured outside of England. Upon returning, he joined the Queen's Chapel in 1771. He additionally substituted for Crosdill as first violoncellist in the 1778 season of the Three Choirs Festival at Gloucester. The other major duty undertaken was that of principal violoncello for the opera, a position relinquished to Crosdill in October 1782.[124] His retirement was undoubtedly tied to his father's final illness and he inherited a substantial fortune upon his father's death in January 1783. Concert reports do indicate that he returned at least briefly to the opera in 1785, as he is listed as performing in Cherubini's *Demetrio*, with the composer himself leading from the keyboard.[125]

Despite his wealth, Cervetto maintained an active schedule, being a frequent member of the Hanover Square concerts, as well as a participant in the private subscription concerts of the nobility.[126] The repertoire of the Hanover Square series included continuo sonatas performed with J. L. Duport in 1783 and advertisements attest to numerous concertos and symphonies concertantes performed by Cervetto.[127] Concert requirements sparked the composition of several sets of sonatas for violoncello, as well as

122 William H. Husk, "Gunn," *A History of Music and Musicians*, ed. George Grove, 4 vols. (London: Macmillan, 1879–89), vol. II, p. 611.
123 Scholes, *The Great Doctor Burney*, vol. I, p. 138.
124 *The Public Advertiser*, October 24, 1782.
125 *The Public Advertiser*, January 10, 1785.
126 "Those very magnificent Concerts at private Houses on Sunday Evenings are established this Winter as usual, – at Lady Archer's – Lady Delme's, – Lord Edgecumbe's, when he returns from Brussels, etc, etc, etc, the Performers, of the same Excellence as usual, Pacchierotti, Cramer, Cervetto, Weiss, Fischer, etc." *The Public Advertiser*, January 1, 1783.
127 *The Public Advertiser*, January 19, 1782; April 4, 1783; February 1, 1785; February 14, 1785.

a set of sonatas for flute and trios for two violins and violoncello. He preferred less public visibility after the success of his student, Robert Lindley,
during the 1790s and little is documented about the remainder of his life.
Cervetto died in London on February 5, 1837.

The story of John Crosdill portrays a man skilled both as a performer
and as a climber of London's social ladder. Born in London in 1755, he was
educated at Westminster School and became a chorister at Westminster
Abbey. His first public appearance was at age nine, when Siprutini, his
probable teacher, presented him in a duo.[128] Crosdill was accepted to the
Royal Society of Musicians in 1768; and during the 1770s, he performed as
principal violoncellist for the Bach–Abel concerts, a position which en-
tailed the execution of solos as well as orchestral parts.[129] He was made a
member of the Chapel Royal in 1777.[130]

Crosdill made the first of many sojourns to Paris in the early 1770s, taking lessons with either Janson or one of the Duports. He soon became close
friends with the Duports and an intimate at court circles. The following
well-known anecdote describing Duport's virtuosity also, of course, implies that Crosdill frequently performed with Duport and Viotti and was a
favorite of Marie Antoinette:

One day in the former queen's small suite, they were waiting for Viotti, to execute
with Krosdell [sic], the famous English violoncellist, whom we have spoken of in
preceding numbers, a duo concertante for violin and violoncello of his own composition and unpublished. Viotti didn't arrive: the queen was just appearing to
notice this, when Duport, who had already played a sonata, demanded to look at
the violin part. Barely having glimpsed the manuscript, he engaged Krosdell to
begin, and played with such superiority that one doubts if Viotti, in executing it on
the violin, could have given as much pleasure.[131]

The 1780s brought Crosdill numerous London successes. In 1782, he was
appointed chamber musician to Queen Charlotte and violoncello instructor to George IV. Through the influence of his royal student, Crosdill
was also given the position in 1784 of Composer and Master of the King's
Band in Ireland by the Duke of Rutland. For this, the violoncellist earned
the enmity of Charles Burney, who had hoped for the appointment himself.[132] London gossip held that the appointment of composer to the Dublin
band should have gone to Burney, Cooke, Jackson, Linley, or Cramer, and
Crosdill's usurpation of the position did not go unnoticed:

128 Pohl, *Mozart und Haydn in London*, vol. I, p. 53.
129 Simon McVeigh, *Concert Life in London from Mozart to Haydn* (Cambridge University Press, 1993),
     pp. 193, 247.
130 James D. Brown and Stephen S. Stratton, *British Musical Biography* (London: William Reeves,
     1897), p. 107.
131 *Correspondance des Amateurs Musiciens*, no. 40 (August 27, 1803), 1.
132 Roger Lonsdale, *Dr. Charles Burney, a Literary Biography* (Oxford: Clarendon Press, 1965), p. 315.

Cordell's [Crosdill's] succession to the Irish band mastership is a very fine sine-
cure to him; the salary is of course subject to the absentee tax, which is 25 per
cent; but when that shall be paid, there will still remain a nett income of above
150l. per ann. and for nothing but composing a couple of annual odes.[133]

This appointment no doubt secured Crosdill the enmity of other musicians
in addition to Burney, for his compositions were not considered on a par
with his performance skills. A review remarks that "though Crosdill is to
be reported for playing thus well, he undoubtedly is not in an equal Degree
select in what he is to play; he undoubtedly does not compose well for the
Instrument."[134]

The multiplicity of Crosdill's London concert reports testifies to his active performance career. In addition to taking Cervetto's position with the
opera in 1782, Crosdill was principal violoncellist for the Concerts of Ancient Music and the Professional Concerts, the latter association requiring
the execution of numerous concertos, continuo sonatas, and chamber music. He also performed for benefit concerts, including annual productions
of *Messiah*, and was principal violoncello for the 1784 Handel commemora-
tive concerts.[135] Private concerts for the nobility were also an important
part of Crosdill's performance schedule, his position as teacher to the
Prince of Wales giving him suitable social cachet. In this guise, he organ-
ised Friday afternoon ladies' concerts for the nobility.[136] During this same
period, Crosdill's work extended to Paris. He was a member of Viotti's
orchestra for the Concert de la Loge Olympique in 1780 and he is listed as
having performed at the Concert Spirituel on August 15, 1784.[137]

Crosdill returned to England permanently in 1785, spending the spring
concert season performing with the Pantheon series. Organized in competition with the Hanover Square series, for which Cervetto played, the Pantheon concerts included numerous performances by the Maras.[138]
Gertrude was one of the great singers of her day and her husband, Johann,
played violoncello. Crosdill became a close friend and, through this relationship, met Haydn in 1791 when the composer was escorted by Salomon
to a dinner party given by Madame Mara.[139] Crosdill later bought the
"Mara" Stradivari in 1802.[140]

133 *The Public Advertiser*, March 9, 1785.
134 *The Public Advertiser*, March 2, 1782.
135 The vast extent of Crosdill's London performances is documented in *The Public Advertiser*
between 1780 and 1785.
136 Pohl, *Mozart und Haydn in London*, vol. II, p. 54.
137 Pierre, *Histoire du Concert Spirituel*, p. 327.
138 *The Public Advertiser*, January 8, 1785
139 Karl Geiringer, *Haydn: a Creative Life in Music* (third edition, Berkeley: University of California
Press, 1982), p. 102.
140 While Johann Mara was considered one of the foremost violoncellists of the day, he is remembered in history primarily for his addiction to alcohol. See Hill, *Stradivari*, p. 133.

The summer of 1785 saw Crosdill raising social eyebrows once again, marrying the seventy-year-old widow Mrs. Colebrooke. Her wealth allowed him to retire from most professional appearances, but did not pass without comment on the society pages:

The particulars of Crosdell's late marriage with Mrs. Colebrooke are to this effect: – She is in the full maturity of almost three-score years and ten. She carries, however, weight for age, having no less than twenty-five thousand pounds in money, and a jointure of 1500l. a year. – The gentleman, per contra, whose good parts are barely thirty, is to give up playing in public, or having any scholars under him but his Royal Highness the Prince of Wales. Of course Mara [Johann] must be accompanied, and the town consoled with the violoncello of Cervetto.[141]

Crosdill did, in fact, largely adhere to the strictures of his marriage contract. Public performances after 1785 were limited to two further years of the Three Choirs Festival in Gloucester and Michael Kelly mentioned that Crosdill performed in Dublin during the summer months of 1787, one of numerous London musicians who were engaged for the season.[142] Crosdill also maintained his position with the court and performed at the coronation of George IV, Lindley acting as his accompanist.[143] It is likely that Crosdill made a later, subsequent marriage, as his only son, Lieutenant Colonel Crosdill, of the East India Company, presented the Royal Society of Musicians £1,000 upon his father's death. Crosdill died in Escrick, Yorkshire in October 1825.[144]

Robert Lindley was born in Rotherham on March 4, 1776. His father, an amateur violoncellist, introduced him to the violin at age five, adding instruction on the violoncello at age nine. Lindley began his public career at age eleven performing concertos. At sixteen, he played for James Cervetto, who generously gave him free lessons. Professionally, Lindley first began playing at the Brighton Theatre, gaining the attention of the Prince of Wales while there.[145] The concert season of 1792 saw him presented to the London public at the Professional Concerts and in the interludes of the oratorio series at the Haymarket Theatre.[146] He was appointed principal with the Opera orchestra in 1794, the same year as Dragonetti, with whom he shared a desk and many solo engagements. Contemporaries found the pair remarkable; Henry Chorley wrote:

There was no escaping from the entrance of Lindley and Dragonetti into the orchestra: a pair of favorite figures, whose sociable companionship for some thirty

141 *The Public Advertiser*, July 26, 1785.
142 Kelly, *Reminiscences*, p. 4.
143 "Rise and Progress of the Violoncello," 475.
144 William H. Husk, "Crosdill," *A Dictionary of Music and Musicians*, ed. Grove, vol. I, p. 420.
145 "Rise and Progress of the Violoncello," 479.
146 *The Public Advertiser*, February 7, 1792; February 17, 1792; February 24, 1792; March 7, 1792; March 9, 1792.

years was as remarkable as their appearance was contrasted – no two faces imaginable being more unlike than the round, good-humoured, comely visage of the Yorkshireman from that of the gaunt Venetian, as brown and as tough as one of his own strings. On what the affectionate regard maintained between them was fed it is hard to say; for both were next to unintelligible in their speech – the Englishman from an impediment in utterance, the Italian from the disarranged mixture of many languages in which he expressed his sentiments and narrated his adventures. They talked to each other on the violoncello and double bass, bending their heads with quiet confidential smiles, which were truly humorous to see.[147]

The two performers were best known for performing Corelli trio sonatas, either with violin, violoncello, and bass, or with two violoncellos and bass.[148] Lindley also played with the orchestras of the Philharmonic Society, the Ancient Music concerts, and with festival orchestras all over England. He was beloved by English audiences as a native-born performer; a contemporary wrote that "there is no concert of any note, and no festival at which Lindley is not a prominent attraction."[149]

Lindley wrote and performed his own concertos and concert pieces, receiving mixed reviews from critics. His technique and sound production were considered superb, but his compositions received fewer accolades. His fame rested with his ability to accompany, particularly in recitatives. In addition to four concertos, concert pieces, a trio and several duos, Lindley published his elementary *Handbook for the Violoncello* and the more demanding op. 15 *Capriccios and Exercises for the Violoncello*. He was appointed to the Royal Academy of Music in 1822 and complimented by the visiting Fétis for having "formed good pupils in the academy."[150] Outliving Dragonetti, who died in 1846, Lindley continued to perform until 1850. He died in London on June 13, 1855.

AUSTRIA, GERMANY, AND EASTERN EUROPE

As in France, the violoncello was introduced into Germany by Italian musicians and, similarly, gained slow acceptance among court musicians because of the preference for the viola da gamba. Unlike France, whose cultural center was to be found only in Paris, Austria and Germany were loosely unified as political entities and, by the mid-part of the eighteenth century, several cities achieved distinction for supporting good-quality vio-

147 Henry F. Chorley, *Musical Recollections* (New York: Alfred A. Knopf, 1926), pp. 56–57.
148 *The Harmonicon*, 1, no. 4 (April 1823), 58; 1, no. 7 (July 1823), 100; 4, no. 42 (June 1826), 130; 6, no. 6 (June 1828), 142; 7, no. 7 (July 1829), 175.
149 "Rise and Progress of the Violoncello," 475.
150 "M. Fétis on the State of Music in London," *The Harmonicon*, 7, no. 9 (September 1829), 219.

loncello performance. Vienna and Berlin were continuing musical centers, reflecting political importance maintained throughout the eighteenth and nineteenth centuries. With the exception of these two capitals, other places of musical significance shifted throughout the centuries, owing to the vagaries of dynastic and political reorganizations. For instance, Mannheim cultivated violoncello playing during the mid-part of the eighteenth century. However, when the Elector Carl Theodor inherited the Electorship of both Bavaria and Mannheim in 1778, Mannheim ceased to be a musical center as the court was removed to Munich. This, of course, resulted in Munich gaining new cultural energy.

Other cities drawing historically significant musicians to their court orchestras were Bonn and Dresden. The Bonn Kapelle, home at one point to Joseph and Anton Reicha, Bernhard and Andreas Romberg, and Ludwig van Beethoven, was dissolved in 1792 during the French invasion, never to be restructured. Dresden was able to maintain greater political and economic continuity and supported a reputable court orchestra during the majority of the eighteenth and nineteenth centuries.[151] Its notability for violoncello performance is due to the participation of Tricklir and the Romberg protégés Dotzauer and Kummer.

The presence of proficient violoncellists within the many Kapellen also fostered the composition of numerous works for the instrument by non-violoncellists. The Bach suites from the early part of the century are the most appreciated example, but concertos were later written in Vienna by Monn and Wagenseil, at Esterháza by Haydn, and in Berlin by C. P. E. Bach and Carl Stamitz. With the exception of publications by Baumgartner (1774) and Kauer (1788), the writing of violoncello methods came after the turn of the nineteenth century. Individual methods were published by J. Alexander (c. 1801), J. Fröhlich (Simrock, 1808), and Bernard Stiastny (1829). Subsequent tutors – Dotzauer (1832), Kummer (1839), and Romberg (1839) – are associated with the Dresden school.

The first German method for violoncello was published by Johann Baptist Baumgartner, who was born in Augsburg in 1723. Remaining in that city until the prince-bishop's death in 1768, he then toured England, Scandinavia, and Germany before settling for a time in Amsterdam, where his method was published.[152] The year following this event, he was offered a position with the royal orchestra in Stockholm, but was forced to resign owing to ill health caused by the cold. He resurrected his peripatetic career, touring cities of the Holy Roman Empire before taking a post at the Bavarian court of Eichstätt, where he died on May 18, 1782. In

---

151 Burney reported in 1775 that both Rousseau and J. A. Hasse considered Dresden's orchestra to be among Europe's finest; see Charles Burney, *An Eighteenth-Century Musical Tour in Central Europe and the Netherlands,* ed. Percy A. Scholes, 2 vols. (Oxford University Press, 1959), vol. II, p. 118. Nineteenth-century conductors included Carl Maria von Weber and Richard Wagner.
152 Herbert Seifert, "Baumgartner," *NG,* vol. II, p. 303.

addition to his method, Baumgartner composed four concertos and works for solo violoncello. He was also reported as being an agreeable singer.[153]

The Mannheim school was initiated by Anton Filtz (Fils). He was baptized in Eichstätt on September 22, 1733. Filtz was the son of Johann Georg Filtz, a violoncellist attached to the court. Anton attended local schools and most likely studied violoncello with his father. He left Eichstätt in 1753; by then both his parents had died and his step-mother was married to another violoncellist at the court. After studying law and theology at the university in Ingolstadt, he joined the Mannheim court in 1754.[154]

At Mannheim, Filtz was employed as second violoncellist under Innocenz Danzi. He also took the opportunity of studying composition with Johann Stamitz. During the following six years, Filtz composed a vast amount of music, including masses, symphonies, concertos, chamber music, and works for violoncello.[155] Well on his way to success within the court, he married in 1757 and was able to buy a house in May of 1759, his wife having given birth to a daughter. Ten months later Filtz was dead: he was buried on March 14, 1760.[156] Four months after his death, La Chevardière in Paris brought out his first symphony, the first of numerous publications which gained Filtz posthumous international attention.

Peter Ritter was a native Mannheimer, born on July 2, 1763. The family trade was music, his father and uncle having been engaged at the court since 1756. Peter studied violoncello with Innocenz Danzi and thoroughbass with Abbé Vogler.[157] He undertook his first concert tour at thirteen, appearing with other family members in Frankfurt. Demonstrating an early flair for composition, he had his first symphony performed when he was sixteen and Abbé Vogler published a string quartet by Ritter in the *Musikalische Monatsschrift* the following year.[158]

The larger part of the court orchestra was moved to Bavaria in 1778, but Ritter remained in Mannheim, sharing a desk in the small opera orchestra with Franz Danzi and then taking the first violoncello position in 1784, when Danzi left to take his father's position in Munich. Ritter continued to travel, visiting J. P. Duport in Berlin in 1785. According to Ritter's own autobiography, included in the biography published by Wilhelm Schulze, not only did he play one of his own concertos for Duport, but his father had the boy entertain his audience by sightreading one of Duport's concer-

---

153 "Rise and Progress of the Violoncello," 479.
154 *Johann Anton Fils (1733–1760): Ein Eichstätter Komponist der Mannheimer Klassik* (Tutzing: Hans Schneider, 1983), p. 55.
155 Gerber, *Lexikon*, vol. I, cols. 409–410.
156 *Johann Anton Fils*, p. 55.
157 Josephine Elsen, "The Instrumental Works of Peter Ritter" (Ph.D. thesis, Northwestern University, 1967), pp. 1–2.
158 Van der Straeten, *History of the Violoncello*, pp. 202–203.

tos with the music upside-down on the music desk.[159] Ritter later composed a set of string quartets dedicated to the Prussian King upon Friedrich Wilhelm II's elevation.

The primary focus of the Mannheim orchestra after 1778 was theater and Ritter gained prominence through the composition of *Singspiele*. He also continued writing concertos for his own use and chamber music, including quartets with violoncello obbligato. The Mannheim Kapelle maintained its reputation for supporting German music and Mozart visited several times, the last time being in 1790 to hear *Le nozze di Figaro*, whose performance was not then allowed in Munich.[160]

The outbreak of war was devastating for Mannheim, whose citizens experienced battles and occupation. Ritter was one of the few musicians to remain at Mannheim, frequently working without pay. He became adept at using amateurs from the community to augment the court's dwindling resources and this success led to his appointment as Kapellmeister in 1801.[161] When Mannheim became part of the Grand Duchy of Baden in 1803, Ritter remained as Kapellmeister. Continuing to compose and perform music with his orchestra, Ritter, with the flutist Appold, was called to perform for Napoleon at Karlsruhe in January 1806. He also took a trip to Paris in May 1809.[162]

French control of the Federation of the Rhine led to the normalization of daily life and the return of touring virtuosos. Louis Spohr visited in 1807 and Carl Maria von Weber stayed in Mannheim through 1810–11, the latter's visit eliciting antagonism from Ritter, who perceived that Weber desired his position.[163] In these later years, Ritter maintained distinction by his stage productions, but he continued to play and teach the violoncello. Apparently he required little practice to retain his performing skills; a student, Alexander von Dusch, described his teacher's ability thus:

His great virtuosity on the cello, which for him in this later time was such a completely indifferent matter of secondary importance, was all the more to be wondered at, since he no longer, with the exception, of course, of almost daily orchestra rehearsals, devoted the least practice to this accomplishment, which was just as much talent as earlier exhausting industry.[164]

159 Gisela Blees, *Das Cello-Konzert um 1800: Eine Untersuchung der Cello-Konzerte zwischen Haydns op. 101 und Schumanns op. 129* (Regensburg: Gustav Bosse Verlag, 1973), p. 38.
160 Aug. Guil. Iffland, *Collection des mémoires sur l'art dramatique* (Paris: Chez Etienne Ledoux, 1823), p. 118.
161 Elsen, "Instrumental Works of Peter Ritter," pp. 16–17.
162 Ibid., pp. 34–38.
163 Carl Maria von Weber, *Writings on Music*, ed. John Warrack, trans. Martin Cooper (Cambridge University Press, 1981), pp. 41–42, 64.
164 Quoted in Elsen, "Instrumental Works of Peter Ritter," p. 28.

Little is known about the end of Ritter's life. He attempted to establish a music conservatory in Mannheim in 1819, but encountered difficulties. He took his retirement on October 1, 1823, ending his composing as well as his performing and conducting career. He died in Mannheim on July 31, 1846.

The Dresden school of violoncello took root from the performance practices of Bernhard Romberg. He was born into a family of professional musicians in Dinklage, Lower Saxony on November 13, 1767. The family left Dinklage for Münster in 1769, both father and uncle taking positions with the orchestra of the Archbishop. It was a tightly-knit family: Bernhard was raised with his cousin Andreas, a violinist, the two musicians being frequently mistaken for brothers.[165]

It is generally believed that Romberg's early training was with his father and the violoncellist Johann Conrad Schlick. Bernhard began touring with Andreas at an early age, appearing in Holland in 1776, Leipzig in 1780, and Frankfurt am Main in 1782.[166] In Frankfurt, they made acquaintance with Christian Gottlob Neefe.[167] The most educational tour of these early years was in the spring of 1785, when the Rombergs traveled to Paris. Coming under the sponsorship of Baron de Bagge, they played for A. Philidor, Viotti, and J. L. Duport. The Rombergs also gave multiple performances in February, March, and April at the Concert Spirituel.[168]

Bernhard and Andreas returned to work alongside their parents at Münster Cathedral until 1790, when Neefe sponsored their employment with the Bonn Kapelle. Bernhard became good friends with the younger Beethoven; both young men played chamber music together and studied composition with Neefe. It is here that they met Haydn for the first time.[169] With the dissolution of the Kapelle in 1792, the Rombergs returned for a short time to Münster, before obtaining employment at Schröder's theater in Hamburg. On a leave of absence in 1795, they toured Germany, Switzerland, and Italy, visiting with Piccini, Paisiello, and Lolli while in Italy.[170] The cousins returned by way of Vienna, coming under the sponsorship of Haydn, to whom both young composers dedicated their op. 1 string quartets.[171] Bernhard also gave the first Viennese performance of Beethoven's

165 *AMZ* (November 1798), col. 126.
166 Lev Ginsburg, *History of the Violoncello*, ed. Dr. Herbert Axelrod, trans. Tanya Tchistyakova (Neptune City, New Jersey: Paganiniana Publications, 1983), p. 16.
167 Irmgard Leur, "Christian Gottlob Neefe und Andreas Romberg," *Zeitschrift für Musikwissenschaft*, 7, no. 137 (1925), 655.
168 Pierre, *Histoire du Concert Spirituel*, p. 328.
169 Franz Wegeler and Ferdinand Ries, *Beethoven Remembered*, trans. Frederick Noonan (Arlington, Virginia: Great Ocean Publishers, 1987), pp. 21–22.
170 *AMZ* (October 1798), cols. 46–48; (November 1798), cols. 111–112; (July 1799), cols. 685–686; (August 1799), cols. 760–764.
171 H. C. Robbins Landon, "Haydn: The Years of 'The Creation' 1796–1800," vol. IV of *Haydn Chronicle and Works*, 4 vols. (Bloomington: Indiana University Press, 1977), pp. 111–112.

op. 5 sonatas with the composer.[172] The Rombergs then left for Hamburg, returning to work at the theater until 1799.

Bernhard resumed touring at this point, traveling to London, Portugal, and Spain, where he visited Boccherini. He then left for Paris; Andreas joined him there. Bernhard was extremely successful in Paris, producing an opera and performing public solos. Although he briefly returned to Hamburg to be married, he returned to France in the fall of 1800, receiving an appointment at the Paris Conservatoire.[173] He stayed for two years, teaching alongside Levasseur, Baudiot, Janson, Kreutzer, Rode, and Baillot. Numerous compositions were also published. All these activities gained him wide attention throughout the musical community.

It is not known why Romberg left the Conservatoire, but he was in Hamburg by the end of 1803, leaving shortly thereafter for Berlin. German concert reports were rapturous about his playing and his compositions, one review stating that he performed with such "ease and unaffectedness that one didn't know whether to be more astonished over the art or the artist."[174] The success of Romberg's Berlin concerts led to an appointment with the Berlin Kapelle. For the next eighteen months he shared a desk with J. L. Duport at the Berlin opera. Romberg also played chamber music with Spohr and continued to perform, publish, and teach. Max Bohrer met with him in Vienna in 1805 and Dotzauer came to study in 1806, living with the Rombergs for six months.[175]

The Berlin Kapelle was disbanded with the French invasion of 1806. Romberg resumed touring, eventually reaching Moscow. Coming under the patronage of Counts Saltikov and Viel'gorsky, and Prince Golitzin, he moved his family there in 1810.[176] While in Russia, Romberg renewed his relationship with a student from his Bonn days, Ferdinand Ries. The two artists performed throughout Russia and Ries composed two sonatas for Romberg. Caught in yet another French invasion in 1812, the two musicians escaped Russia via Sweden, almost drowning in their crossing of the Gulf of Finland.[177]

Romberg continued his travels, performing in Sweden, Hungary, Germany, and Vienna. Ries had left for England, where Romberg joined him in 1814; the two gave a concert with Ries and Sir George Smart at Willis's Rooms in London on June 27.[178] Romberg was back in Berlin by October, giving performances that continued to amaze critics. E. T. A. Hoffmann wrote of a January 1815 concert:

---

172 Wegeler and Ries, *Beethoven Remembered*, p. 157.
173 Pierre, *Conservatoire*, p. 478.
174 *AMZ* (May 1804), col. 588.
175 *AMZ* (December 1806), col. 204.
176 Ginsburg, *History of the Violoncello*, pp. 28–29.
177 "Memoir of Ferdinand Ries," *The Harmonicon*, 2, no. 15 (March 1824), 33–35.
178 *The Times*, June 23, 1814.

The total freedom of his playing and absolute mastery of his instrument obviate any struggle with the mechanical means of expression and make the instrument an immediate, unfettered organ of the spirit...Romberg possesses all the qualities one customarily extols in cellists to such a high degree that for the present at least he is unsurpassed.[179]

Romberg returned to a position with the Berlin Kapelle in 1816, as second Kapellmeister. He held this position until 1819, when Spontini was appointed. Concentrating on opera production during this period, a genre in which he had continually aspired for distinction, Romberg directed the first performance of E. T. A. Hoffmann's *Undine* in 1816 and produced his own final opera, *Rittertreue*, in 1819.

After leaving Berlin, Romberg resumed touring and composing. Performing from Paris to Russia, frequently with his son and daughter, he was dubbed "the Hero of all Violoncellists, the King of all Virtuosos."[180] His concerts earned record receipts and he commanded international acclaim. Numerous young performers worked with him, including Nicolaus Kraft, Merk, Mendelssohn, and Moscheles. Residing in Hamburg during the summer months when he was not on tour, Romberg opened a piano factory, which he operated with success.[181]

Romberg continued to mesmerize audiences with long, demanding performances through 1836. A Viennese report from 1833 reads:

Bernhard Romberg, the king of violoncellists, introduced himself to the public in the *Hof-Operntheater*, with two concertinos, a fantasia on Norwegian mountain airs, and a humorous melodic tableau, under the title of the *Masked Ball*...Even those who are not particularly fond of the picturesque in music, could not help being pleased with the characteristic conception of the individual component parts of this medley, their ingenious combination into a consistent whole, and lastly, with the high skill and unique talent displayed by the master; for Romberg, although advanced in years, still continues to be the same great artist as hitherto, his instrument sings as sweetly as before, he playfully dallies with the most deterring difficulties, and will probably remain unexcelled for a long time to come.[182]

Romberg spent his retirement writing his violoncello method, which was published in 1839 in France and England, and in Germany in 1840. The method was accepted by Cherubini and Norblin for use at the Paris Conservatoire and was sponsored in England by Moscheles.[183] Romberg died in Hamburg of a lung ailment on August 13, 1841.

Justus Johann Friedrich Dotzauer was born in the small Thuringian town

---

179 *AMZ* (January 1815), cols. 19–20; trans. in *E. T. A. Hoffmann's Musical Writings*, ed. David Charlton, trans. Martyn Clarke (Cambridge University Press, 1989), pp. 389–391.
180 *AMZ*, no. 9 (February 1822), col. 146.
181 Schäfer, *Romberg*, p. 95.
182 *AMZ*, no. 24 (June 1833), col. 393, reprinted in *The Harmonicon*, 9, no. 9 (September 1833), 202.
183 Schäfer, *Romberg*, p. 108; Moscheles, *Recent Music and Musicians*, p. 254.

of Häselrieth on January 20, 1783. His father was a church pastor and encouraged his son to study piano, violin, violoncello, double bass, French horn, and clarinet. Young Dotzauer also studied theory and composition with Rüttingen, a student of J. S. Bach's pupil Johann Kittel.[184] Choosing to devote himself to the violoncello, Dotzauer moved to Meiningen in 1799 to study with J. L. Duport's student J. J. Kriegck. He remained for two years and then took a position at the court of Coburg until 1805, when he moved to Leipzig. Dotzauer was an active performer during these years, playing solos and chamber music, in addition to his orchestral work.[185]

Concert reports indicate that Dotzauer left for Berlin in 1806, studying and living with Romberg for six months.[186] It is also probable that he met the Duports during this period. This study time initiated new successes for Dotzauer, for he gained increased recognition for his solo and chamber music appearances, and for his published music. He left Leipzig for a position at Dresden in 1811, the year that Tricklir retired.

Dotzauer remained at Dresden for the remainder of his life, being appointed principal violoncello in 1821. In his capacity as an orchestra musician, he worked under both Carl Maria von Weber and Richard Wagner. He continued to tour as a soloist, although reviewers varied in their assessment of his performances. At times he was criticized for intonation problems in double-stop and octave passages, while other performances elicited praise for his skill, sensitivity, and beautiful sound.[187] Dotzauer's chamber music recitals were given general acclamation; his performances of this genre were numerous owing to his position at the court.

Dotzauer's greatest recognition, however, came for his abilities as a composer, teacher, and writer of teaching material. The most prolific violoncellist/composer of his era, he wrote copiously for violoncello and chamber music ensembles, and composed orchestral and vocal music, including religious works. He was also one of the first violoncellists to make an edition of the Bach suites. Dotzauer published his first violoncello method in 1832. An amalgamation of the methodology of Romberg and J. L. Duport, it was followed by three other teaching works. This material was lauded by contemporaries who considered that "there is no man who is as known and as loved by both teachers and students, as Dotzauer."[188] He died in Dresden on March 6, 1860.

Max Bohrer was born in Munich in 1785. His father was the principal contrabass player with the Munich Kapelle and he was raised with three older brothers who studied violin and viola. Trained in Mannheim traditions by Franz Danzi and violoncellist Anton Schwartz, Max made his first

184 Van der Straeten, *History of the Violoncello*, p. 240.
185 *BMZ*, no. 88 (1805), 350; no. 1 (1806), 4; no. 2 (1806), 8.
186 *AMZ* (December 1806), col. 204; (December 1806), col. 217.
187 *AMZ* (January 1818), col. 53; (February 1815), col. 94.
188 *AMZ*, no. 56 (September 1841), cols. 739–730.

tour at age ten, when he and his brothers were promoted as a prodigy string quartet.[189] The death of two of his brothers in 1805 left him and his brother Anton as an inseparable violin/violoncello duo, much like the Romberg cousins.[190] The two brothers toured continually and Max made Romberg's acquaintance while in Vienna in 1805. According to Fétis, who seems to have known the Bohrers while the brothers were in Paris, this event had a significant impact on Max's style of playing. Concert reports were laudatory: the duo's strength rested on Max's virtuosity and Anton's talent as a composer. Their success as performers led to both publishing concertos, duos, and chamber music.

A tour in 1811 found them in Vienna, Hungary, Poland, and Russia. While in Kiev, Anton became ill and they were forced to stay there for four months. Finally able to leave for Moscow, they came directly into the path of the invading French and the defending Russian armies. Taken prisoner by the Cossacks, according to Fétis, they were only saved from being sent to Siberia by the fact that General Seblowsky, the commanding officer, was a passionate musical amateur. He had them escorted to St. Petersburg, where they remained until 1814.

The brothers left Russia by way of Sweden and Holland, traveling next to England. They stayed in England for one season, "during which, they were much admired for the neatness of their execution, and for the accuracy that the habit of playing together had produced."[191] In 1816 the Bohrers arrived in Paris, where they stayed for two years. Max performed on a Concert Spirituel program in which J. L. Duport was a member of the orchestra. The review noted that the beautiful playing of the older violoncellist was not suitably appreciated because "the playing of the young Bohrer, this wonderman" had not yet died away in the ears of the audience.[192] Bohrer did not, however, sustain his popularity with the Parisian critics, who began to complain that his playing had little emotional depth and was too "German." [193]

The Bohrers returned to Germany for a short time, during which Max replaced Romberg as principal violoncellist in Berlin.[194] Concert reports indicate that they returned to Paris in 1819, where they remained until 1830, albeit making numerous tours. In Paris, they participated in soirees and gained special popularity for their performances of the late Beethoven quartets.[195] Both brothers also composed and published, performances of their new compositions continuing to generate venomous, parochial re-

189 Fétis, *Biographie universelle*, vol. I, pp. 477–478.
190 Van der Straeten, *History of the Violoncello*, p. 244.
191 "Diary of a Dilettante," *The Harmonicon*, 6, no. 5 (May 1828), 110.
192 *AMZ* (February 1817), col. 150.
193 *AMZ* (May 1818), cols. 345–346.
194 Fétis, *Biographie universelle*, vol. I, pp. 477–478.
195 For Berlioz's ecstatic opinion, see *The Memoirs of Hector Berlioz*, ed. and trans. David Cairns (New York: Alfred A. Knopf, 1969), p. 345.

views from French critics. This attitude incensed at least one English writer, who remarked on French bias in a report from Paris for *The Harmonicon*. "[A] celebrated" French critic is quoted as having written about the Bohrers' new Fantasia for violin and violoncello as follows:

An eternal wandering from subject to subject, adopted without design, and abandoned without motive, can have no other effect than to excite weariness and disgust, which all the ability of these performers is unable to dispel. The MM. Bohrer are sadly mistaken if they imagine that they can succeed in Paris with music like this: in England, where these gentlemen have resided for some time, and *where a taste for futile music is so predominant*, such things may do; but we have too many persons of taste among us, of sufficient influence to prevent the introduction of such charlatanism here![196]

One detour took them home to Munich, where they each married a daughter of the renowned piano maker Johann Ludwig Dülken. They returned to London in June 1828, gaining the patronage of members of the Royal Family. Notwithstanding this influential support, it was remarked that in two concerts given on the 13th and 16th, their audiences were very small. Performing under the baton of Moscheles on the 16th, "the two brothers played in a most delightful manner," according to the reviewer.[197]

The brothers finally separated after leaving Paris. Max and his wife joined Nicolaus Kraft at the Kapelle in Stuttgart in 1832, but, by 1837, he was again on tour. In this year he was in Russia, performing under the patronage of Count Viel'gorsky. He was also in England and Vienna, before embarking for the Americas in 1842–43.[198] In 1847, Bohrer returned to Russia, assisting Berlioz with his Moscow concert.[199] Although he was acclaimed for technical accomplishments all of his life, reviews were less kind to Bohrer in these last years, critical of music deemed cold, scientific, and overly virtuoso.[200] Leaving the concert stage after this final tour, he retired in Stuttgart, where he died in 1867.

Friedrich August Kummer was born on August 5, 1797 in Meiningen, where his father was the court oboist. Friedrich began his studies on his father's instrument, but when the family moved to the court of Dresden in 1805, he took up the violoncello. It is not known if he began his studies with Tricklir or one of the other court violoncellists, but Kummer did study with Dotzauer after his arrival in 1811.

Kummer entered the court orchestra as an oboist in 1814, but continued his violoncello practice with rehearsals of the opera orchestra. Weber ap-

196 "Extracts from the Diary of a Dilettante," *The Harmonicon*, 6, no. 5 (May 1828), 110.
197 *The Harmonicon*, 6, no. 7 (July 1828), 168.
198 *Allgemeine Wiener Musik-Zeitung*, no. 32 (March 14, 1844), 138.
199 *Memoirs of Berlioz*, p. 430.
200 Ginsburg, *Istoriya violonchel'nogo*, vol. II, pp. 560–561.

pointed him to fill a violoncello vacancy with the court orchestra in 1817. Kummer soon gained attention with the quality of his solo performances and for his compositions. One reviewer considered that his works "show much talent and fire," and that "he played with great precision and skill." However, this same critic was of the opinion that "if he could have the benefit of instruction from the famous Romberg, he would probably become one of the best artists of his instrument."[201]

Kummer's relationship with Romberg is unclear. Fétis states that he did study with the older violoncellist while Romberg was in Dresden, but exact details are lacking. Kummer evidently did further his technical abilities, for reviews from his tours of the 1820s were unified in their acclaim. Successful publications followed, which became popular with amateur musicians.[202] In the 1830s he began a new relationship with the violinist Franz Schubert; the two musicians toured as a duo and collaborated on works for publication.[203] Kummer also performed extensively as a chamber musician, a duty that went with his appointment as first violoncello following Dotzauer's retirement in 1850.

Kummer, like his teacher, became especially respected for his teaching. He was appointed professor of violoncello at the Dresden Conservatory upon its founding in 1856. His pedagogical writings included several sets of etudes, teaching duets, an innovative book of orchestral studies, orchestration charts, and the *Violoncell-Schule* op. 60, which was first published in 1839 and then later re-edited by the author.[204] Kummer continued his orchestral and chamber music duties until the fiftieth anniversary of his membership in the Dresden Kapelle was celebrated in 1864. He died on August 22, 1879.

Violoncello playing was introduced into Austria by Italian musicians and was highly cultivated, but little is known about individual personalities before Anton Kraft. He was born in Rokitzan, Bohemia on December 30, 1749. Anton learned violoncello as a child, but was sent to the University of Prague to study law. While there, he furthered his instrumental studies with a violoncellist by the name of Werner. Through Werner's connections, Kraft obtained an orchestra position at the Imperial Hofkapelle in Vienna.[205] In Vienna Kraft made the acquaintance of Haydn, who then secured him a place with Prince Esterházy, which commenced in January 1779.

While employed at Esterháza, Kraft studied composition with Haydn, and performed his own compositions as well as his teacher's. He also made

201 *AMZ* (July 1819), cols. 460–461.
202 *AMZ*, no. 40 (October 1831), col. 668.
203 *AMZ*, no. 26 (June 1832), col. 429; (1836), col. 224; (1840), col. 52.
204 Joseph Eckhardt, *Die Violoncellschulen von J. J. F. Dotzauer, F. A. Kummer, und B. Romberg* (Regensburg: Gustav Bosse Verlag, 1968), p. 14.
205 Othmar Wessely, "Kraft," *MGG*, vol. VII, cols. 1679–1680.

occasional tours, at times without permission, transgressions for which he was fined.[206] On one tour in 1789, he and his son, Nicolaus, met Mozart in Dresden; the elder Kraft performed the trio K563 with the composer on April 13.[207] The Krafts remained in Dresden until the end of May and then went to Berlin, where they met with J. P. Duport.

With the dissolution of the Esterháza Kapelle in 1790, the Krafts moved to Vienna. Anton joined the Kapelle of Prince Anton Grassalkovics, but was allowed to tour and to publish his compositions. In 1793, he was also engaged by Prince Lichnowsky to perform in Friday morning chamber music concerts. Haydn was sometimes in attendance and it was here that Beethoven first introduced his op. 1 trios.[208] The following year, Kraft joined violinists Ignaz Schuppanzigh and Louis Sina and violist Franz Weiss in establishing a regular quartet to work closely with Lichnowsky's protégé, Beethoven.

Prince Grassalkovics died in 1794 and Kraft and his son, Nicolaus, obtained positions with Prince Lobkowitz. Kraft was the premier violoncellist in Vienna, regularly performing chamber music in addition to solo engagements. He maintained a good relationship with Beethoven, and it was for Kraft that the younger composer wrote the violoncello part of the op. 56 triple concerto.

Kraft maintained this position within Viennese musical circles until 1808, when animosity between him and Schuppanzigh reached a point where the two could no longer work together. Beethoven's letters indicate that when made to choose between them, he decided that Schuppanzigh was the indispensable performer.[209] Kraft's career disintegrated from this point on, his difficulties acerbated by the financial devastation experienced by Vienna's nobility toward the end of the Napoleonic Wars. He lived with the Lobkowitz family for the remainder of his life, although he probably received little renumeration after 1809. The year before he died, he was given one final honor: an appointment as violoncello teacher to the newly instituted Conservatorium der Gesellschaft der Musikfreunde. He died in Vienna on August 28, 1820.

Nicolaus Kraft was born at Esterháza on December 14, 1778. He began touring with his father at age nine. Upon moving to Vienna in 1790, he was enrolled at the Josephstädter-Gymnasium, but continued to perform.[210] Having visited Berlin as a youngster, he returned in 1801 to study with J. L.

206 János Harich, "Das Haydn-Orchester im Jahr 1780," trans. Eugene Hartzell, *The Haydn Yearbook*, 8 (Bryn Mawr, Pennsylvania: Theodore Presser Co., 1971), pp. 61–62.
207 *The Letters of Mozart to His Family*, ed. and trans. Emily Anderson, 3 vols. (London: Macmillan, 1938), vol. III, p. 1373.
208 Wegeler and Ries, *Beethoven Remembered*, p. 74.
209 *The Letters of Beethoven*, ed. and trans. Emily Anderson, 3 vols. (London: Macmillan, 1961), vol. I, pp. 226–227.
210 Wessely, "Kraft," col. 1681.

Duport, with whom he remained for one year. Kraft then returned to Vienna, and for the following fifteen years worked side by side with his father. He frequently substituted in Schuppanzigh's quartet and was active in Vienna as a soloist, often performing works by Romberg, to whom he later dedicated two of his own concertos.[211] Kraft also worked with Beethoven, and premiered his A major sonata op. 69 in 1809. Released from Prince Lobkowitz's employment this same year, Kraft found a position as solo violoncellist with the Kärntnertortheater.

Nicolaus now began to emerge from the shadow of his father. He continued to be a popular soloist and was offered a position in Stuttgart (which he accepted) during the Congress of Vienna in 1814. Spohr intimated that the Stuttgart Kapelle was a difficult place to work, owing to the despotic nature of the Württemberg kings, Friedrich I (1754–1816) and Wilhelm I (1781–1864), but the position did have advantages for Kraft.[212] He performed with fine professionals, such as bassoonist Anton Romberg and pianist J. N. Hummel, and when Bernhard Romberg visited in 1820, the two violoncellists played together.[213] Furthermore, Kraft's new contract allowed him to tour, which he did from 1815 to 1824. The success of these concerts led to publishing opportunities and he composed numerous violoncello works during these years. Unfortunately, Kraft injured a finger while tuning his violoncello in 1824 and, over the course of time, it proved to be a debilitating problem. He ceased touring, but continued to perform at Stuttgart until 1834. He died in Cheb, Bohemia on May 18, 1853.

Joseph Lincke was born in Trachenberg, Silesia on June 8, 1783. He studied violin and violoncello as a child. A poorly treated sprain from a childhood injury left him permanently lame.[214] After his parents died in 1793, Lincke earned his keep as a music copyist until the Dominican Friars accepted him as a violinist at the monastery in Breslau. There he studied organ, harmony, and violoncello. When his teacher, Lose, retired, Lincke was given the first violoncello position at the theater, whose Kapellmeister from 1804 to 1806 was Carl Maria von Weber.[215] Breslau was occupied by the French in 1808 and in this year Lincke decided to move to Vienna.

In Vienna, Lincke was immediately engaged by Schuppanzigh to replace Anton Kraft in his string quartet, now under the patronage of Count Rasoumowsky. Through this relationship, Lincke became a familiar member of Vienna's musical life, both publicly and privately. The violinist

211 Mary Sue Morrow, *Concert Life in Haydn's Vienna: Aspects of a Developing Musical and Social Institution* (Stuyvesant, New York: Pendragon Press, 1989), pp. 322, 338, 341, 344, 345; Blees, *Das Cello-Konzert um 1800*, p. 178.
212 *Spohr's Autobiography*, vol. I, p. 250.
213 *AMZ*, no. 9 (March 1820), col. 152.
214 *Grove's Dictionary of Music and Musicians*, ed. Eric Blom, 9 vols. (fifth edition, London: Macmillan, 1954), vol. V, p. 238.
215 Fétis, *Biographie universelle*, vol. V, p. 310.

Michael Frey, visiting from Mannheim in 1815, described Lincke's playing thus:

Linke treats his instrument as well as anyone in a quartet can ever manage it. He overcomes all difficulties, fits in so smoothly into the whole, and plays with so much feeling and expression, that one could not wish for him to give more.[216]

Lincke also presented solo concerts, in which – like many other young violoncellists – he performed the works of Romberg.[217] He also gave the first performances of Beethoven's op. 102 sonatas. Frey considered the op. 102 sonata he heard to be "so original, that with only one hearing it was impossible to understand."[218]

Lincke's Viennese life was interrupted in 1815, when Schuppanzigh had to disband the quartet because of the financial problems of the Rasoumowskys and other noble families. Lincke left Vienna for a period with the Erdödy family, but returned by 1818 to take a position as first violoncellist at the Theater an der Wien. He was later employed at the Kärntnertortheater and with the Court opera, where he shared a desk with Joseph Merk. Lincke married in 1818, an occurrence that was greeted with enthusiasm by such friends as Carl Czerny, who described his previous existence as "always so disorganized".[219]

Schuppanzigh returned to Vienna in 1823 and regrouped his quartet. They continued to perform Beethoven's works, but also began introducing the compositions of Schubert to Viennese audiences. Lincke was a close friend of both composers and took upon himself the distressing duty of organizing anniversary concerts after the death of each. Schuppanzigh then died in 1830; thereafter Lincke performed with Joseph Böhm, Carl Holz, and Leopold Jansa. He remained active until 1835 and died on March 26, 1837.

Joseph Merk was born in Vienna on January 18, 1795. The son of a Viennese merchant, Merk began his studies on the violin, performing in public by the time he was fifteen. His promising career as a violinist had to be abandoned when, during a vacation at the family's country home, he was mauled by a dog. The injuries to his left arm were so severe that it remained permanently shorter than the right arm. Transferring his skills to violoncello, Merk undertook a short period of study with Philip Schindlöcker, a member of the Imperial Kapelle.[220]

Merk left Vienna for two years, touring through Hungary, Bohemia, and Austria before returning in 1815. In that year, he accepted the first violon-

216 Joseph Schmidt-Görg, "Das Wiener Tagebuch des Mannheimer Hofkapellmeisters Michael Frey," *Beethoven Jahrbuch*, 6 (Bonn: Beethovenhaus, 1969) pp. 138–139.
217 *AMZ* (April 1811), col. 293; (March 1812), col. 211.
218 Schmidt-Görg, "Tagebuch Frey," p. 182.
219 Ludwig van Beethoven, *Konversationshefte*, ed. Karl-Heinz Köhler and Gita Herre, 9 vols. (Leipzig: VEB Deutscher Verlag für Musik, 1972), vol. I, p. 375.
220 "Joseph Merk," *AMZ*, no. 10 (March 1836), cols. 149–152.

cello position in the opera orchestra. Like Lincke, Merk moved into the mainstream of Viennese musical life, performing as both a soloist and a chamber musician. Considered a more dynamic soloist than Lincke, he continued to tour outside of Vienna. Merk performed his own compositions and those by Romberg. The two violoncellists mutually admired each other, having met under the auspices of Nicolaus Kraft.[221]

Merk was named to the Austrian Imperial Kapelle, in addition to his duties with the opera, in 1819. In 1822, he followed Anton Kraft as Professor of Violoncello at the Conservatorium der Gesellschaft der Musikfreunde. As one of the most respected performers in Vienna, Merk, like Lincke, became associated with the works of Beethoven and Schubert. Merk became close friends with Schubert, often accompanying the composer to private recitals.[222] His relationship with Beethoven commenced in 1825, when the quartet in which Merk performed with Joseph Mayseder was entrusted with a performance of the op. 127 string quartet. Merk also entertained Chopin, who spent time in Vienna in 1829. Chopin composed the op. 3 *Introduction and Polonaise* for Merk's performance.

Merk continued to accumulate performance honors throughout the next decade, being named chamber virtuoso to the Emperor in 1834. He also gained recognition for his publications: his numerous works for violoncello include *20 Exercises pour violoncello* op. 11 and a set of variations on a favorite waltz of Schubert, both of which were dedicated to Schubert. Merk made his final concert tour in 1836 and retired from the Conservatorium in 1848. He died in Vienna on June 16, 1852.

Violoncello performance in Bohemia is ably represented by the Stiastny brothers, Bernard and Jan. Their father was an oboist with the Prague theater orchestra. Bernard was born in 1760 and Jan in 1764. Bernard remained in Prague, joining the theater orchestra in 1778 and becoming the first instructor of violoncello at the Prague Conservatory upon its foundation in 1811. He retired in 1822.[223] His compositional output was centered upon teaching material, while that of his younger brother was composed for public performance.

Jan studied violoncello with Bernard and joined the theater orchestra for a short while. Probably wishing to strike out on his own, he left Prague, working in Mainz from 1789 to 1797, Frankfurt am Main during the 1820s and Mannheim after Ritter's retirement in 1826.[224] At some point, he visited Paris and London. He published a total of thirteen works: op. 3 is

221 Affection on Romberg's part is demonstrated in a letter of introduction for Merk to August Prell at the court of Brunswick. See Schäfer, *Romberg*, appendix.
222 *Schubert: Memoirs by His Friends*, collected and ed. Otto Eric Deutsch, trans. Rosamund Ley and John Nowell (London: Adam & Charles Black, 1958), p. 262; Otto Eric Deutsch, *Schubert: a Documentary Biography*, trans. Eric Blom (London: J. M. Dent & Sons, Ltd., 1946), p. 220.
223 Milan Postolka, "Stiastny," *NG*, vol. XVIII, p. 84.
224 Van der Straeten, *History of the Violoncello*, pp. 346–347.

dedicated to the students of the Paris Conservatoire, op. 7 to Robert Lindley, and op. 10 to John Crosdill. W. H. Husk referred to Jan as the "Beethoven of the violoncello" and stated that Lindley considered the op. 7 Concertino for violoncello to be "the finest piece ever written for the instrument."[225] Husk, Vidal, and Van der Straeten all report that Jan had a nervous disposition which limited his ability to perform.

The development of the Russian school of violoncello is identified with Karl Davydov in the latter part of the nineteenth century, as most professional posts were filled with foreign musicians before this point. However, Davydov's achievements are a legacy of events that occurred earlier in the century. During the Napoleonic Wars, Russia was an especially inviting destination for violoncellists as they were richly supported by Prince Golitzin and Count Matvey Viel'gorsky (Wielhorsky), both amateur violoncellists. Viel'gorsky, in particular, stands out as one of the dominating influences in the development of violoncello playing in Russia.

Viel'gorsky was born in St. Petersburg on April 26, 1794. Professionally, he served in the military from 1812 to 1826, but his avocation was music. This was a passion he shared with his brother, Mikhail, who was a violinist and composer. Matvey first studied violoncello with Adolph Meinhardt, but his most important association was with Bernhard Romberg.[226] The German virtuoso became his teacher and very close friend and Viel'gorsky maintained relationships with Romberg's son, Karl, and nephew, Cyprian. The Romberg family first stayed with Viel'gorsky from 1810 to 1812, but numerous visits occurred in the years following and the younger Rombergs eventually took court positions. Bernhard Romberg and Viel'gorsky maintained correspondence until the older violoncellist's death.[227]

Viel'gorsky was an active and accomplished performer, giving concerts both privately and publicly in Moscow, St. Petersburg, and various European cities. He and Mikhail sponsored the visits of numerous luminaries including Liszt, Berlioz, Bohrer, Servais, and the Schumanns. The respect which Matvey engendered is demonstrated in the many violoncello compositions dedicated to him. These include works by Romberg, Bohrer, Servais, Mendelssohn, and Piatti. Together with Prince Golitzin, he founded the Society of Lovers of Music in 1828 and, in 1859, Viel'gorsky helped to inaugurate the St. Petersburg branch of the Russian Musical Society. He died in Nice on March 5, 1866.[228]

225 William H. Husk, "Stiastny," *A Dictionary of Music and Musicians*, ed. Grove, vol. III, p. 713.
226 Gerald Seaman, "Viel'gorsky," *Biographical Dictionary of Russian/Soviet Composers*, ed. Allan Ho and Dmitry Feofanov (New York: Greenwood Press, 1989), p. 580.
227 Schäfer, *Romberg*, appendix.
228 The most comprehensive biography of Viel'gorsky appears in Ginsburg, *Istoriya violonchel'nogo*, vol. II, pp. 278–330.

2

Development of the violoncello, the bow, and notation

Music-making of the years 1740 to 1840 is intrinsically connected with innovations in instrument and bow design. Individual theories regarding construction techniques and sometimes vehement rebuttals to these same ideas multiplied as interest in scientific inquiry increased.[1] While a certain amount of experimentation was generated by the desire for novelty and the attending financial rewards enjoyed by the most celebrated innovators, serious performers continually searched for methods to make their instruments more responsive to changes in musical taste. There is something of the chicken and the egg with the many modifications which took place, for when one aspect of instrument design was altered, often a change to the bow or another part of the instrument became necessary. That change, then, would spark another alteration, and so on.

By the turn of the nineteenth century, experimentation had become so widespread, with such variation in the sophistication of those interested in making and rebuilding instruments and bows, that many performers became concerned about damage to instruments. At this point, players and teachers began working towards a total codification of instrument and bow design. This is documented in violoncello methods and through the many published articles and books written to instruct amateurs about "correct" construction techniques.

THE VIOLONCELLO

Musicians of the era 1740 to 1840 considered the violoncello, as they knew the instrument, to be an eighteenth-century product. This viewpoint re-

---

1 See, for instance: Antonio Bagatella, *Regole per la costruzione de' violini* [1786], also translated by J. O. H. Schaum as *Ueber den Bau der Violinen, Bratschen, Violoncells und Violons* (Leipzig: Kühnel, n.d.); "Noch etwas über den Bau der Geige," *AMZ* (October 24, 1804), col. 49; "Nochmalige Untersuchungen über den Bau der Violin," *AMZ* (January 30, 1811), cols. 69–82; J. A. Otto, *Ueber den Bau und die Erhaltung der Geige und aller Bogen-Instrumente* (Halle, 1817).

flects the experiences of players who actually witnessed the codification of the instrument's physical dimensions nevertheless, it needs to be qualified: it was the violoncello used for playing solos that was an eighteenth-century creation. Smaller than many seventeenth-century forms, this was the instrument described in La Borde's *Essai sur la musique ancienne et moderne* (1780). Although the solo violoncello became the instrument commonly used by the end of the eighteenth century, it is not possible to specify when collateral instruments stopped being played.

For most of the eighteenth century, there were two distinct categories of instruments within the violin family, smaller solo instruments and the larger ones of the orchestra.[2] In 1752, Quantz was unequivocal in his discussion of the violoncello, writing that orchestral players must use larger instruments with thicker strings because "if a small instrument with thin strings were employed for both types of parts, the accompaniment in a large ensemble would have no effect whatsoever."[3] Leopold Mozart gave information of a similar nature in 1756, stating that a variety of sizes was common for the violoncello and "although some are larger, others smaller, they differ little from each other excepting in the strength of their tone, according to the fashion of their stringing."[4]

A similar reference to violin playing implies that use of two differing instruments was still common later in the century. A report in the *Musikalische Real-Zeitung* of 1788 specified that "Tardini [Tartini], Holzboger [Holzbauer] and other thorough solo players knew this well, and always played on two kinds of instruments," because "the orchestra violin must penetrate, the solo violin sound gently."[5]

Most organological evidence of orchestra violoncellos disappeared long before researchers became interested in the subject. For this reason, the number of sources from which information can be gleaned is limited. Primary research was accomplished by the Hill luthiers, who refer to larger-sized violoncellos as "church basses," on the grounds that many such instruments were constructed for use in church orchestras. They documented the dimensions of several surviving specimens, whose measurements are as follows:[6]

---

2 This same practice may also be observed of the viol family: see Henry Burnett, "The Bowed String Instruments of the Baroque Basso-Continuo (ca. 1680–ca. 1752) in Italy and France," *Journal of the Viola da Gamba Society of America*, 8 (1971), 36–37.

3 Johann Joachim Quantz, *On Playing the Flute*, trans. Edward R. Reilly (London: Faber & Faber, 1966), p. 241.

4 *Leopold Mozart's Treatise on the Fundamentals of Violin Playing*, ed. Editha Knocker (second edition, Oxford University Press, 1951), pp. 11–12.

5 "Anmerkungen über die Violin und den Violinspieler," *Musikalische Real-Zeitung* (July 30, 1788), cols. 38–39.

6 Hill, *Stradivari*, pp. 297–298.

Francesco Rugeri, 1667

Length	30 $^5/_{16}$ inches
Width	18 $^3/_8$ "
"	14 $^7/_8$ "
Sides	4 $^5/_8$ "
"	4 $^1/_2$ "
Stop	16 $^5/_8$ "

Antonio Stradivari, 1690
"The Tuscan"

Length	31 $^3/_8$ inches
Width	18 $^1/_2$ "
"	14 $^1/_2$ "
Sides	4 $^3/_4$ "
"	4 $^1/_2$ "
Stop	16 $^3/_4$ "

Antonio Stradivari, 1701
"The Servais"

Length	31 $^1/_8$ inches
Width	18 $^1/_2$ "
"	14 $^3/_8$ "
Sides	5 "
"	4 $^7/_8$ "
Stop	16 $^3/_4$ "

"Church basses" were constructed by makers past the mid-part of the eighteenth century. Roman luthier David Tecchler made such instruments until his death in 1747 and American maker Abraham Prescott utilized larger patterns into the nineteenth century.[7] Instructions for endpin use (p. 98 below) also suggest that "church basses" were common in Germany at least through the end of the eighteenth century. There were also other forms of collateral instruments made during the eighteenth and nineteenth centuries, most being hybrids whose designs incorporated attributes of both the viola da gamba and the violoncello. Instruments of this type were made by numerous builders in the seventeenth century and the intellectual creativity engendered by the Enlightenment led some luthiers to continue this avenue of exploration. Models include the five-string violoncello, built during the early decades of the eighteenth century, the later *harmonicello* of J. C. Bischoff, the *heptacorde* devised by Raoul and Vuillaume, and Johann Staufer's *arpeggione*. In addition, luthiers also became adept at converting viols into violoncellos and Milliot affirms that Claude Boivin attained a certain popularity with his hybrid "arched viols."[8] One example of this

---

7 Ibid., p. 115. A Prescott violoncello is in the collection of The Shrine to Music Museum.
8 Milliot, *Le violoncelle en France*, p. 50.

kind, belonging to the Marquis de Lusignan de Lezay, was listed in the inventory of instruments seized by the *Commission temporaire des arts* in 1795.[9] It was described as "Une basse faite d'une viole, sans nom d'auteur, n'y archet, n'y étuy, estimée 150 francs."[10]

Both Leopold Mozart and Quantz remarked on the correlation between the use of an instrument and its stringing. Thicker strings were placed on larger instruments. This produced a more resonant sound, but thicker strings lay high off the fingerboard and were more difficult to make respond. Solo instruments were strung with thinner strings, making for a quicker response, but also a more delicate tone quality. This divergence in the stringing of orchestral and solo instruments remained even after players stopped using "church basses." For this reason, writers at the beginning of the nineteenth century still considered it important to explain the difference between the "basse" and the "violoncello," and in what context they were using the terms. Bréval wrote in 1804 that

The Basse, which for us is the same instrument as the violoncello, is nonetheless treated with this difference: that by Basse is understood the section which accompanies, incorporating a limited register, and by violoncello, the same section, which incorporates a more extensive register and which is at the same time accompaniment and solo part. But we will admit here a clear understanding that Basse and violoncello shall be the same thing.[11]

The professors at the Paris Conservatoire also wanted to make clear in their method the difference between the two differing uses:

In this work, the Basse has been considered from two different points of view: first, as the solo part called *Violoncello* and [secondly] as the accompaniment section which is commonly called Basse.[12]

Terminology used to list the instruments seized by the *Commission temporaire des arts* also suggests that a differential existed between *basse* and violoncello. While Bruni gave no indication in his list of what the two differing designations might refer to, the two terms do not appear to have been applied interchangeably and, since bass viols and contrabasses were listed separately, these non-violoncellos do not fall into the general cat-

---

9 The *Commission temporaire des arts* was formed on May 3, 1794, superseding the 1791 *Commission des monuments*. Its purpose was to collect and catalogue books, instruments, and other objects of science and art suitable for public instruction. It was subdivided into eleven committees, the eleventh of which dealt with musical instruments and was headed by Bernard Sarrette and Antonio Bruni. Sarrette was director of the music of the National Guard, soon to be the Paris Conservatoire, and Bruni was first violinist of the Théâtre-italien. The actual inventory was drawn up by Bruni.

10 Jules Gallay, ed., *Un inventaire sous la terreur. Etat des instruments relevés chez les émigrés et condamnés par Bruni* (Paris: Georges Chamerot, 1890), list CI.

11 J. B. Bréval, *Traité du violoncelle*, op. 42 (Paris: Imbault, [1804]), p. 2.

12 P. Baillot, J. H. Levasseur, C.-S. Catel, and C.-N. Baudiot, *Méthode de violoncelle et de basse d'accompagnement* (Paris: A l'Imprimerie du Conservatoire, [1805]), p. 1. (Quotations are reproduced by permission of The Music Library, University of California, Berkeley.)

egory of *basse*. It seems more likely that the distinction is between orchestral instruments, which would have been the majority of instruments seized, and solo instruments.

The first listing for a violoncello-type instrument is for May 11, 1795, when "une basse de Castagnery, année 1751" was taken from the household of Louis-Jean Josset Saint-Laurent.[13] The instruments appropriated on May 29 lend a clearer picture to Bruni's use of the two terms by reason of Bruni's uncertainty as to what kind of instrument he was taking. In the first household, that of the Bertier residence, he was diffident, the list describing "une basse ou violoncelle par Bassot à Paris, année 1781." However, at the mansion of J. B. Tavernier de Boulogne, visited on that same day, Bruni was clear, listing "un violoncelle de Castagnery, année 1757" and "un violoncelle de Cabresy, année 1725."[14] In total, Bruni's inventory contains fourteen *basses*, seven violoncellos, one instrument that is either a *basse* or a violoncello, one viola da gamba, one hybrid, and one contrabass.

Most knowledge about the two types of violoncellos comes from instructions to amateur players. Stringing the instrument for each use was a major consideration. The *Correspondance des Amateurs Musiciens* provided advice for choosing the proper string thickness and corresponding bridge height, solo instruments using a lower bridge:

> What is extremely essential to observe is that when one strings a basse [violoncello] for the orchestra, for a symphony, there should be four lines of distance between each string and the end of the fingerboard towards the bridge. If one strings a basse for quartets or solos, this distance must not be more than two lines.[15]

Dotzauer likewise observed that the height of the strings from the fingerboard was greater on the instrument of an orchestral player than on that of a solo player. Stressing the individuality of each instrument, he recommended choosing the thinnest possible strings that would give a full sound.[16] German musicians recommended string gauges to measure the thickness of strings.[17] Using a scale device, a more scientific approach to assessing string quality was recommended in the *Correspondance des Amateurs Musiciens*. Calibrated by tension, strings were measured in order to select those which achived an equal level of tension at the required pitch, this uniformity being an important attribute in obtaining consistent string response from the action of the bow. The writer explained:

13 Galley, *Inventaire sous la terreur*, list II.
14 Ibid., list IX and list XIII.
15 "Le violoncelle," *Correspondance des Amateurs Musiciens*, no. 42 (September 10, 1803), 1.
16 J. J. F. Dotzauer, *Violonzell-Schule* (Mainz: B. Schott, [1832]), p. 60.
17 "Anmerkungen über die Violin," *Musikalische Real-Zeitung* (October 11, 1788), col. 106; *Spohr's Violin School*, ed. Henry Holmes, trans. Florence Marshall (London: Boosey & Co.), p. 7; Bernhard Romberg, *A Complete Theoretical and Practical School for the Violoncello* (London: Boosey & Sons Foreign Musical Library, [1839]), p. 5.

The method of weighing the strings is very simple. The thing is to have a scale or a balance. One adjusts at one end [of the scale or balance]. It represents the bottom of the violoncello. One attaches a string to it, under which a bridge is placed at the ordinary distance. Further along, a small raise should be made to give the effect of the saddle, and then a peg, inserted into a hole in a board, with which one sets the string to orchestra pitch. Once this has been achieved, the space [on the gauge] of the balance or the scale indicates the weight of this pressure on this same string. One may therefore test a certain quantity, which one records gradually in proportion, in order to find by means of different settings replacements for those that break.[18]

This source intimates that pitch standards also affected the thickness of the strings employed. Differences in pitch were substantial during the eighteenth and nineteenth centuries and were one more difficulty that musicians, especially those who toured, had to contend with. Low pitch required the use of thicker strings, while higher pitch allowed for the stringing of an instrument with thinner, tauter strings. Leopold Mozart discussed this specifically, explaining that not only did one need to determine string thickness corresponding to the size of the instrument one was using, but that

with sharp or flat pitch one has to accommodate in the same manner. Just as the thicker strings give a better result with the flat pitch, so the thinner strings will serve better with the sharp pitch.[19]

Data compiled by Arthur Mendel suggests that pitch varied not only among regions, but also within specific cities and regions. Mendel begins by citing La Borde, who, in discussing the variability of pitch within Paris, wrote of the adjustments necessary to wind instruments playing at different venues. La Borde stated:

as the pitch which one actually adopts in varying types of music, and particularly at the Concert Spirituel, is much higher than the diapason, which was used when the bassoon was first used, it is necessary to reduce the length of this instrument in proportion...Normally in cathedral churches, the pitch of the organ is very low, as that at the Church of the Innocents was formerly, and as those at the Sainte-Chapelle of Paris and the Chapel of the King at Versailles are still.[20]

The low pitch which La Borde used for comparison at the Chapel of Versailles was indeed very low; Mendel gave it as $a^1 = 396$, two semi-tones below $a^1 = 440$.[21] While the pitch used at the Concert Spirituel was stated as

18 "Le violoncelle," *Correspondance des Amateurs Musiciens*, no. 43 (September 17, 1803), 1.
19 *Mozart's Treatise on Violin Playing*, p. 16.
20 La Borde, *Essai sur la musique* (1780), vol. I, p. 328, quoted in Arthur Mendel, "Pitch in Western Music since 1500," *Acta Musicologica*, 50 (1978), 75.
21 Mendel, "Pitch in Western Music," p. 28.

being higher than this, other reports quoted by Mendel indicate that Parisian pitch was lower than that used in Berlin and, by way of comparison, Berlin pitch was also lower than that used in Vienna. This is important because strings used by performers using Parisian pitch had to be thicker than those used by musicians playing with a higher pitch.

Although the diapason altered significantly between 1785 and 1840, Mendel concluded that regional differences remained similar, even while the general standard of pitch rose. Giving figures for c. 1834, Mendel stated that in Paris, the pitch used by the Théâtre-italien was $a^1 = 435.2$ and the Paris Opéra was $a^1 = 434$, while the pitch of the Berlin opera orchestra was $a^1 = 441.8$ and Viennese pitch was as high as $a^1 = 445$.[22] Some of Mendel's information was drawn from remarks left by Sir George Smart. Smart traveled Europe with a tuning fork pitched at $a^1 = 433$, the pitch used in London for the Philharmonic concerts.[23] He noted that in 1825, the orchestra of the Palace Theater in Vienna was pitched higher than his fork, as was the Schuppanzigh string quartet.[24] In Paris two months later, Smart recorded that, while the pitch used at the Opéra was slightly higher than his fork, the pitch used at the Théâtre-italien and by Baillot at a private soiree matched his fork.[25]

Strings were the major component leading to the evolution of the solo violoncello. The development of the wire-wound string occurred in the 1660s and from that point onward, it became possible to build a violoncello of smaller dimensions which maintained a richness of sound equal to that of the larger "church bass."[26] Eighteenth- and nineteenth-century violoncellos were strung with silver- or copper-wound strings on the G and C strings and with plain gut on the A and D strings.[27]

Solo instruments underwent continuous alterations in construction until the mid-point of the nineteenth century, as makers and players continued to search for instruments that were increasingly responsive to rapidly changing performance demands. The first step in this process was the codification of the solo violoncello's dimensions. Although he was not the first to make instruments of smaller measurements than the "church bass," the work of Antonio Stradivari did become a dominating influence throughout Europe, particularly in the second half of the century when his instruments gained wide popularity among virtuosos. Stradivari codified his dimensions for the smaller violoncello in 1707 and, at that time, ceased making

22 Ibid., p. 86.
23 Ibid., p. 87.
24 *Leaves from the Journals of Sir George Smart*, ed. H. Bertram Cox and C. L. E. Cox (London: Longmans & Co., 1907/R 1971), p. 110.
25 Ibid., p. 230.
26 Bonta, "A Question of Strings," 64–99.
27 This stringing is noted for violoncellists in "Schreiben eines Dilettanten an den Herausgeber," *BMZ*, no. 45 (1805), 178.

the larger instrument.[28] The measurements of the "Duport" violoncello, considered by the Hills to be the most beautiful of Stradivari's instruments, serve as an example.[29]

The "Duport" Violoncello, 1711

Length	29 $^7/_8$ inches
Width	17 $^3/_8$ "
"	13 $^5/_8$ "
Sides	4 $^5/_8$ "
"	4 $^1/$ "
Stop	15 $^3/_4$ "

Instruments of even smaller dimensions were built by other makers. A "processional" violoncello (with modern neck and fingerboard) from the early part of the seventeenth century is held in the collection of The Shrine to Music Museum (Plate 1). Of Brescian provenance, it has a flat back with small holes cut so that a strap could be attached to facilitate marching. At 28 inches in length, it is slightly smaller than an English violoncello by William Baker dated 1672, which has a body length of $28\frac{3}{8}$ inches (73 cm).[30] Baker's dimensions correspond to those recorded by James Talbot *c.* 1695, the instrument used for Talbot's measurements being that of Jacques Paisible, a French violoncellist employed at the English court.[31] Also of this genus is a 1679 Venetian instrument by Martin Kaiser, built as a violoncello inclusive of slinging holes, but having a viol-type rose carved in the face and fret marks on the neck. It has a body length of $28\frac{1}{8}$ inches (71 cm).[32]

Acceptance by makers of Stradivari's dimensions was a gradual process, but ultimately led to the belief that all violoncellos had to generally conform to the measurements of his smaller pattern. As a result, from the latter part of the eighteenth century onward, most violoncellos of larger size were cut down. This procedure was done indiscriminately and by luthiers of varying qualifications. The Hills describe how the Stradivari violoncello of the Spanish court was rebuilt, quoting an account book kept by Dom Ascensio, the court luthier. Although the instrument was cut down to its present size at a later date by Ascensio's successor, the process was begun in 1783. Ascensio's entry of August 6 reads:

The violoncello, which is of very large proportions – larger than those Stradivari usually adopted – I wished to reform [*sic*] ... I pieced the centre, replaced the bar

28 Hill, *Stradivari*, pp. 125–128.
29 Ibid., p. 298. The fifth fraction in the list is incomplete in the original.
30 John Dilworth, "Mr Baker the Fidell Maker," *The Strad*, 106, no. 1261 (May 1995), 475–481.
31 Robert Donington, "James Talbot's Manuscript," *The Galpin Society Journal*, 3 (March 1950), 30; Peter Trevelyan, "A Quartet of String Instruments by William Baker of Oxford (*circa* 1645–1685)," *The Galpin Society Journal*, 49 (March 1996), 74.
32 Anthony Baines, *European and American Musical Instruments* (London: B. T. Batsford, 1966), p. 10.

Plate 1   Violoncello, Brescian school *c.* 1625 (The Shrine to Music Museum, Vermillion, South Dakota)

by one adjusted to mathematical proportions based on that of Stradivari. I corrected the thicknesses, pieced the four corner-blocks, took the back off and inserted a piece in the centre, as it was too thin. I had to replace the neck, which I did in the most careful manner. I then adjusted the instrument, the tone of which was rendered excellent by all these changes. It took me three months to do...[33]

The reduction of instruments by those who had individual ideas of how this should be accomplished was a major concern to many performers. Nineteenth-century writings are replete with horror stories of "repairs" performed by those wishing to "improve" instruments, the spirit of scientific inquiry leading to numerous excesses. That this was a continuing problem for violoncellists was testified to by both Dotzauer and Romberg. In Dotzauer's words:

Lucky is he who owns an unspoiled genuine Italian violoncello. He is to be envied! Most of these instruments have already fallen into the hands of bunglers, and the great value of their sound, which each ancient excellent master knew how to create, is lost.[34]

Romberg, who owned a 1703 Tecchler and a 1711 Stradivari, devoted a section of his violoncello method to the discussion of the optimum dimensions for the violoncello.[35] The Stradivari was originally built to the measurements of the "small pattern," but it is likely that Romberg had the Tecchler reduced to its nineteenth-century length of 75.8 cm.[36] His writings attest to a familiarity with reducing instrument size and a concern with indiscriminate cutting. The remarks contained in his tutor read:

In reducing the size of Instruments, every Maker has his own peculiar ideas on the proper length and breadth of the Violoncello; but since few among them are players, and since, consequently they cannot know from their own experience the correct proportions that a Violoncello should have, in order that it be played upon with ease, the opinion of a connoisseur may perhaps be not unacceptable to them.

　How many valuable Instruments may not have been already ruined by the injudicious treatment of ignorant pretenders![37]

THE FITTINGS

As the eighteenth century progressed, experiments with the dimensions of the violoncello body became less common as, concurrently, luthiers and

33 Hill, *Stradivari*, pp. 77–78.
34 Dotzauer, *Violonzell-Schule*, p. 58.
35 The 1711 Stradivari was used as the basis for the measurements provided by Romberg. The 1703 Tecchler was certified by the Parisian luthiers Caressa & Français in 1910. Certificate provided by Raymond Rosen, Chicago.
36 According to the Hills, only four of the fifty Tecchler violoncellos with which they were familiar were originally constructed in a small pattern. Hill, *Stradivari*, p. 115.
37 Romberg, *School*, p. 5.

performers became aware that changes to the fittings yielded more flexible and responsive instruments. Changes inside the instrument included the insertion of increasingly longer and thicker bass-bars and larger sound-posts. Such alterations were made in response to several variables, all of which stemmed from the desire by audiences and performers for an increased volume of sound. Rising pitch levels and the canted neck contributed to the need for stronger bass-bars, as did the use of bow sticks of concave design, the properties of which allowed for greater leverage to be placed against the string and instrument.

The insertion of a new soundpost was a relatively minor alteration, eliciting little comment from contemporary musicians. The replacement of a bass-bar, however, was a major repair, as the statement from Dom Ascensio affirms. Another example of this repair is preserved in the Esterháza archives. A repair bill of J. J. Stadlmann of Vienna, dated April 4, 1766 and countersigned by Haydn, recorded that, "first, a Pasetl [violoncello] repaired, newly strung, the neck repaired, the bas-bar [*sic*] reinforced."[38]

As with many aspects of instrument construction, the dimensions and shapes of bass-bars varied greatly among makers. Variations in length, depth, width, and taper attest to the unstandardized nature of this fitting throughout the eighteenth century. There are even intimations that some luthiers did not use bass-bars, instead leaving the top-table wood thicker at the bass-bar position. The Hills stated that this form of construction was usual for sixteenth-century instruments, but the practice prevailed among some luthiers into the following centuries. This form of reinforcement is found on the Baker viola[39] and Fred Lindeman has observed this construction method in Flemish violins of the eighteenth century.[40] A 1788 German article on violin construction also testifies to the practice:

In examining the preparation of the part of the violin that is called the bass-bar, the opinions of instrument makers are not the same. Some leave so much standing on the bass-bar side in the interior of the top table by the manner in which they plane the wood, that this can be substituted in place of the bass-bar; others and indeed most glue the bass-bar separately.[41]

The components of the violoncello which underwent more visible changes were the neck and fingerboard. The necks of early instruments were inserted perpendicular to the body of the instrument, the neck usually being

38 Landon, "Haydn at Esterháza," p. 120.
39 Dilworth, "Mr Baker the Fidell Maker," 479.
40 Fred Lindeman, "Dutch Violin Making Down the Centuries," *The Strad*, 106, no. 1264 (August 1995), 782–783.
41 "Anmerkungen über die Violin und den Violinspieler," *Musikalische Real-Zeitung* (July 23, 1788), col. 30.

affixed into the neckblock by nails or dowels. Some makers did carve the neck and block in one piece, while others made a heel extension which they inserted through the neck block.[42] On most instruments, a wedge was then placed on the neck, on top of which was glued the fingerboard. The cant of the fingerboard was determined by the angle of the wedge. Based on construction techniques devised at the time the wire-wound string was developed, and in contrast to the plain or inlaid hardwood fingerboards preferred before the advent of overspun strings, early eighteenth-century fingerboards were generally made from a composite of woods. Owing to its lightness, fruitwood was often the main component, while a veneer might be ebony, black-stained fruitwood, or, as on one example housed at The Shrine to Music Museum, rosewood.[43]

The demands of increasing virtuosity and greater sound production led to the following changes in construction practices taking place over the course of the second half of the eighteenth century: neck length was increased by approximately one inch (2.5 cm), while width was gradually thinned to ease fingering; the angle of the fingerboard above the instrument body was increased to match bridges being raised for greater string tension, thereby making higher pitches playable; the fingerboard wedge was reduced and then abandoned as luthiers devised the technique of mortising the neck into the shoulder, the neck tilting backwards; the fingerboard was lengthened over the course of the eighteenth century, ebony becoming the wood of choice because of its inherent strength.

One of the singular features of eighteenth-century string technique is the continuous addition of accessible notes. The range of the violoncello was relatively stable for the first three decades of the eighteenth century, musicians experimenting with additional strings and hybrid instruments to yield higher pitches.[44] Performance repertoire and iconographic sources suggest that the violoncello fingerboard of this period was long enough to allow the half-string harmonics to be played. The earliest measurement for a violoncello neck comes from the Talbot manuscript of *c.* 1695, in which the fingerboard length was given as 13 inches (33 cm).[45] However, Italian violoncellists eventually found that playing with thumb-position techniques facilitated more virtuosity and fingerboards began to lengthen accordingly.

---

42 Ian Watchorn, "Baroque Renaissance," *The Strad,* 95, no. 1139 (March 1985), 824.
43 The Shrine to Music Museum, Witten collection #SA-1, Violoncello fingerboard (Italian) – rosewood veneer on pear with remainder of walnut wedge; length 53.2 cm.
44 Such instruments were made at least until the mid-part of the eighteenth century, as demonstrated by a *violoncello piccolo à cinque corde* by Giuseppe Gaffino which bears a label indicating it was made in Paris in 1748. See C. Van Leeuwen Boomkamp and J. H. Van Der Meer, *The Carel Van Leeuwen Boomkamp Collection of Musical Instruments* (Amsterdam: Frits Knuf, 1971), ex. 19.
45 Donington, "Talbot's Manuscript," 30.

Fingerboard length become an increasingly personal matter after the third decade of the eighteenth century, the range exhibited by individual players varying greatly. Corrette demonstrated notes only to the B above the half-string harmonic b^1, but suggested that pitches in thumb position could go higher. Lanzetti had already taken solo playing to b^2 in the 1730s: his op. 1 sonatas (1736) are unique in rising to that pitch. The Mannheim works of Filtz, composed between 1754 and 1760, demonstrate that he was another who pushed violoncello tessitura above the norm. Filtz's B♭ major concerto rises to c^3, while a series of harmonics in the D major sonata actually extends the range to g^3.

The majority of compositions from the 1760s stayed beneath the c^3 used by Filtz, but by the next decade, Janson was utilizing harmonics up to a^3, with a stopped pitch of f^3 incorporated into the sixth concerto of his op. 6 collection. The lengthening process stabilized by the turn of the century. Dotzauer and Romberg both stipulated in their methods that the fingerboard length for stopped notes extended to d^3, but Hus-Desforges' concerto op. 23 (c. 1828), like the earlier works of his teacher, Janson, reaches to f^3. This is the range of most modern fingerboards.

Discussion of the fingerboard is incomplete without remarking on the use of frets with the violoncello. Fret markings on the necks of such existing instruments as the "Kaiser" violoncello (1679) intimate that it was not unusual for seventeenth-century players to use frets on violoncellos or hybrid instruments.[46] Although this practice compromised the violoncello's ability to make fine adjustments in tuning – an important reason for the instrument's increasing popularity – it died out very slowly. During the first half of the eighteenth century, violoncellists who were also gambists may have felt more secure with frets and suggestions for fret usage are found in some elementary tutors. Corrette recommended that beginning players apply a form of surrogate frets to the violoncello fingerboard, inlaying the fingerboard with ivory or mother-of-pearl to mark finger placement.[47] Quantz wrote of violoncellists using frets in 1752 as if it were a common occurrence. In discussing the execution of correct pitch, he instructed that "if the violoncello has frets, as is customary upon the viola da gamba, the violoncellist must, in playing notes marked with flats, depress the strings a little above the frets, and apply a little more pressure with his fingers…"[48]

Writing in 1765, Crome suggested that frets be inlaid into the fingerboard for those commencing their violoncello studies. "Tho the Learner may have a good Ear," he wrote, "it will be some time before he can stop

46 Baines, *European and American Musical Instruments*, ex. 54.
47 Michel Corrette, *Méthode théorique et pratique pour apprendre en peu de temps le violoncelle dans sa perfection. Ensemble de principes de musique avec des leçons*, op. 24 (Paris: 1741/R 1972), p. C.
48 Quantz, *On Playing the Flute*, p. 247.

the Notes perfectly in tune, and therefore it will be a great help to him at first to have his Finger board Fretted, like that of the Guittar, and when the Fingers are acquainted with the Finger board, have the Fretts filed down."[49] A tied fret was used by Crome to facilitate accurate tuning, "a piece of Fiddle String tight on the Neck under the Strings" placed where fourth-position E–A–D–G lie. Crome instructed the student to sound the higher string, "then screw up the Second till by putting the Finger just below the frett on the Second String it has the same sound as the first String open."[50]

Interest in and acceptance of these changes to the neck and fingerboard varied greatly among regions and players. Violinists were at the forefront of technological innovation; some violoncellists adopted the design modifications, while others seemed to think that altering their instruments was unnecessary. Research so far indicates that Paris was the center of innovative violin construction, with manufacturers from other countries following suit after being introduced to reconstructed fittings by traveling virtuosos. The exact time of these occurrences is difficult to pinpoint. Early advocates of the redesigned neck appear to have introduced its use at about the same time as the "Tourte" bow was devised, c. 1785. Contemporary articles document that such fittings were familiar to European players by the turn of the nineteenth century. Italian construction is reported by Vincetto Lancetti in *Biographical Notices* (Milan, 1823):

about 1800 the Brothers Mantegazza of Milan were restorers of instruments who were often entrusted by French and Italian artists to lengthen the necks of their violins after the Paris fashion, an example which was followed by amateurs and professors all over North Italy.[51]

An article on the violin which appeared in *AMZ* in 1804 indicates that the redesigned fittings were known in Germany at this time. This article states:

In modern times everything that has happened to improve [the violin] consists of a further setting back and lengthening of the neck, a longer fingerboard and a somewhat raised position of the tailpiece over the edge.[52]

An early advocate for the use of "modern" fittings on the violoncello was Bernhard Romberg. An innovative player, Romberg also offered his own contribution to the design of the fingerboard. Impelled by his use of a "Tourte" bow in conjunction with the low standard of pitch used in Paris at the beginning of the nineteenth century, Romberg devised a violoncello

---

49 Robert Crome, *The Compleat Tutor for the Violoncello* (London), p. 6.
50 Ibid., p. 4.
51 Quoted by Kenneth Skeaping, "Some Speculations on a Crisis in the History of the Violin," *The Galpin Society Journal*, 8 (March 1955), 10.
52 "Noch etwas über der Bau der Geige," *AMZ* (October 24, 1804), col. 50.

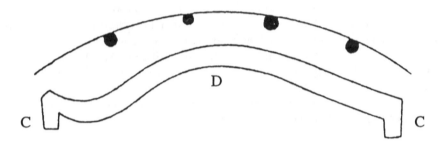

Fig. 2.1 Recommended shape of the end of the fingerboard as illustrated by Romberg

fingerboard which was recessed under the C string. The shape of this fingerboard was pictured in Romberg's *School* and is shown in Fig. 2.1. Romberg's compositions exploit the virtuoso possibilities of the upper register of the C string, and this alteration was necessary to accommodate the wider vibrations of the thicker, low-tension string he would have used while living in Paris. Louis Spohr transferred this design to violin fingerboards in 1807.[53]

Opposition to the shape of the grooved fingerboard was widespread, continuing even to the end of the century. In 1885, Edward Heron-Allen wrote that "my experience of this vagary is that it is a worrying and useless eccentricity, whose superfluity is only equalled by its unsightliness."[54] Although adopted by Romberg's protégé, Dotzauer,[55] the grooved fingerboard was disliked by numerous violoncellists. Romberg was aware of this:

Many players find it inconvenient to play with grooves in the fingerboard, and yet without them, the strings G,D,A cannot lie in proper proportion. The C string should lie higher, otherwise it would jar when played on with a strong bow.[56]

Dr. J. C. Nicolai, a violoncello and contrabass player from Rudolstadt, also disliked the redesigned fingerboard. In an article on construction procedures, he recommends the slimmer neck design and attests that Romberg introduced progressive instrument fittings into Germany:

Since the rise of B. Romberg, and since the method and manner has become known of how he treats the violoncello and how he writes for this instrument, one has also found, that it is almost impossible to play his compositions on instruments

53 *Spohr's Violin School*, p. 5.
54 Edward Heron-Allen, *Violin-Making as It Was and Is* (London: Ward Lock & Co., Ltd., 1885), p. 191.
55 See Dotzauer, *Violonzell-Schule*, p. 59.
56 Romberg, *School*, p. 2.

that have been fitted in the old manner, that is to say with short, thick necks, and where the fingerboard is low, or lying quite close to the body of the instrument. Many who have seen Romberg play and have had the opportunity to examine his instrument closely have now – if they have been in the company of a clever instrument builder – replaced their fittings with fittings like his. This fitting consisted of the insertion of a longer and thinner neck that projects nearly two inches above the body, and the introduction of a groove on the fingerboard that runs down on the side where the C string is. This last one I have not imitated, because I am not convinced of the advantages of this groove...[57]

However, numerous sources from the beginning of the nineteenth century imply that violoncellists were hesitant to adopt the slimmer dimensions of Romberg's neck fittings. The representations of violoncellos from Aubert's (Fig. 2.2) and Bréval's (Fig. 3.1) methods both show instruments having shorter, thicker necks.[58] Duport's portrait (Plate 7) likewise illustrates a similar construction, while a reference to the performance of cadences in his *Essai* alludes to familiarity with the discomfort of performing on an instrument with a thick neck:

The cadences in E major and minor on the first string are perhaps the most difficult on the violoncello because the hand finds itself set at the place where the neck is joined to the instrument and if the neck is short, they become very tiring.[59]

Information about Joseph Lincke likewise suggests that the adoption of redesigned fittings did not immediately occur in Vienna. Descriptions of Lincke's playing refer to his lack of sound projection. For example, when he performed a concerto and a set of variations by Romberg in 1813, one reviewer wrote:

It is a pity that the performance of this excellent virtuoso lost its effect in this hall through the weak tone of his instrument.[60]

Physical evidence supporting the idea that Lincke played on an instrument without redesigned fittings comes from the instrument case of the violoncello bought by Prince Lichnowsky for his string quartet. In the care of Carl Holz until 1827 and Carl Böhme until 1855, the violoncello used by Lincke is now in the collection of the Staatliches Institut für Musikforschung Preussischer Kulturbesitz in Berlin. The instrument's construction and history have been analyzed by Irmgard Otto for the institute.

57 Dr. J. C. Nicolai, "Wichtige Erfindung für das Violoncell," *AMZ*, no. 22 (May 1823), cols. 354–356. A portion of this article was reprinted in *The Harmonicon*, 1, no. 8 (August 1823), 111–112 and 1, no. 11 (November 1823), 161. Nicolai's writing additionally promotes the invention of a detachable neck, "invented" by Johann Staufer in Vienna. Staufer also built the *arpeggione*.
58 Pierre François Olivier Aubert, born in Amiens in 1763, was a violoncellist in the orchestra of the Opéra-comique.
59 Jean-Louis Duport, *Essai sur le doigté du violoncelle, et sur la conduite de l'archet* (Paris: Janet et Cotelle, [1806]), p. 128.
60 *Wiener Allgemeine Musikalische Zeitung*, no. 19 (May 8, 1813), cols. 293–294.

Fig. 2.2 Violoncello illustration by Aubert

Originally an instrument of larger dimensions, it has been cut down to a smaller pattern and the fittings have been "modernized." The printed label inside the violoncello "Andreas Guarnerius fecit Cremone Anno 1675" is a forgery. Otto speculates that the alterations to the fittings occurred after Beethoven's time. This opinion is due, in part, to the fact that a tailpiece of eighteenth-century design was found tightly connected to a short endpin inside the case.[61] Because of his crippled leg, Lincke probably used an endpin.

Violoncellists' acceptance of the redesigned fittings was gradual for several reasons. The expense of major reconstruction was certainly a consideration. Another problem associated with having the neck of the instrument replaced was discussed by Nicolai:

These longer, projecting necks are so beautiful and comfortable, but it is disagreeable, that, in time, they are apt to warp, even if they are made of the best wood. I myself have had to have two changed on both my violoncellos, even though the wood of the neck is as hard as a bone, and I was even at the point of having my best violoncello changed a third time.[62]

Another alteration to the fingerboard – possibly, like Romberg's, in response to pitch differentials – is reported, though in the vaguest manner, in a review of 1818. Max Bohrer is described as having drilled his fingerboard after the instructions of the Saxon instrument maker Elias Schlegel. Although no indication of what this might have accomplished is given, the review states that the Bohrers performed with a high pitch and, because of this, had to forgo some Parisian engagements:

Of all musicians who whistle and bow, or clap with their hands (one formerly said, strike the organ, the piano), the cellist Bohrer is inclined to be perhaps the one who ranks the highest now in possessing the greatest artistic and mechanical skill; he drills, after the instructions of Schlegel, the fingerboard where it is thickest. Curiously, these brothers always tighten the strings too high: when they arrived in Paris they tuned their instruments a half tone higher than the orchestra of the Théâtre-italien, and now they cannot tune once more with Mr. Valabrègue, even though they were offered five thousand francs if they had deigned to be heard with him in five *Concerts-Spirituels* during Easter week.[63]

Accuracy of tuning and improvement of tone quality through control of string vibration was a goal of numerous innovators. The *microcosme musical* was invented by Jean Tricklir in 1785. This was a device attached to the instrument that purported to prevent atmospheric change from affecting the tuning. Tricklir published his theories on this subject in his treatise *Le microcosme musical ouvrage: phylosogéometry musical fondé sur l'indiscordabilité, invention concourant avec le present système à la perfection de la musique.* Further discussion regarding this device appeared in two articles in Cramer's *Magazin der Musik.*[64]

Another device designed to facilitate the vibrations of the violoncello

61 Irmgard Otto, *Katalog für Streichinstrumente* (Berlin, 1975), p. 250.
62 Nicolai, "Wichtige Erfindung," cols. 354–355.
63 *AMZ* (March 1818), cols. 181–182.
64 Gerber, *Lexikon*, vol. I, cols. 682–683.

strings was invented by one of the members of the Forster family in London. Reported in the *Revue Musicale*, this invention was described as a brass bracket which was attached to the tailpiece. It had four vertical sections through one of which each string passed, and which were connected together at the bottom. The device was said to purify the tone of individual notes, particularly the A and B, and may have been a forerunner of the modern wolf-stop.[65]

The fittings of the bridge and tailpiece were also necessarily altered in order to accommodate modifications to the fingerboard. The bridge, especially, demonstrates much regional variation before the shape, pattern, and setting were standardized towards the end of the eighteenth century. The representation of Boccherini (Plate 2) portrays one example of Italian design, and extant bridges are held in the collections of the Museo Stradivariano Collection, Cremona, and the Museo Luigi Cherubini, Florence. Bridges of Viennese and English design are found in the Schreiner Collection, Germanisches Nationalmuseum, Nuremberg.[66] A variety of designs from the Witten Collection of The Shrine to Music Museum are illustrated in Plate 3.

Tailpieces of the eighteenth and early nineteenth centuries were formed to match the fingerboard of the instrument. Examples can be seen in the representations used by Aubert and Bréval. As the fingerboard was lengthened and narrowed, the tailpiece underwent similar modifications. Like the fingerboard, eighteenth-century tailpieces were frequently veneered fruitwood, sometimes inlaid with decorative elements. Tailpieces were affixed by either gut or wire. The solid ebony tailpiece appeared after 1800. Narrower in design, this tailpiece was raised to a greater angle to match higher fingerboard and bridge settings.[67]

THE BOW

J. M. Raoul summarized the condition of the bow in 1802: "like the bow of the violin, the bow of the violoncello has been endlessly modified," for "essentially the charm of these two instruments lies in the conduct of the bow."[68] Violoncello bows of the eighteenth century demonstrate rich diversity, in keeping with regional differences in musical style, variations in bow grips, and distinctions between bows used for the orchestra and those designed for soloists.

---

65 "Nouveau tirant pour le violoncelle," *Revue Musicale*, 8, no. 14 (April 6, 1834), 110–111.
66 Watchorn, "Baroque Renaissance," 826.
67 Ibid.
68 J. M. Raoul, *Méthode de violoncelle* (Paris: Pleyel/R 1972), p. 2.

Plate 2 Luigi Boccherini c. 1764–67 (Italian, eighteenth century, oil on canvas 133.8 × 90.7 cm, Everard Studley Millet Bequest 1961, National Gallery of Victoria, Melbourne, Australia)

Plates 3a–c Bridges of the eighteenth and early nineteenth centuries (The Shrine to Music Museum, Vermillion, South Dakota)

For the first part of the century, performers alternated between performing dance music, accompaniments, and solo works, each genre requiring a bow suitable to the violoncello and its stringing. The bow used for playing dance music was the shortest in design; it was abandoned first by Italian musicians and had outlived its usefulness by the mid-point of the century.[69] However, bows having distinctive qualities for orchestral or solo playing remained necessary. Corresponding to the lighter stringing of solo instruments, solo bows were thinner than those used for the more heavily-strung orchestral instruments. Discussing this necessity for the violin, the *Musikalische Real-Zeitung* specified that:

69 Boomkamp, *Collection of Instruments*, pp. 55–56.

A violin that only allows a thin setting, because it will lose tone with a thicker one, will also have a thinner bow. And with a violin of a thicker setting the opposite is the case. There is, although seldom, a bow that follows the middle way between thin and thick, heavy and light, so that one can use it on almost all violins.[70]

Earlier in the century, Quantz had recommended the use of two different types of bows for the violoncello. He additionally advised that solo bows be strung with white hair, while orchestral bows should have black hair, "with which the strings may be struck more sharply than with white ones."[71] Similarly specific, a repair bill to the Esterháza estate of March 3, 1767 states that the bow has been rehaired with white hair.[72]

Precise dating of extant historic bows is difficult, since most eighteenth-century bows were not stamped by their makers. Iconographic sources provide some assistance, but many purportedly historical pictures and descriptions by eighteenth- and nineteenth-century historians are inaccurate. It must also be noted that little is documented about bows used by players who retained the underhand grip used by gambists. For these reasons, the evolution of bow making in Europe in the eighteenth century can only be painted in the broadest terms. Notwithstanding these limitations, however, certain trends in design alterations are discernible throughout the century.

Bow makers modified their products in response to the demands of musical style, many being influenced by virtuoso violinists such as Corelli, Tartini, Cramer, Fränzl, and Viotti. As solo music became more legato and slur lengths increased, the bow stick was lengthened to correspond. When performers desired a bow capable of placing greater leverage against the string, necessary for the execution of sudden dynamic changes, the camber of the bow stick was given a concave shape and flexible pernambuco wood replaced the stiffer snakewood. As the stick became increasingly concave, alterations to the tip were made to increase the distance between the stick and hair. The elongated "pike" or "swan's head" tip, such as that seen in the Boccherini portrait, gave way to the "battle axe" or "hatchet" shape of the transitional Dodd bow pictured in Plate 4. The extra weight of these tips made more weight at the frog necessary for balance. The frog was then elongated and filled with decorative elements to increase the weight. When performers wanted more hair attached to the frog without its bunching up, the ferrule was devised.

The progression and adoption of these various elements of bow design took place over the course of the eighteenth century, varying among locations and makers. The centers of development were Mannheim, Paris, and London, the cities in which virtuoso violinists were working. By the later

70 "Anmerkungen Ueber die Violin," *Musikalische Real-Zeitung* (July 30, 1788), col. 37.
71 Quantz, *On Playing the Flute*, p. 241.
72 Landon, "Haydn at Esterháza," p. 136.

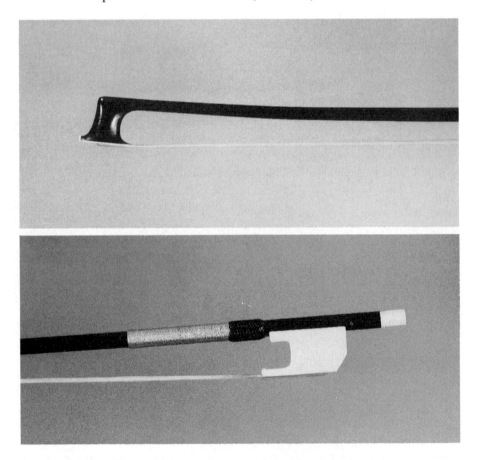

Plates 4a–b Transitional bow by Edward Dodd *c.* 1770–80 (The Smithsonian Institution, Washington, D.C.)

part of the century, individual bow makers were gaining renown for their skills and the family names of Tourte, La Fleur, Meauchand, Dodd, and Tubbs became singled out for the excellence of their work. The search for improvement also produced numerous innovations tried and discarded. Such is the "horseflesh" stick of Edward Dodd, with its experimental frog, shown in Plate 5. The fact that this bow was made as an experiment probably accounts for the maker's use of the cheapest brazilwood (the term "horseflesh" was used to describe the porous, heavily grained wood).[73]

Tradition states that the optimum design for a bow usable on both solo and orchestral instruments, yet responsive to the stylistic requirements of soloists, came from Paris. Created by the Tourte family during the 1780s,

---

73 I am indebted to Anthony Elmsly for his analysis of various grades of brazilwood/pernambuco and bow making. Letter to the author, October 14, 1995.

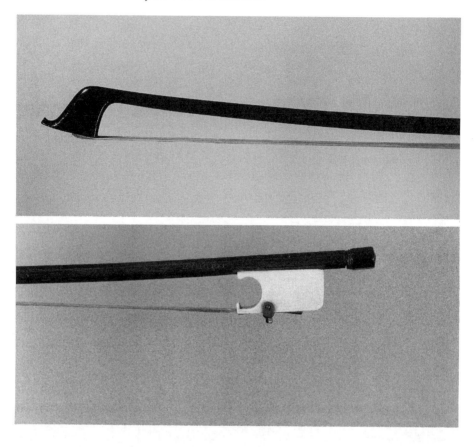

Plates 5a–b Experimental bow with "horse-flesh" stick by Edward Dodd (The Smithsonian Institution, Washington D. C.)

the "Tourte" bow, the end result of the many alterations and experiments undertaken throughout the century, is believed to reflect the influence of the violinist G. B. Viotti. Viotti lived in Paris between 1782 and 1792 and the bowing techniques favored by him and his protégés Rode, Kreutzer, and Baillot are contingent upon the characteristics inherent in the "Tourte" design.[74]

There is general agreement as to what the Tourte family accomplished with their bow design. Tourte *père* developed the ferrule, while his son, François Tourte, devised the method of shaping the camber of the stick by

74 Studies which investigate this relationship include Chappell White, "Giovanni Baptista Viotti" (Ph.D. thesis, Princeton University, 1957); Pat Bryan Curry, "The François Tourte Violin Bow: Its Development and Its Effect on Selected Solo Violin Literature of the Late Eighteenth and Early Nineteenth Centuries" (Ph.D. thesis, Brigham Young University, 1968); Mary Frances Boyce, "The French School of Violin Playing in the Sphere of Viotti: Technique and Style" (Ph.D. thesis, University of North Carolina, 1973).

heating the wood, thus preserving the natural elasticity and resilience of the wood fibers. Bows before this point had been shaped by carving the wood. In addition to maximizing the natural flexibility of the bow stick, Tourte *le jeune* established a uniformity of shape, length, and weight. Pernambuco was chosen as the preferred wood for all but the cheapest bows, the head was given a "hatchet" shape to give sufficient distance between the hair and the stick, and the frog was standardized as to shape, with increased weight being added by the use of a metal mechanism and assorted decorative additions to achieve the desired balance.[75] The length of the violoncello stick was set at 72.2 cm. to 73.6 cm., with a hair length of 60.3 cm. to 61 cm. The center of gravity was placed about 18.2 cm. from the frog.[76]

Experimentation with bow design did not cease with the development of the "Tourte" bow. Tourte's bows were originally constructed without a metal underslide on the frog and, to prevent undue wear on the component parts, the underslide was later added. This addition is attributed to François Lupot II, younger brother of the Parisian luthier Nicolas Lupot.[77]

Although a great admirer of Tourte, J. B. Vuillaume carried out further innovative designs. He also offered his own design modifications to the Tourte bow. Although Lupot had added the metal underslide, Vuillaume noticed that after several years of wear, the frog did not adhere firmly to its position on the stick. Vuillaume subsequently worked with carving a recess in the stick so that the frog rested in, instead of on, the stick. The recess was rounded rather than being left octagonal. Vuillaume was not able to incorporate this idea with complete success into his own bow manufacturing because he also rounded the ferrule at the top of the frog, thereby narrowing the width of usable hair. However, his concept of a recessed stick was later explored by the Hill bow makers with success.[78]

A manufacturing innovation which had greater success at the time was Vuillaume's hollow steel bow. Production of this model, which incorporated a more elongated head, began in 1834 and continued for about sixteen years, with approximately eight thousand bows being produced.[79] The use of steel was, in part, an attempt to overcome the difficulty of obtaining quality pernambuco wood, but the bow was also intended to be lightweight and supple. A bow of this design is pictured in Plate 6.

Another innovative bow introduced by Vuillaume was the 'self-

75 David D. Boyden et al., *The New Grove Violin Family* (London: Macmillan, 1989), p. 213.
76 F. J. Fétis, *Antony Stradivari*, trans. John Bishop (London: William Reeves, 1864/R 1964), pp. 117–118.
77 Mark Reindorf, "Authentic Authorship," *The Strad*, 101, no. 1203 (July 1990), 546–550.
78 Roger Millant, *J. B. Vuillaume: sa vie et son œuvre*, trans. Andrew Hill (London: W. E. Hill and Sons, 1972), p. 108.
79 Reindorf, "Authentic Authorship," 548.

rehairing' design.[80] The idea behind this bow was that the amateur could change the hair as easily as he changed a string on his instrument. Developed in the early 1830s, the concept was popular during this decade, Etienne Pajeot also making bows of this type. Pajeot's self-rehairing bows were exhibited at the 1834 Exposition Universelle.[81]

Although the Tourte-design bow came into being shortly before the French Revolution, its general adoption throughout Europe was as gradual as the acceptance of instrumental alterations. First used by performers who had associations with Paris, Tourte's bows are documented as being the bows of choice for J. L. Duport and Romberg and were also probably used by Janson and Lamare.[82] Demonstrations of the excellence of Tourte bows were frequent during the years of the Napoleonic Wars, as Lamare and Romberg toured throughout Europe. Romberg's compositions, in particular, were dependent upon the leverage inherent in the bow design.

Writing about the contrabass in 1816, Dr. Nicolai made reference to the fact that the "so-called Paris" bow had been introduced into Germany by Rode, Spohr, "and similar masters." He stated that, in his opinion, this design was also the best for the contrabass and that, at this point in time, its use had already been introduced to violoncellists.[83]

NOTATION

As with other aspects of eighteenth-century violoncello performance, the writing of notes and fingering directions in printed music was varied and sometimes confusing. The rapidly expanding range of the instrument, in particular, led to diverse methods of using clefs, as composers and publishers worked to determine the most convenient method of notation. While bass clef was used most commonly to write notes within the first two octaves, C to c^1, pitches of the third octave came to be notated with movable C clefs in the early part of the eighteenth century. In 1741, Corrette stated that Italian players preferred tenor clef, while French players used alto clef.[84] However, the development of thumb-position fingerings soon led composers to expand notation beyond such consistency.

As Italian performers were at the forefront of technical development during the first half of the century, it is natural that these same composer-

80 A "self-rehairing" bow by Vuillaume is held in the collection of the Smithsonian Institution.
81 Paul Childs, "The Bows of Etienne Pajeot," *The Strad*, 104, no. 1136 (April 1993), 374.
82 J. L. Duport recommended Tourte's bows in his *Essai*. Romberg is known to have owned two Tourte bows, now in the private collection of Edmund Kurtz.
83 Dr. Nicolai, "Das Spiel auf dem Contrabass," *AMZ*, no. 16 (April 17, 1816), cols. 259–260.
84 Corrette, *Méthode*, p. 1.

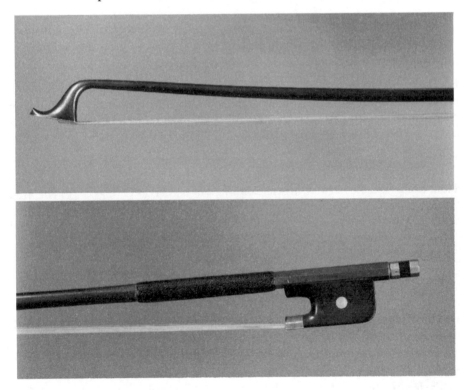

Plates 6a–b   Hollow-steel bow by J. B. Vuillaume (The Smithsonian Institution, Washington D. C.)

performers devised a manner of notating music complementary to the placement of notes on the fingerboard. Following the pattern of adhering to vocal clefs, in addition to tenor clef, Italian composers adopted the use of other movable C clefs, writing all notes to be played at the written pitch. This system was adopted by many violoncellists of other nationalities until about 1760, but the exceptions provide further evidence of how individual-istic violoncellists were during this period. A case in point is Filtz, whose works were composed over a relatively short period of time before his death in 1760 and are notated in a variety of ways. To take three manuscript solo sonatas as examples, that in A major is written in the bass, tenor, and G clefs at pitch, while the sonata in D major uses the bass and G clefs, the G clef played one octave lower than notated. The C minor sonata, on the other hand, is written using bass, soprano, and G clefs, the bass and so-prano clefs read at pitch, the G clef read down one octave.[85]

85 These sonatas are held in the Staatsbibliothek zu Berlin, KHM 1267, 1268, and 1269.

According to Romberg, the system of using movable clefs could conform to the placement of the thumb in setting fingering patterns. Discussing Boccherini's use of clefs, Romberg explained:

Boccherini has used all the clefs employed in Music with the greatest precision. In his works, it is immediately perceived what position the thumb should occupy in playing the Thumb-passage. Thus he noted his music in the Bass-clef as high as the D above the first leger line in the common position. He wrote in the Tenor-clef as high as the upper D, but always without using the thumb. For the Thumb-passages he began with the Contr'alto in B as far as C , he used the Soprano-clef from D to F , and the Violin-clef from G and upwards . In the Tenor-clef he wrote as far down as the G .[86]

Earlier Italian composers did not utilize the G clef, limiting themselves to the bass clef and movable C clefs. As seen in Lanzetti's sonatas op. 1, published in Amsterdam, this system of notation was in use as early as the mid-1730s. Such clef usage is also found in violoncello compositions published in Paris during the 1740s and 1750s, and in London through the 1770s. However, during the 1760s, as seen in the sonatas of J. P. Duport, publishers increasingly sought to make violoncello music adaptable for both violoncello and violin. They therefore regulated notation to two clefs, the bass and G clefs, notes written in the violin clef being played one octave lower on the violoncello. Writing at the beginning of the nineteenth century, J. L. Duport remarked that such notation had been in place for the previous thirty years.[87]

By the 1780s, this system had become the predominant method of writing the solo voice in violoncello music, accompaniments being written in bass and tenor clefs. As the range of the instrument continued to increase, however, it became practical to consistently write notes at pitch in the G clef, necessitating further instruction to avoid confusion. Such was the purpose of a letter from Beethoven to Sigmund Steiner, in which he outlined the common system of notation using the G clef:

So as to avoid all errors you must know that in all those works of mine where in the violoncello part the treble clef is used, the notes should be played an octave

---

86 Romberg, *School*, p. 65.
87 Duport, *Essai*, p. 4.

lower, i.e. this passage

must sound as follows:

But if 'in 8va' is written over it, as here,

then it should sound like this:

If 'loco' is written,

then the notes are in the same position as in the treble clef, namely:

Players eventually began to view both systems of notation as flawed. Romberg stated that Boccherini, himself, began to find too many movable clefs confusing and eventually adopted the sole use of the bass, tenor, and G clefs.[89] This method of notation is also found in the last two concertos of Tricklir, who began publishing his compositions at pitch in the three clefs in the 1780s. Following in Tricklir's footsteps, Romberg became a vocal advocate for this system. He defined his opinion on the subject in an 1807 letter to Friedrich Kunst, specifying that in his works and in those of his cousin, Andreas, violin, tenor, and bass clefs were always written to be read at pitch.[90] Bemoaning the French system of notation, still in use in Germany throughout the nineteenth century, Romberg wrote in his method:

A practice has hitherto prevailed, of playing those notes which are written for the Violoncello in the Violin-Clef, an octave lower than the pitch of the Violin. Far from being inclined to sanction such a practice, I am decidedly and strongly opposed to it...Unfortunately, however, several celebrated Composers have noted

---

88 *Letters of Beethoven*, vol. II, pp. 594–595.
89 Romberg, *School*, p. 65.
90 Schäfer, *Romberg*, appendix, letter no. 2.

the Violin-clef in Violoncello-music, an octave higher than it should be played. We cannot with justice reproach these great Masters with ignorance of their art, but we may certainly reprove them for their adoption of a bad habit.[91]

All of Romberg's compositions were published at pitch. Such was his impact on other European violoncellists that movable C clefs and the French system of notation were generally avoided by the 1820s.[92] Romberg also codified other indicators, heretofore unstandardized. Notation designating the open string varied throughout the eighteenth century in accordance with language. The French used "a" for *à vide*, while English and German performers generally wrote "0". "0" was also employed by many performers to designate the thumb, and by some to mark natural harmonics. Other signs used for harmonics were Raoul's "har:," "∧," found in the music of Berteau and J. L. Duport, and "∨," Bréval's symbol. Some composers simply marked *flautino* or *flageolet* over the appropriate notes, a method suitable for a series of pitches played as natural harmonics. Signs for the thumb, in addition to the "0," include "C," used by Lanzetti and Filtz, Gunn's "×," Breval's sign "ss," the "e" of Kauer's method, "+" in Crouch's tutor, and Alexander's "–".

As an introduction to Romberg's op. 2 concerto, published in Paris in 1802, a written explanation was included to define the applied notation. At this time, a system was introduced that would eventually be adopted internationally. In Romberg's works, 1, 2, 3, 4 represent finger numbers, "0" signifies the open string, "♀" is used for the thumb, and 2<u>da</u>, 3<u>da</u>, and 4<u>da</u> refer to the specific string utilized.[93] His designation for harmonics, the "0" placed on top of the finger number "$\frac{0}{3}$," appeared in the op. 3 concerto, published the same year. Directional markings for down-bow "⊓" and up-bow "∨" followed the system introduced by Parisian violinists.

---

91 Romberg, *School*, p. 65.
92 Baudiot, as one example, writes of notating passages at pitch "in the style of Romberg." Charles Baudiot, *Méthode pour le violoncelle*, op. 25, 2 vols. (Paris: Pleyel, [1826, 1828]), vol. II, p. 51.
93 Bernhard Romberg, *Grand Concerto pour Violoncelle*, op. 2 (Paris: Erard).

3

The bow grip and instrument hold

The foundation of all further performance characteristics is laid by the bow grip and instrument hold, for these define accessibility and leverage in drawing the bow against the strings. Far from being stagnant techniques, customary holds changed throughout the eighteenth century in response to alterations in musical style and to accommodate ever-changing bow and instrument designs. Changes, however, were not uniform but, as with other performance traits, evolved through regional preferences.

THE UNDERHAND BOW GRIP

The underhand bow grip was historically used by gambists and was adopted by numerous early violoncellists, many of whom played both instruments. This bow grip is described by Georg Muffat as being in use in Italy at the end of the seventeenth century and later references specify that some Italian and German violoncellists continued to play this way through the beginning of the nineteenth century.[1] Quantz indicated in the middle of the century that, among German players with whom he had contact, the underhand bow grip was as common as the overhand grip. His preference, however, was for the overhand grip and he noted that the Italian players of his acquaintance played like violinists, that is with an overhand bow grip.[2]

Despite indications that many Italian violoncellists played with an overhand grip, regional variations in Italy existed for the better part of the eighteenth century. Charles Burney wrote that Vandini, a frequent accompanist for Tartini, played with an underhand grip, as did all the players he

---

1 Georg Muffat, *Florilegium secundum für Streichinstrumente*, ed. Heinrich Rietsch in *Denkmäler der Tonkunst in Österreich*, vol. IV (Graz: Akademische Druck- u. Verlagsanstalt, 1959), p. 21.
2 Quantz, *On Playing the Flute*, p. 241.

witnessed in Padua.[3] Diversity was also true of German players and was remarked upon to the end of the century. While touring Germany, Burney noted that Marcus Grauel, a violoncellist at the Berlin court, played with an underhand grip.[4] The same was true of Johann Schetky, of whom a most detailed description was reported in the *AMZ*:

Usually the bow is managed with the thumb under, and with four fingers over the stick, as with the violin, except that with the violoncello the arm hangs down and the bowstroke goes downwards…With Schetky it was different. The thumb lay on the frog of the bow, the forefinger alone on the stick and the three other fingers underneath on the hair. Through the pressure of that [the fingers] lying below, especially of the little finger, he increased or decreased the power of his bow stroke, and thereby brought the maximum strength to the lower parts, or the loveliest oboe tones to the higher parts![5]

THE OVERHAND BOW GRIP

The practice of holding the bow from above the stick developed under the influence of violinists. During the first part of the seventeenth century, there were several differing methods of finger placement for an overhand bow grip. Muffat stated that French violoncellists held the bow similarly to French violinists, with the fingers on top of the stick and the thumb under the hair.[6] This method of playing was still accepted by French players when Corrette wrote his method. He illustrated this bow grip as a second recommendation, in addition to two other overhand methods. His first method of holding the bow overhand is above the frog, places the thumb on the stick, and is noted as being used by many Italian players; a third method places the hand at the frog. His explanation reads:

De la maniere de tenir et conduire L'Archet.

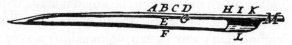

One takes the bow in the right hand. There are three different ways to hold it: the first being the manner most used by the Italians, is to place the 2nd, 3rd, 4th, and 5th fingers on the wood ABCD, and the thumb under the 3rd finger E.

3 Burney, *An Eighteenth-Century Musical Tour in Central Europe and the Netherlands*, vol. I, p. 104.
4 Ibid., vol. II, p. 203.
5 *AMZ*, no. 5 (October 16, 1799), cols. 33–34.
6 Muffat, *Florilegium secundum*, p. 21.

The second manner is to place also the 2nd, 3rd, and 4th on the wood ABC, the thumb on the hair F, and the little finger placed on the wood opposite the hair G.

And the 3rd manner to hold the bow is to place the 2nd, 3rd, and 4th fingers next to the frog HIK, the thumb under the hair L, and the little finger next to the wood M. These three different ways of holding the bow are equally good...[7]

Only the first of Corrette's bow grips, the Italian method, was taught after the mid-part of the century. Boccherini's portrait (Plate 2, p. 68) illustrates Italian practice, while English adoption of this style is delineated in Crome's 1765 tutor, in which it was advised that the bow is held "near the Nutt with the Thumb and fore Finger, and supported with the other Fingers near the end at a small distance from each other."[8] In France, Cupis recommended this same hold in 1772:

The bow is held in the right hand close to the frog, the four fingers on top of the stick and fairly advanced so that the index and the ring finger may easily touch the hair; as it is the index which gives all the force to the bow, it must be more advanced than the others on the hair. The thumb is found on the other side of the stick between the index and the ring finger...[9]

Cupis' admonition regarding the importance of the forefinger is repeated by J. L. Duport, whose instructions for the bow grip, like those of Aubert, Raoul, Bréval, Bideau, and the Conservatoire, duplicate those of Cupis. Once codified, the French bow grip changed little during the course of the nineteenth century, even though the design of the bow changed significantly. While most French tutors omit references to specific bow design preferences, Duport was one of the earliest exponents of the "Tourte" bow, recommending it as the finest bow available.[10]

Although Duport stated that the choice of bow model and bow grip were individual matters and varied greatly among players, he was very specific in explaining his own methodology, warning against a bow grip in which the hand was slanted too far forward in the manner of a violinist:

The thumb should lie flat on the stick; the middle finger should be on top of the hair; the index finger should be forward on the stick a short distance from the middle finger; it should be mobile, because the more it is moved away from the middle finger, the better the bow's grip on the string: This mobility, sometimes great, sometimes average, or even almost imperceptible, according to the circumstances, is very necessary for expression. The little finger should be placed on top of the stick and the ring finger finds itself, therefore, naturally placed. It is necessary that this ring finger only touch the hair lightly, otherwise the bow would be

---

7 Corrette, *Méthode*, p. 8.
8 Crome, *Compleat Tutor*, p. 11.
9 François Cupis, *Méthode nouvelle et raisonnée pour apprendre à jouer du violoncelle* [1772] (facsimile edition, Arnaldo Forni, Civico Museo Bibliografico Musicale di Bologna), p. 1.
10 Duport, *Essai*, p. 175.

Plate 7 Jean-Louis Duport (Portrait attributed to Madame Vigée-Lebrun. Dimitry Markevitch collection)

placed too much forward in the hand, which could, it is true, increase the grip on the bow but which would destroy all the mobility or the play of the fingers (which is very useful). When I say that the ring finger must not touch the hair, I mean to speak of an average hand; for those who have long fingers, this finger must some-what touch the hair, without the bow being too far forward in the hand. With this hold of the bow, the thumb is placed between the middle finger and the ring finger.[11]

Visual evidence of Duport's bow and bow hold exists in the portrait from the school of Madame Vigée-Lebrun (Plate 7), a copy of a 1788 painting by Rémy-Furcy Descarsin and presently in a private collection. The details of Duport's playing attitude have been exactly duplicated from the original.[12]

Although unified in the method of holding the bow, not all French violoncellists of J. L. Duport's generation adopted the use of the Tourte bow: for example, Bréval's representation of correct violoncello practices shows a player using a pre-Tourte stick (Fig. 3.1).

Tourte-design bows were consistently employed by the following generation of French players, as was Duport's recommended bow grip. Baudiot's tutor is explicit in this regard, his illustration (Fig. 3.2) supplementing these instructions:

The right hand holds the bow, with the fingers placed naturally on the stick, close to the frog and without stiffness. The index or first finger is stretched, slightly separated from the other fingers and embracing the stick at the knuckle of the second joint, where it usually forms a callus; the median or second finger reaches the hair of the bow only with its tip; the third finger or ring finger comes very close to the hair without touching it, remaining slightly bent against the stick; finally the little finger rests pressed against the stick, above the beginning of the frog, from the extremity of the bow, while the thumb is placed opposite and between the second and third fingers, gripping the stick with the interior fleshy part and slightly close to the nail.[13]

According to Baudiot's student O. C. Vaslin, this bow grip was the cause of extensive damage inflicted upon the right side of Baudiot's Stradivari instrument. French violoncellists before Baudiot used the C string infrequently in solo compositions and the change to the Tourte bow with its heavier frog had had little effect on their treatment of this string. Baudiot, however, was much influenced by Romberg's use of the C string but did not adopt his bow grip; consequently, he frequently hit the bout of his violoncello while playing. Vaslin described the problem thus:

---

11 Ibid., p. 156.
12 Letter to the author from Sylvette Milliot, February 26, 1996. The Descarsin painting is reprinted in *Instrumentalistes et luthiers parisiens XVIIe–XIXe siècles* (Paris, 1988).
13 Baudiot, *Méthode*, vol. I, p. 9.

Fig. 3.1 Illustration from the method of J. B. Bréval

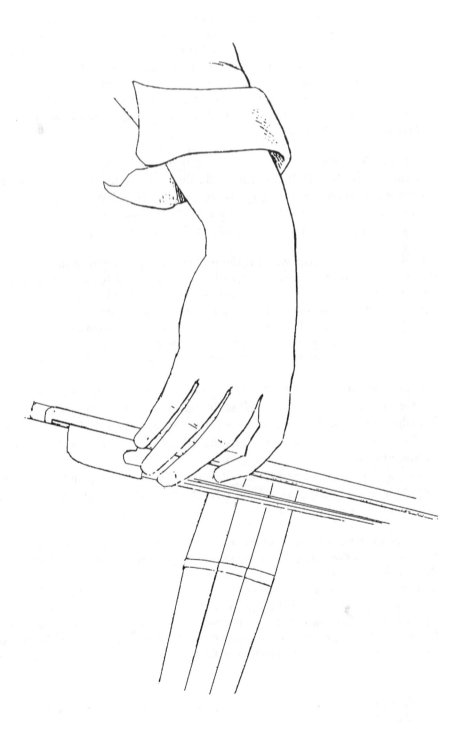

Fig. 3.2 Bow grip as illustrated by Baudiot

As to the bow, the proper hold had been demonstrated to me by the professor, but there remained the management of it through which, with care and reasoning, one might hope to achieve all possible effects. A misdemeanor which had disastrous consequences was for me one of the best lessons I received. The sight of my teacher's mutilated Stradivarius, the edge of the C string side cracked, the rib so much damaged as to need repair, to the disgust of the celebrated luthier Lupoz [Lupot], caused it to become the subject of serious reflections, made privately, discussion being forbidden.[14]

Vaslin's reflections resulted in a bow grip which amalgamated Baudiot's teaching with that of the violinist Baillot, whom he greatly esteemed. Vaslin maintained the bow grip above the frog, but slanted his fingers at a greater angle towards the tip, raising his wrist in compensation. Sensitive to the criticism he must have encountered, Vaslin instructed:

I do not allow a bow hold with the thumb flat and especially with the little finger descending as far as the frog; not that it is an absolute obstacle, but because, in allowing the bow to be only supported and not carried, it leaves much to be desired in the thousand details that one encounters in chamber music, and because lastly the very people who practice this hold pronounce its condemnation when they declare it impossible to achieve on the violoncello both a clean and clear détaché and also all the effects of the bow which are heard from violinists.[15]

Baudiot's students were not the only players of the following generation of Conservatoire-trained violoncellists to maintain a bow grip above the frog. Norblin's students likewise followed the traditions of J. L. Duport, as seen in the 1878 portrait of Franchomme (Plate 8), playing with an ivory-mounted bow.

    The use of an overhand bow grip above the frog remained common in other parts of Europe as well. In England, Gunn's instructions echoed those of Cupis and J. L. Duport:

The bow must be held betwixt the second finger and thumb, in such a manner, that the first and second joint of the thumb shall form an angle, and the point of the thumb be opposite to the middle of the second joint of the second finger; the hair of the bow will be then pressed by the middle of the first joint of that finger, or by the point of it: the first finger should be separated about half an inch from the second. The pressure is in a great measure given to the bow by the first finger; but, at each turning of the bow, this pressure on it is to be taken off, by the first and second joint of that finger advancing farther from the second. The third and

---

14 Olive Vaslin, *L'art du violoncelle: conseils aux jeunes violoncellistes sur la conduite de l'archet* (Paris: Richault, [1884]), p. I.
15 Ibid.

Plate 8 Auguste Franchomme with the Alard string quartet, by F. Hillmacher

fourth fingers are to lie on the bow, at nearly the same separation, but without any pressure on it, their office being only to keep the bow properly balanced.[16]

The anonymous method printed by Clementi & Co. during the first decade of the nineteenth century similarly explained the bow hold: "the Bow must be held a small distance from the Nutt, & the greater part of the first joint of all your Fingers, except the fourth, must reach over, but not so far as to touch the end of your Thumb."[17]

Instructions from Crouch and Lindley indicate that an above-the-frog bow grip was still common to English violoncellists through the mid-part of the nineteenth century; Crouch placed the little finger about half an inch above the frog.[18] While Lindley's description is less restrictive than the teachings of earlier tutors, his methodology was also strongly influenced

16 Gunn, *Theory and Practice*, first ed., p. 60.
17 *New and Complete Instructions for the Violoncello* (London: Clementi, Banger, Hyde, Collard & Davis, [before 1810]), p. 7.
18 Frederick W. Crouch, *A Compleat Treatise on the Violoncello* (London: Latour, [1827]), p. 7. Crouch was a violoncellist with the King's Theatre. His method, which plagiarizes substantial portions of the Paris Conservatoire tutor, was reviewed in *The Harmonicon*, 5, no. 1 (January 1827), 28–29.

by that of J. L. Duport. He is, however, the only author to advocate a slight inclination of the tip of the bow towards the bridge, a recommendation made to facilitate an even, full sound:

The Bow is held between the thumb and the first joint of the first finger, which gives the necessary pressure. The little finger must be placed upon the Nut - or near it, and the other fingers must assist in governing the Bow without impeding the freedom of the wrist. The Bow should be drawn across the strings with the point inclining a little downwards, the hair must be turned slightly towards the fingerboard.[19]

A grip above the frog was also the method by which Belgian players held the bow. The transmitter of French technique was Nicolas Platel, a student of J. L. Duport and Lamare, and the first violoncello instructor at the Royal School of Music in Brussels. The bow grip above the frog was still in evidence at the conservatory in 1889, illustrated in the violoncello tutor of Jules De Swert.[20] A photograph of Pablo Casals from 1907 indicates that this type of bow grip was also common to the Spanish school of violoncello performance during the nineteenth century.[21]

Likewise, an absence of contradictory documentation suggests that Austrian and Bohemian players of the eighteenth and early nineteenth centuries played with the bow held above the frog. Bernard Stiastny recommended this bow grip:

The bow is held in the right hand, close to the frog between the thumb and the second and sometimes third fingers. It is placed on the strings about two to three inches from the bridge, and it is pushed and pulled parallel to the bridge with the wrist.[22]

Stiastny's prescribed position of the bow on the string was approved by most violoncellists, irrespective of performance school. Players generally agreed that the bow had to be set on the string two to three inches from the bridge, the stick angled slightly towards the fingerboard, and drawn perpendicular to the bridge. The majority of instructions also state that control of dynamic variation was affected by the position of the bow in relationship to the bridge. Lindley presented a concise description of how sound production could be influenced by bow placement:

The place for the Bow is about two inches from the Bridge, but this distance varies according to the quality of the tone required. A reedy tone is produced by placing

19 Robert Lindley, *Lindley's Handbook for the Violoncello* (London: The Musical Bouquet Office, [before 1855]), p. 5. (No. b.160; quotations are reproduced by permission of The British Library.)
20 Jules De Swert, *The Violoncello* (London: Novello, 1927), p. 4.
21 *Joys and Sorrows: Reflections by Pablo Casals as Told to Alfred E. Kahn* (London: Macdonald and Co., Ltd., 1970), p. 112.
22 Bernard Stiastny, *Violoncell-Schule*, 2 vols. (Mainz: Georges Zulehner), vol. I, p. 2. (Quotations are reproduced by permission of The Music Library, University of California, Berkeley.)

the Bow closer to the Bridge, and a mellow tone is gained by using the Bow nearer to the fingerboard. An inch from the Bridge gives the extreme of metallic or reedy tone, two inches will give a medium quality, and three inches, with moderate pressure, will ensure a soft and Fluty effect. With some Instruments these distances may require to be increased, and even lessened, but in most cases they will be found correct.[23]

Other aspects of bow management to gain uniform agreement were the relationship of wrist movements to changes in bow direction and string crossings. J. L. Duport provided careful instructions about these techniques:

There are two quite distinct movements…when one wants to pull or push the bow completely horizontally on the string, as I said previously, it is necessary that the wrist respond, like a mechanical hinge, otherwise the point of the bow will face the floor when pulled, and the sky when pushed…

The second movement of the wrist, of which I spoke above, serves to change the string. I assume that the bow is resting on the second string: one only has to raise the wrist a little, and the bow finds itself placed on the first string; if, on the contrary, one has it [the wrist] a little lower, the bow would have found itself on the third string; the arm has nothing or almost nothing to do with this; one should make this movement each time one changes to another string.[24]

THE ROMBERG BOW GRIP

For German violoncellists, the bow hold remained an individual choice. Dotzauer affirmed that "concerning the hold [of the bow], the experts are not in agreement, and one finds amongst the best players those that hold it as close as possible against the frog and others that grasp it further away."[25] He did not mention the underhand bow grip, which was still illustrated in some iconographic sources at the beginning of the nineteenth century.[26] His description is of two distinctly different overhand grips, one above the frog, the other at the frog. Consistent with the methodology of other European violoncellists, a bow grip above the frog was taught by Kauer and Alexander and was presumably employed by other German players who followed this tradition.[27] However, despite the prevalence of this bow hold, other strategies evolved after the turn of the nineteenth century, and, as

---

23 Lindley, *Handbook*, p. 5.
24 Duport, *Essai*, pp. 159–160.
25 Dotzauer, *Violonzell-Schule*, pp. 6–7.
26 See Fig. 16 in Tilden A. Russell, "The Development of the Cello Endpin," *Imago Musicae*, 4 (1987).
27 F. Kauer, *Kurzgefasste Anweisung das Violoncell zu Spielen* (Vienna: Johann Cappi, [1788]), p. 5; *Jos. Alexanders Anleitung zum Violoncellspiel* (Leipzig: Breitkopf und Härtel, [c. 1801]), p. 1. Alexander was a violoncellist at the court of Duisburg.

with many aspects of violoncello technique, the instigator of change was Bernhard Romberg.

Virtually nothing is known about Romberg's training, but his concertos, the first of which was composed in 1791, emulate the style of the French violin school of Viotti, Rode, Kreutzer, and Baillot. The works use techniques dependent upon intense leverage against the lower strings, a recognized trait of Viotti's playing.[28] The desire for a leveraged bow stroke was one of the deciding factors in the formulation of the Tourte bow, and with the advent of this bow design many Parisian violinists began to play with a consistently lower grip.

The lower bow grip of the French violin school allows greater pressure to be placed against the string, a practice not embraced by French violoncellists. The differing relationship of the fingers to the frog evident from a comparison of French violin and violoncello bow grips is documented in articles on both instruments published in the *Correspondance des Amateurs Musiciens*. Instructions for violinists follow the method advocated by the Conservatoire violin tutor of Baillot, Kreutzer, and Rode:

The bow is held in the right hand. The little finger is placed immediately above the end of the frog, half an inch from the screw, the other fingers equidistant, but only slightly spread, so that those four occupy a distance of about four inches; the thumb below between the first and second finger...[29]

Instructions for the violoncello bow grip place the little finger next to the frog, rather than by the screw:

The bow is held in the right hand. The little finger is next to the frog, the two following straight, so that they rest on the hair; the fourth, or index, should wrap around the stick, and the thumb is placed perpendicularly opposite the center of the four fingers...[30]

Romberg's tenure in Paris gave him the opportunity to familiarize himself with the Tourte-design bow. He owned at least two made by Tourte, stamped Romberg 1 and Romberg 2 on the ferrule.[31] Like the French vio-

---

28 One of the hallmarks of Viotti's style was use of the fourth string. This was discussed by Baillot in a Conservatoire discourse at the 1812 *Distribution des Prix*. Baillot explained, "violin playing has become more varied, more intense, more majestic, that is to say, since the celebrated Viotti has extended its limits and increased its potential by introducing into his noble and grandiose music the frequent use of the fourth string, a use which one did not find consistently in the works of composers who preceded him." Quoted in Pierre, *Conservatoire*, p. 911. Eugène Sauzay, Baillot's son-in-law, remarked that Baillot, himself, "pulled the sounds of a contrabass from the fourth string." See François-Sappey, "Mémoires d'Eugène Sauzay," 168.
29 *Correspondance des Amateurs Musiciens*, no. 14 (February 26, 1803), 1.
30 *Correspondance des Amateurs Musiciens*, no. 46 (October 8, 1803), 1.
31 These bows are in the current possession of Edmund Kurtz. According to Mr. Kurtz, they are a twin set of identical bows which have never been parted. He considers that they were made at the same time, while Romberg was living in Paris, and were constructed from the same stave of pernambuco wood. The frogs are ebony, with mother-of-pearl and silver mountings and are con-

linists, Romberg, too, was playing with a grip at the frog by the early years of the nineteenth century. The first existing description of his bow grip comes in a letter written on April 25, 1807 to his friend Friedrich Kunst, a Viennese civil servant and amateur violoncellist. Kunst had presumably enquired about Romberg's technique, perhaps because it differed from that of the Viennese players. Romberg wrote two letters giving specific instructions as to how to hold the violoncello and bow.

I hold the bow close to the frog and indeed so that the thumb lies on the upper and the middle finger on the under side of the frog. The stick of the bow lies in the middle of the top joint of the thumb. The third finger lies next to the middle finger so that it covers the beginning of the frog; the little finger lies next to the third finger. The first [finger] is placed so that the stick of the bow rests in the first joint. All must rest firmly lying on the bow and not move while bowing.[32]

The instructions presented in Romberg's method thirty years later echo those given to Kunst; they include illustrations of Romberg's Tourte bow and the method by which the bow was held. This bow grip is shown in Fig. 3.3.

Although Romberg concurred with other violoncellists that wrist motion played a part in changes of bow direction and string crossings, his wrist and finger action was much stiffer than that of other virtuosos. As seen in the upper drawing of Fig. 3.3, Romberg's wrist rigidly dipped downwards as the bow tip was approached. Flexibility of the small joints was not a concern; rather, his emphasis was on the use of a relaxed arm motion, with the movement of the bow originating from the forearm. Romberg described his reasons for this manner of playing as follows:

The knuckles of the hand should run parallel to the stick of the bow, which position should always remain, as much as possible, unaltered, for it is only by placing the hand firmly on the bow, that a strong, powerful tone can be drawn from the Instrument, without employing the force of the arm. On the other hand, if the strength of the tone proceed from the arm, the Instrument must be played with the arm held stiff; which entirely prevents a fine execution, and this is the cause that so few players arrive at perfection, they play with the arm, and not with the hand.[33]

Romberg's lower bow grip was adopted by his Russian and German protégés. These players include Matvey Viel'gorsky and the Hamburg student J. N. Prell, who then transferred the technique to his student Sebastian

structed without a metal underslide. The two bows are slightly shorter than normal, the hair of the first bow measuring 59.9 cm. and the second measuring 59.7 cm. The bows were owned in succession by Romberg, A. Piatti, Robert von Mendelssohn, Hammig (a Berlin dealer), Max Adler (a Chicago amateur), and Kurtz.

32 Romberg's correspondence to Kunst was published in Schäfer, *Romberg*, appendix, letter no. 2.

33 Romberg, *School*, p. 8.

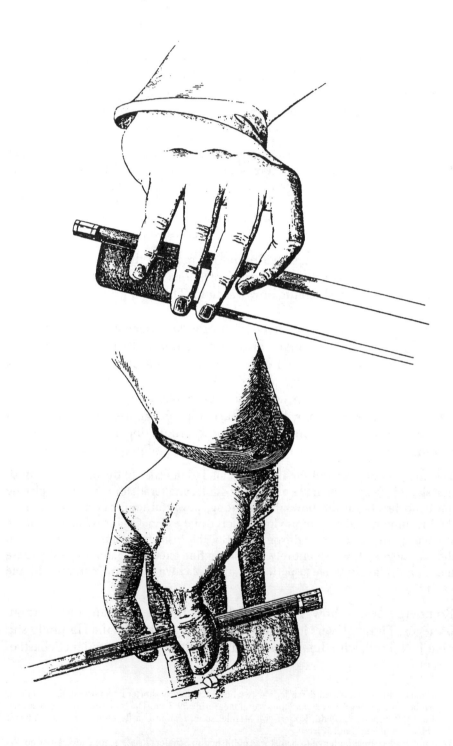

Fig. 3.3 Illustration of Romberg's bow grip

Lee. The Dresden school, led by Dotzauer, similarly followed Romberg's teachings, but with one notable difference. Drawing on what he considered to be the most appealing characteristics of both Romberg's and J. L. Duport's methodology, Dotzauer developed a bow grip at the frog that incorporated rounded, relaxed wrist and finger motions. Stressing the relationship between an outwardly bent thumb and mobility, he gave directions for the bow grip which are easily recognizable to modern players:

One places the thumb as close as possible sideways against the stick and places it on the first joint opposite the nail. If one bends the first joint too far inwards, the hand loses its flexibility. The upper part of the arm is not held too high, because this appears affected. The inner part of the hand should be rounded without force, held slightly protruding over the bow stick. The index finger should be somewhat bent, but less than the others. The middle finger rests on the hair; the fourth and little finger rest without pressure on the stick; in general one should place the fingers without force, neither too far from nor too close to each other.[34]

Dotzauer's position with bow and instrument is illustrated in Fig. 3.4.

THE INSTRUMENT HOLD FOR SOLO PERFORMANCE

Dotzauer's representation portrays the most common violoncello hold for solo performers of the eighteenth and early nineteenth centuries; the instrument was raised from the floor and placed between the calves of the legs. Comparison of written descriptions shows minor variations in the placement of the feet, and eighteenth-century players tended to hold the instrument a little lower than nineteenth-century performers, probably because of the shorter playing length of the fingerboard. However, the size of the violoncello in relationship to the human body allowed for little individuality in cradling the instrument, although slender, long-legged players certainly had an advantage over short, stout ones. The main issues influencing the violoncello hold were nicely summarized by Gunn:

The end to be answered, in holding the instrument is, that it shall be steady, and admit of the action of the bow without being impeded by the left knee or the right thigh. The first of these purposes is best answered, by pressing the upper edge or rim of the Violoncello against the side of the calf, or thickest part, of the right leg; and the side of the instrument against that of the left: and, for the latter purpose, it is necessary that the right leg be perpendicular to the ground, and that the left leg be extended in an oblique direction until the left foot be four or five inches more advanced from the body than the right; and it is also necessary, that the instrument be raised sufficiently to admit of the free action of the bow, on the fourth string, near three inches from the bridge, without touching the right thigh.[35]

34 Dotzauer, *Violonzell-Schule*, p. 7.
35 Gunn, *Theory and Practice*, first ed., p. 60.

Fig. 3.4 Dotzauer's position with bow and instrument

Most nineteenth-century teachers were concerned that two aspects of the instrument hold be particularly addressed. Firstly, the instrument had to be held so that the bow could be moved without hitting either knee. Secondly, the player had to sit with a straight back so that chest pain could be avoided and breath could be drawn with ease. The instructions of J. L. Duport and Romberg are thorough yet concise on these issues. Duport advised that the left leg be placed slightly ahead of the right:

One should first be seated on the front part of a chair; then place the left foot forward away from oneself, and bring the right nearer; then place the instrument between the legs, so that the lower left bout at the bottom rests against the joint of the left knee, so that the weight of the instrument is carried on the calf of the left leg; and the left foot turned outward. If the knee were, by contrast, placed in this bout, it would prevent the bow from passing easily when one sought to use the Chanterelle or the first string. The right leg should be placed against the lower ribs of the instrument to maintain a secure hold.[36]

Romberg, whose illustration of the instrument hold is shown in Fig. 3.5, played with the violoncello higher and straighter than most other players. He also drew the distinction that the legs had to adjust slightly to accommodate instruments of different widths, and instructed the player to keep the violoncello upright and immobile, with feet parallel rather than the left foot ahead of the right:

The best posture to be adopted for sitting, is that which is most conducive to bodily health. In playing the Violoncello, the chest should not be bent in, nor the shoulders pushed forward, as such a posture is sure to produce a crooked back. This must be avoided, and that posture be adopted, in which the Instrument can be played freely and with ease. During play, no change of posture should take place; least of all, any thing like an affected attitude, which may betray the trouble employed in playing. The player then, is seated on his chair, in such a posture that his thighs do not cover the seat of the chair; his legs should fall in a straight line to the ground, his feet turned a little outwards, but not too much. The heels may be six inches apart, and one foot not more advanced than the other. If the lower part of the Instrument be rather small, the feet should be brought a little closer together; if too broad, the feet must stand farther apart. The chair upon which the Player sits should not be too high. The round side of the lower part of the belly of the Instrument should be pressed into the calf of the right leg, and the round part of the back, into the left calf, so that the Instrument may rest on both legs, without being closely pressed by either.

  The player should arrange his posture as nearly as possible in such a manner that the back of the Instrument may rest on his chest. The Instrument should be so held, that the lower part of the scroll (the C peg) may be in an exact straight line with his left eye, and that, between the scroll and his eye, there may be a distance of two fingers-breadth.[37]

36 Duport, *Essai*, p. 5.
37 Romberg, *School*, p. 7.

Fig. 3.5 Romberg's hold of the violoncello

Greater flexibility of positioning was advocated by Lindley. Unlike other teachers, he recommended rotating the violoncello to accommodate the placement of the bow on individual strings, and required a firmer hold than that of Romberg:

The performer should sit forward upon a chair, with the left foot a little in advance of the right foot.
     The Instrument should be supported by the calf of the left leg, whilst the right leg affords the pressure requisite to keep it in its place. The Instrument must be under the control of the right leg, so that it may be made to slant either one way or the other, as the first and second, or third and fourth strings may be most required.[38]

Method books written before the end of the nineteenth century universally omitted references to the endpin for those engaged in solo playing. However, one of the results of holding the violoncello without an endpin is that the vibrations of the instrument body are dampened by the legs. This concern is mentioned by mid-nineteenth-century performers. Like Romberg, both Kummer and Vaslin warned of pressing the legs too tightly against the ribs.[39] Kummer also instructed the player to place the left foot slightly ahead of the right, but to maintain a straight back:

The violoncellist sits on the forward part of the seat; the feet must be extended forwards a little, but the left somewhat more than the right, while the upper body stays in a straight and natural position. The instrument is held between the legs, so that the lower front edge on the right touches the right calf, and the left rear edge touches the left calf of the player. But avoid, as much as possible, covering the surface of the ribs, because in doing so the vibrations of the sound would be hindered. One holds the violoncello inclined somewhat backwards, far enough on the left side so that the C peg is about an inch away from the face; the upper part of the body comes to lie easily against the chest. The instrument is always held high enough for the movement of the bow not to be restricted through bumping against the left knee.[40]

The use of an endpin facilitated a gentler grip of the legs around the instrument, thereby accomplishing the aims of both Kummer and Vaslin. Adrien Servais is credited with introducing this device – necessary to him because of his girth and the fact that he played on an uncut, larger Stradivari – during the second half of the nineteenth century. However, use of an endpin was not unknown before Servais: Lincke most likely used one because of his crippled leg. In the previous century, Crome had recommended its use for beginning students, who then discontinued the practice when they became comfortable with the instrument. In his words:

38 Lindley, *Handbook*, p. 5.
39 Vaslin, *L'art*, pp. 2–3.
40 F. A. Kummer, *Violoncell-Schule*, op. 60 [1839], ed. Hugo Becker (Leipzig: Peters), p. VIII.

This instrument may be Consider'd as a Large Fiddle only held the contrary way, and the fourth string is next to the Bow-Hand, as the Body is turn'd downward, the lower part is to rest on the Calves of the Leggs supported with the Knees, but for the greater ease of a Learner we wou'd advize [sic] him to have an hole made in the Tail-pin and a Wooden Peg to screw into it to rest on the Floor which may be taken out when he Pleases.[41]

Notwithstanding the influence of Servais, the endpin did not become a standard fitting for soloists until the beginning of the twentieth century. Among nineteenth-century players, its use had decidedly amateur or womanish overtones and professional musicians probably regarded it as an affront to their male pride. Even after it gained more general acceptance, many later nineteenth-century violoncellists, including Alfredo Piatti, W. E. Whitehouse, Friedrich Grützmacher, and Robert Hausmann, refused to play with one.[42]

THE INSTRUMENT HOLD FOR ACCOMPANYING

During the period in which larger violoncellos were used for accompaniment, the width of the instrument required that most players either place it on the floor, or in a minimally raised position for either sitting or standing. Eighteenth-century sources demonstrate that various lifting-and-holding devices were fairly common, use of an endpin being an option for some accompanists.[43] Corrette remarked that the endpin was sometimes employed with larger violoncellos if the violoncellist stood to play[44] and two German music primers provide evidence that, as late as 1786, this was an orthodox method of handling the instrument. Johann Samuel Petri, who published *Anleitung zur praktischen Musik* in 1782, confirmed that some ripienists stood to play. He viewed this position as outmoded, preferring to accompany in a seated position because of the increased demands that "modern" music placed on shifting. However, the anonymously written *Musikalisches Handwörterbuch* (Weimar, 1786) advocated the standing position with endpin, the author arguing that a proficient violoncellist could successfully execute any passage, including those in the higher registers, as well as a seated player. This author included specific instructions for endpin construction and mentioned that some German luthiers routinely fitted violoncellos with endpins.[45]

---

41 Crome, *Compleat Tutor*, p. 1.
42 Russell, "Development of the Cello Endpin," 342.
43 Ibid.
44 Corrette, *Méthode*, p. 7.
45 Tilden A. Russell, "New Light on the Historical Manner of Holding the Cello," *Historical Performance*, 6, no. 2 (Fall 1993), 73.

Use of an endpin is not alluded to by the French school which followed Corrette. However, two methods of holding the violoncello for accompanying were offered by several teachers. While the preferred method was to hold the instrument between the legs as for solo playing, a lower setting remained a second option well into the nineteenth century. Rather than rest the instrument on the floor or on an endpin, the recommendation was made to place the violoncello on the instep of the left foot. Precise instructions for this method are found in the tutors of Aubert, Raoul, and the Conservatoire.[46] Those of the last-named read:

One sometimes rests the violoncello on the left foot, leaning [the foot] towards the left and turned inward. The upper end of the lower bout then rests on the top of the left knee; the right leg should be vertical and not stretched back as is often the case. This position may be conveniently used by skillful masters in an orchestra because the instrument placed in this manner occupies less space.[47]

Writing twenty years later, Baudiot also referred to this positioning of the violoncello, similarly recommending it as a second option. He remarked that placing the instrument on the left foot was not only convenient for orchestral playing but necessary for people who were too small to grip the violoncello between their legs.[48]

The player most noted for this instrument hold was Lamare, who placed the violoncello on his left foot both when accompanying and when performing solos. His playing was described in detail subsequent to Viennese appearances in 1805. The author, who considered Lamare's quartet accompaniments to be superior to his solo playing, explained that "he does not hold it [the violoncello] as others, firmly between the legs, but rather he places it on the left forefoot, supported by the left knee, placing the right foot back, next to the stool upon which he sits, and holds it so that the instrument is tight against the right knee."[49]

THE OBLIQUE LEFT HAND POSITION

For much of the eighteenth and nineteenth centuries, there existed two opposing methods of placing the left hand on the neck of the instrument. The more established but increasingly less popular of these was to slant the hand in an oblique fashion. Gunn, who considered this method of playing to be antiquated, illustrated the two opposing hand positions (Fig. 3.6).

In spite of Gunn's opinion, a select group of virtuosos continued to teach

---

46 P. F. O. Aubert, *Methode ou nouvelles etudes pour le violoncelle*, op. 9 (Paris, [1802]), p. 2; Raoul, *Méthode*, p. 4.
47 Baillot, *Méthode*, p. 5.   48 Baudiot, *Méthode*, vol. I, pp. 5–6.
49 "Etwas über Lamare," 102.

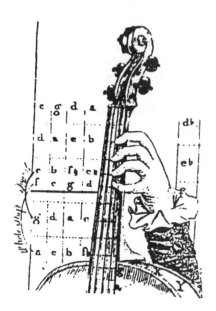

Fig. 3.6 Left hand positions as illustrated by John Gunn

and play with this hand position, several voicing strong opinions as to why it was superior to a perpendicular one. These players include Tricklir, Janson, Romberg, and Vaslin. Tricklir's hand position is inferred by fingerings contained in his concertos, but Janson's is reported in a contemporary journal, where it is negatively compared with that of J. L. Duport:

In Janson's school, the thumb is not placed horizontally; but it is upright, or perpendicular to the back of the fingerboard. Consequently it dominates the whole hand. We admit that this may result in a stronger pressure, but also in less ease in playing the B♭ and the D♯ on the highest string.[50]

Strength of finger pressure, resulting in increased sound production, was the main reason cited by Romberg and Vaslin for their choice of this hand position. The thumb was brought upward against the side of the neck and the fingers were curved, the string being pressed with the fingertips. Because of the slant of the hand, the fingers would not buckle if a finger was

50 *Correspondance des Amateurs Musiciens*, no. 45 (October 1, 1803), 1.

double-jointed. Romberg, whose left hand position is illustrated in Fig. 3.5, described it thus:

The hand should so hold the neck, that the 1st finger should clasp it round, the 2nd should be bent so as to form three sides of a square, the 3rd should be bent half round, and the 4th held straight. The thumb should lie exactly opposite to the 2nd finger, placed so as not to project beyond the finger-board, but on a line with its surface.

The palm of the hand should not be pressed close to the neck, but should be kept hollow, nor must the hollow of the thumb be pressed close to the 1st finger. The neck also must remain quite free in the hand, with all the fingers placed upon the 1st string, and the string lying straight under the fingers.

The more curved the fingers, when placed upon the strings, the firmer will be the tone; the flatter they lie, the weaker, and more dull. The truth of this fact is confirmed by experience; the pressure of the fingers, however, should not be excessive, or else the sinews of the fingers will suffer.[51]

Vaslin's attitude is of particular interest because, having a double-jointed third finger, he adopted the oblique setting in opposition to Baudiot's teaching. Here he explains how he came to use this position, much to the amazement of his classmates:

In 1808, arriving in Paris at the age of 14 years, and having been accepted at the Conservatoire in Baudiot's class, I joined the "Orchestre des Variétés" at 15. I worked with ardor, but without much discernment, aiming above all for agility, which progressed despite the faults and the shortage of means. There I met M. Ropiquet Sr., a modest violinist who became impressed by my eagerness. He was struck by the defects of my left hand; it was no trouble for him to make me understand that the dimensions of a large instrument were no reason to exclude the logical and rational principles of the smaller one, its brother. Therefore, I abandoned the placing of the thumb opposite the second finger, so it was only the very end of the fingers which pressed down on the string. At the same time I had to set right, with some pain, the third finger, which was inclined to collapse in the former defective position, rectifying this by perseverance with the encouragement of this good counselor whose advice concerned only this left hand; it was a step forward which in fact surprised my fellow students.[52]

Vaslin believed that this hand position, in which "the thumb encircles the neck and the fingers are all arched and consequently present only the tips to the strings," allowed him to play with greater clarity and uniformity of sound.[53] This was due to the fact that the left hand shape was the same when playing in any of the first four positions. He also considered that his

51 Romberg, *School*, p. 7.
52 Vaslin, *L'art*, p. I.
53 Ibid., p. 3.

execution was more rapid and that he obtained greater force from his fingers, particularly the weak third and fourth fingers.

THE PERPENDICULAR LEFT HAND POSITION

As violoncello fingerings became increasingly idiomatic, the majority of players became convinced that a perpendicular left hand position was the most natural and yielded the purest, most dependable intonation. There are numerous citations giving instructions for this hand setting, many of which warn against slanting the hand in an oblique manner. John Gunn, referring to his illustration (shown in Fig. 3.6), wrote:

It will then be necessary to place the fingers of the left hand, on the finger-board, in the position at *Fig. 16*, separating the fingers at about an inch asunder, and raising them into the form of an arch; the fingers will then be at about the interval of a semitone from each other, but the first at that of a tone from the nut; and the fingers will, by the most simple movement, in crossing the strings, come to the proper distances for any of the notes on the other strings; a great advantage which this position of the hand has over that formerly is use (see *Fig. 18*), where the natural tendency of the fingers would be to move in the oblique direction, shown by the dotted lines; a tendency which can be counteracted but with great trouble.[54]

J. L. Duport similarly railed against this "terrible hand position," which he considered made the interval between the first and second finger too large for correct intonation.[55] Duport's colleagues at the Conservatoire dismissed Janson's playing techniques after his death in 1803 and rejected his slanted hand position. Their instructions molded the hand by wrist and thumb placement, while stressing that the neck must not lie against the fleshy part of the base of the thumb:

The hand should be placed above the neck, the first joint of the thumb resting under the neck, which should be barely squeezed and against which the part of the hand which joins the thumb to the index must not rest. The wrist should be slightly away from the neck in order that the fingers be well-positioned and slightly rounded.

The middle of the first joint of the thumb should be opposite the middle finger.[56]

Another succinct description was provided by Hus-Desforges, who stressed a rounded hand position:

---

54 Gunn, *Theory and Practice*, first ed., pp. 60–61.
55 Duport, *Essai*, p. 8.
56 Baillot, *Méthode*, p. 5.

One should not grip the neck of the violoncello, but hold it loosely, and place the thumb slightly sideways towards the opposing space between the first and the second finger: nor should one stretch the fingers, but firmly press the tips on the strings, and form a kind of arch with the hand, while avoiding touching the strings with the fingernails, in order to obtain a beautiful quality of sound.[57]

Although Romberg's playing was an overwhelming influence on German players, few adopted his oblique hand position; most followed the lead of French and Italian players. The Dresden school, reflecting the influence of J. L. Duport upon Dotzauer, played with a perpendicular left hand position. This is demonstrated in Dotzauer's illustration (Fig. 3.4) and attested to by Kummer:

The left hand encloses the neck of the instrument in [a] hollow form. The thumb lies on the under side of the neck, opposite the forefinger and middle finger, and serves the hand as a base. In order to obtain a good strong sound, the fingers must always fall on the strings like hammers and with their tips firmly pressed.[58]

Stiastny, likewise, advocated this method of playing. He wrote:

The thumb of the left hand is gently placed four fingers away from the head of the violoncello; however this must not be held sideways, but firmly in the middle of the neck, and the tip of each finger on the string must be always firm and strong...[59]

Lindley, too, chose a perpendicular left hand setting. His eminently practical instructions address the importance of the thumb against the back of the neck, tone production, and the issue of fingernail length:

The thumb must be placed at the back of the Neck of the Violoncello, opposite the interval between the first and second fingers. The top of the thumb acts as a kind of pivot for the whole hand, so that if it be placed improperly, there will be an uncertainty in the fingering. The fingers must be curved sufficiently to bring the tops of them upon the strings, which must be pressed very firmly, or the tone will be husky and coarse. The nails should be kept closely pared, in order that the touch may be full and decided; long nails not only lead to a sideways stopping of the fingers, but they also cut the strings.[60]

THE HAND SETTING FOR THUMB POSITION

Instructions for playing in thumb position are less frequently found than those for other hand settings, most violoncello methods being written for

57 Pierre-Louis Hus-Desforges, *Méthode de violoncelle* (Paris, [1829]), p. 2.
58 Kummer, *Violoncell-Schule*, p. X.
59 Stiastny, *Violoncell-Schule*, vol. I, p. 3.
60 Lindley, *Handbook*, p. 5.

beginning students or adult amateurs. Even the Conservatoire method, while giving explicit exercises in fingering technique, refers only briefly to the shape of the hand. The authors remarked that the thumb works as a movable bridge whose use could begin with the D on the A string, although it was more usual to place it in fingering patterns beginning with the G on the A string. The thumb was to be placed on its right side parallel to the bridge. The authors instructed that, because the string increases in height as notes approach the bridge, the thumb must be firmly pressed against the strings.[61] Pictorial evidence of French playing technique is supplied by the portrait of Duport (Plate 7).

More graphic discussion was provided by Romberg, who considered thumb-position passages as natural to the instrument as any other type of playing. As Fig. 3.7 shows, Romberg achieved the rounded shaping of the hand by inserting a bottle cork underneath the palm. His explanation is as follows:

The mode of holding the hand in playing thumb-passages is less difficult than that required where the thumb is held under the neck. When the hand is once accustomed to a good position, it is not easily lost, and I shall here lay down a very simple means by which it may be attained. Take a thick bottle-cork, and hold it between the thumb and 1st finger, close to the muscle, and so placed that both the fingers may lie asunder, and the other fingers be very little curved, so that they may meet the strings conveniently. The thumb should be bent neither out nor in, but should make a straight line with the hand. Care should be taken that the fingers in playing, be not bent too much inwards, but that they fall on the strings with a slight curvature. The nails of the left hand should be cut short, otherwise the strings will be touched by them instead of by the ends of the fingers. The strings must be pressed down by the fore-joint of the Thumb, but only two strings at a time, so as to make a fifth across the strings. One string must exactly cross the joint of the thumb and the other lie under the middle of the nail...

The pupil must play with the Cork in his hand, until he has accustomed his fingers and thumb to retain the same position without it; for nothing is more injurious than to press the thumb together with the fingers upon the strings. He must endeavour to acquire a sufficient strength in the thumb, as to make it a firm bridge across the strings, without any support from the fingers. The arm must lean gently against the edge of the belly and the elbow must not be pushed forward, but should be held free and kept back.[62]

Romberg ended his instructions with admonitions about instrument position, the inference being that numerous players pushed the violoncello outward, the instrument slipping closer to the floor. He maintained that the violoncello must remain upright, in order that the student "not follow the

---

61 Baillot, *Méthode*, p. 80.
62 Romberg, *School*, pp. 51–52.

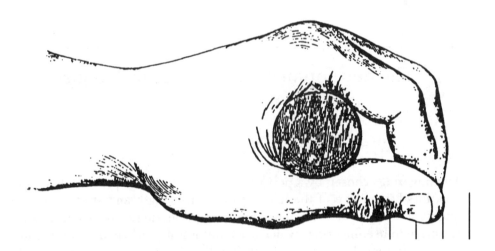

Fig. 3.7 Romberg's hand shape in thumb position

example of many Violoncellists who place the neck of the Instrument upon their shoulder, to play as they imagine, with greater convenience, or stretch forward their feet to see where to place their fingers."[63]

63 Ibid., p. 52.

4

The development of fingering techniques

The fingerings chosen by a performer are determined by a variety of factors. Firstly, the size of the left hand and the length and strength of the fingers and finger joints influence fingering preferences, given that all players strive to use fingerings which are comfortable and yield accurate intonation. Violoncellists with a large hand or long fingers will frequently choose differing patterns from those players whose hand is smaller. Hand position is also an issue, and was especially so during the eighteenth and nineteenth centuries, when some performers preferred an oblique left hand position, others a perpendicular one (see Chapter 3, pp. 99–103). Additional factors are the length and thickness of the fingerboard and neck joint, the length of the instrument's stop and, to some degree, the type of bow used: here, there was notable diversity in the eighteenth century, construction practices for both instruments and bows being varied, with dimensions continually changing. Finally, accepted fingering patterns are always subject to fashion, the vagaries of musical style, and the enthusiasm of youthful quests. Every generation has the tendency to look back on its predecessors and bemoan "the old-fashioned" fingerings previously considered sacrosanct, while touting "modern" fingerings newly devised.

CONCEPTS IN FINGERING WITHOUT USE OF THE THUMB BEFORE 1785

The initial concept of playing the violoncello fingered all notes within one hand position. Additional pitches were gradually added until the half-string harmonics were reached; the use of thumb technique was not yet necessary for the majority of players. This range was sufficient for the execution of accompaniment parts for a very long period of time and only the most virtuoso players grappled with notes above the half-string harmonics before 1750. The few fingered lines of music which exist from the first half of the eighteenth century suggest two fundamentally different methods of addressing fingering patterns which fall below the half-string harmonics – diatonic fingerings versus those which follow the premises of violin or viola da gamba technique.

    Few musicians before the mid-part of the eighteenth century performed exclusively on one instrument and this was especially true of those who took up the violoncello. As intimated in Corrette's tutor, those learning the violoncello were frequently familiar with either the violin or the viola da gamba; accordingly, Corrette devised violoncello fingerings which correspond to fingering patterns used on those instruments.

    For those thinking in terms of violin fingerings, where whole-tone intervals are encompassed with each digit, Corrette substituted the fourth finger for the third finger in the lower positions of the violoncello (Ex. 4.1). When, upon ascending the fingerboard, the intervals between notes become sufficiently close for the third finger to be used, Corrette dispensed with use of the fourth finger (Ex. 4.2).

Ex. 4.1 Corrette, *Methode*, p. 21

Ex. 4.2 p. 33

Corrette also included pattern charts helpful to gambists learning violoncello fingerings, although it must be noted that there are printed inconsistencies. These fingerings include more frequent use of the fourth finger to the exclusion of the third finger and require a change of fingering on select enharmonic notes. These enharmonic finger replacements are made so that pitches comprising a note name using a common letter, i.e. F♭, F♮, F♯, will be played with the same finger (Ex. 4.3).

Ex. 4.3 p. 22

For those wishing to learn fingerings conceived more diatonically, Corrette provided a first-position fingering chart wherein each semi-tone is fingered with a different digit (Ex. 4.4). Although this system is more idiomatic to the violoncello, Corrette advised that violinists would find such fingerings more difficult to become accustomed to owing to the differences between instruments.

Ex. 4.4 p. 42

In defining diatonic fingerings for notes which fall between first position and the half-string harmonics, Corrette divided the fingerboard into the customary four positions, as shown in Ex. 4.5. The first and second positions display stricter diatonic structure than the higher positions, third-position fingerings including notes also considered to form the fourth position.

Ex. 4.5 p. 33

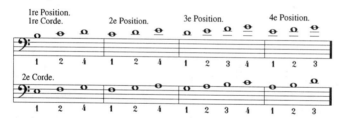

Fingerings for double-stops and *arpeggios* were also diatonically oriented, although the reasoned application of the third and fourth fingers was far from absolute (Ex. 4.6). Corrette recommended that double-stops be played only on the upper three strings, remarking that the low pitches of the C string were too vague for precision.

Ex. 4.6 pp. 38–39
(a) double-stops on the A and D strings

Ex. 4.6 pp. 38–39
(b) *arpeggio* fingerings

Although Corrette demonstrated fourth finger usage for the antecedent notes to the half-string harmonic in third position, he did not recommend the use of the fourth finger for notes above third position. Exclusion of the fourth finger was due to the increasing width of the fingerboard as the bridge was approached and the shortness of the finger itself. Implying the use of an oblique hand position to accommodate the thickness of neck joint and fingerboard wedge, the uppermost notes on Corrette's violoncello are illustrated with 1–2–3 fingerings consistent with violin patterns (Ex. 4.7).

Ex. 4.7 p. 34

Basic concepts in shifting were also addressed by Corrette. He remarked that when one moved from one position to another using consecutive notes, the shift was often accomplished with the same finger (Ex. 4.8a). However, when note patterns were structured with two notes on the same degree, finger-replacement shifts were preferred (Ex. 4.8b).

Ex. 4.8 p. 34
(a)

(b)

The logic behind Corrette's fingerings was common to many eighteenth-century violoncellists, including the Italian virtuoso Lanzetti. Although far from being a comprehensive treatise on all aspects of fingering technique, Lanzetti's *Principes* demonstrates the consistent application of specific fingering patterns.[1] For notes which fall beneath the half-string harmonic, patterns used within half, first, and second position differed from those applied to subsequent positions. Within the first two positions, diatonic fingerings were used, with necessary extensions being placed only between the first and second finger (Ex. 4.9).

Ex. 4.9 Lanzetti, *Principes*
(a) half-position pattern, p. 13

(b) first-position pattern, non-extension, p. 2

(c) first-position extension patterns

A-major pattern, p. 5

E-flat-major pattern, p.11

(d) second-position extension pattern, p. 8

Lanzetti's fingerings for third and fourth position duplicate those of Corrette: whole-tone extensions are permissible between the first, second, and third fingers (Ex. 4.10).

1 Salvatore Lanzetti, *Principes ou l'application de violoncelle, par tous les tons de la manièr la plus facile* (Amsterdam: J. J. Hummel, [c. 1756–67]). (No. 1201/Schulen; quotations are reprod ced by permission of the Gesellschaft der Musikfreunde in Wien.)

Ex. 4.10 p. 2

However, Lanzetti's fingerings in patterns ascending from fourth position do not show the cohesiveness of the 1–2–3 fingerings illustrated by Corrette. Lanzetti demonstrated little regularity in his higher sequences. Most exceptional was the inclusion of the fourth finger in patterns moving beyond the half-string harmonic (Ex. 4.11).

Ex. 4.11
(a) p. 9

(b) p. 10

Note patterns for the lower half of the violoncello entail that, commencing with a stopped first finger, the hand encompasses the interval of either a minor or a major third; three versus four semi-tones. The principal consideration in choosing idiomatic fingerings is the question of when to use a finger to cover each semi-tone and when to reach the distance of a whole tone by extension. As demonstrated by Corrette's discussion of diatonic fingerings, some prescient violoncellists did adopt first-position fingerings which placed a semi-tone under each finger inclusive of the third and fourth digits. After the mid-part of the century, such patterns were commonly, although not exclusively, used for the half, first, and second positions, with necessary extensions executed only between the first and second fingers. However, the latter half of the century witnessed continued disagreement over such systematization in the third and fourth positions, the fingering of which requires working around the neck joint.

Interesting disparities are apparent when the fingerings employed by the French school of Tillière and Cupis are compared to their German contemporary Baumgartner. Baumgartner clearly adopted the use of diatonic systematization when executing notes placed within half, first, or second position. Several of his recommended scale fingerings, such as those used for A♭ major (Ex. 4.12), even provide a choice between using extended fingerings or half-position patterns for notes played next to the nut.

Ex. 4.12 A♭ major scale as illustrated by Baumgartner

However, as with Corrette and Lanzetti's fingerings, whole-tone extensions between the second and third fingers are evident in many of Baumgartner's third- and fourth-position fingerings. His top fingering for the A♭ major scale places whole-tone extensions between the first, second, and third fingers in fourth position. The fingering for the G major scale (Ex. 4.13) similarly duplicates the conjunct third-/fourth-position pattern illustrated by Corrette and Lanzetti, although Baumgartner did provide an additional choice of excluding the third and fourth fingers from the final two notes.

Ex. 4.13 G major scale as illustrated by Baumgartner

Like Corrette and Lanzetti, Baumgartner consistently omitted the fourth finger from third position, a fact observable in the fingerings for the F major scale (Ex. 4.14).

Ex. 4.14 F major scale as illustrated by Baumgartner

Baumgartner altered his fourth-position fingerings for select sequences to include the fourth finger, while consistently omitting this same finger in third position (Ex. 4.15). In many sequences, Baumgartner used 1–2–3 fingerings for notes above fourth position.

Ex. 4.15 Note sequence of Baumgartner

While the use of 1–2–3 fingerings for whole-tone intervals placed above fourth position became a codified concept among French players, Baumgartner, like Lanzetti, was not averse to using the fourth finger with notes adjacent to the half-string harmonic. This is demonstrated in fingerings for the A♭ (Ex. 4.12) and B♭ major scale (Ex. 4.16).

Ex. 4.16 B♭ major scale as illustrated by Baumgartner

The refinement of extended fingerings became a technical focal point for French players of the second half of the eighteenth century. The rejection of extensions between the second and third fingers in patterns within the first four positions of the fingerboard is evident in the methods of Berteau's students Tillière and Cupis. Likewise subtracted from French violoncello technique was the sequence of three semi-tones played with the same finger, evident in Corrette's earlier analogy to viola da gamba fingerings. Tillière explained his choice of fingerings by their relationship to the major or minor third encompassed within one hand position. Limiting extensions to the interval taken between the first and second finger, the following example demonstrates half-, first-, third-, and fourth-position fingerings idiomatic to the violoncello (Ex. 4.17).

Ex. 4.17 Tillière, *Méthode*, p. 11

The choice of 1–3–4 for the minor third hand setting in third position was also demonstrated by Cupis, whose excerpt (Ex. 4.18) contradicts that of Baumgartner (Ex. 4.15). Neither Tillière nor Cupis used the fourth finger above fourth position, transferring instead to fingerings of 1–2–3 to play notes above the half-string harmonic.

Ex. 4.18 Cupis, *Méthode*, p. 8

CONCEPTS IN FINGERING WITHOUT USE OF THE THUMB
AFTER 1785

The systematization of diatonic fingerings inclusive of extensions between the first and second fingers came to be codified by the generation of violoncellists who followed Tillière, Cupis, and Baumgartner. The need to demonstrate idiomatic violoncello technique was, in fact, the premise for the publication of numerous tutors during the first decade of the nineteenth century. The majority of methods demonstrate agreement on the fundamental issues of fingering technique for note patterns lying below the half-string harmonics.

The most common method of organizing fingering patterns was to subdivide the fingerboard into four major positions, each position then further subdivided into fractions of semi-tones; the chart provided by J. L. Duport (Fig. 4.1) succinctly illustrates the major positions. The universality of this premise is observable through the instructions of other contemporary publications, one example being Alexander's "table of fingerings in C major" for second, third, and fourth positions (Fig. 4.2).

In demonstrating the subdivisions inherent in each major position, some teachers organized the fractions into categories by position, while others preferred systematization by key signature. J. L. Duport defined his fingerings by position, the following extract (Ex. 4.19) showing his division of first position.

Ex. 4.19 Duport, *Essai*, p. 147

Alexander explained variations in fingering patterns by key signature, as seen in the fingerings for second-, third-, and fourth-position note patterns in Db major (Ex. 4.20).

Des quatre premières Positions.

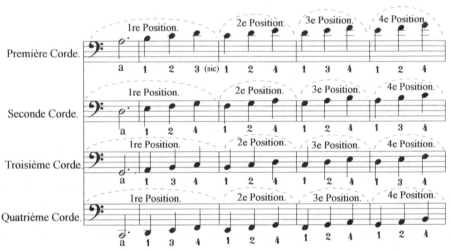

Fig. 4.1 The first four positions as illustrated by Duport

A) Tabelle zu den Applikaturen in C dur.

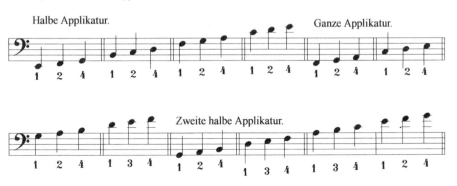

Fig. 4.2 Second, third, and fourth position as illustrated by Alexander

Ex. 4.20 Alexander, *Anleitung zum Violoncellspiel*, p. 22

The majority of violoncello methods written after 1785 demonstrate general acceptance of the concept that idiomatic fingerings could be formed using one finger for each semi-tone in a note pattern encompassing a minor third, with an extension taken between the first and second fingers for those of a major third. However, opinion differed on the inclusion of extensions in minor third patterns. Many players considered it logical to maintain an extended position throughout an entire passage, even if the extension was unnecessary. Such fingerings were chosen either to maintain continuity in the use of extensions, or to avoid using a weak or short fourth finger. Such is the case in the D major scale of Gunn, who recommended extended 1–2–3 fingerings on the A and D strings in conformity with the extended fingerings of the lower strings (Ex. 4.21).

Ex. 4.21 Gunn, *Theory and Practice*, second ed., p. 43

Bréval included alternative fingerings based on this same premise, as seen in his second-position fingering of the E♭ major scale (Ex. 4.22).

Ex. 4.22 Bréval, *Traité*, p. 55

Duport, by contrast, did not countenance the use of unnecessary extensions. His fingerings for all first-position fractions are shown in Ex. 4.19, with those for third position illustrated in Ex. 4.23. The cohesion of Duport's diatonic fingerings was likewise applied to double-stop configurations.

Ex. 4.23 Duport, *Essai*, p. 151

The use of non-essential extensions was a vestige of violin technique, especially those fingerings which placed a whole tone between the second and
third fingers. Both Bréval and Duport confirmed that violin and viola da
gamba technique continued to influence the learning process of many
players.[2] Supplementary evidence is found in the existence of non-idi-
omatic fingerings in other contemporary publications, the extended
fingerings supplied for the G major scale in the English publication of
Clementi & Co. (Ex. 4.24) being one example.

Ex. 4.24 *New and Complete Instructions for the Violoncello*, p. 6

Another example is supplied by Kauer (Ex. 4.25), who used corollary
extensions between the second and third fingers for the Ab and Db major
scales.

Ex. 4.25 Kauer, *Kurzgefasste Anweisung*, p. 7

In addition to extensions taken between the first, second, and third fingers,
as seen in Tricklir's selections, some performers included extended
fingerings between the third and fourth fingers. That Tricklir, a respected,
innovative performer and composer, differed from his French contemporaries in much of his fingering methodology is a possible reason why J. L.
Duport published an edited version of Tricklir's fourth concerto. A carefully notated passage from Tricklir's first concerto illustrates extensions
taken between the third and fourth fingers in second- and third-position
note patterns (Ex. 4.26). These fingerings suggest that Tricklir played on an
instrument with a short neck and used an oblique hand position.

2 Bréval, *Traité*, pp. 4–5; Duport, *Essai*, pp. 144–146.

Ex. 4.26 Tricklir, op. 1, Concerto I, *Allegro*, bars 153–156

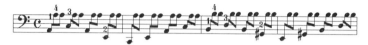

Violoncello methods aimed at students wishing to supersede elementary fundamentals solved the intrinsic problems of extended fingerings by teaching fingering patterns formulated with frequent shifts. Among those teachers who published tutors during the first decade of the nineteenth century, there were two schools of thought on such fingerings: those who recognized that there existed many individual ideas about fingering and considered violoncello patterns, unlike those of the violin, to be inherently inconsistent; and those who wished to impose complete consistency.

Although ascribing to the fundamental systematization of Berteau, Bréval was one who forthrightly countenanced many contradictions in violoncello technique for both fingering and bowing. One illustration of his perception that violoncello fingerings did not yield to consistency was his demonstration of the appropriate use for the third finger following an extension between the first and second fingers: Bréval stated that this fingering could not be employed because such a pattern belonged to violin technique, but an identical pattern could be used on notes falling a semi-tone lower .Uncomfortable with presenting inviolate rules, Bréval believed that fingerings for the lower part of the fingerboard should be devised to avoid tiring the hand.[3]

Bréval allowed for individual preferences by presenting different fingerings for the same note pattern, choices being made between extensions and shifts. His fingerings for A minor patterns (Ex. 4.27) demonstrate alternative methods of playing G♯ on the second, third, and fourth strings.

Ex. 4.27 Bréval, *Traité*, p. 14

3e 4e
Cordes.

3 Bréval, *Traité*, p. 5.

Another violoncellist whose teachings reiterated the difficulties of devising consistent fingerings, and who therefore made a point of providing alternative fingerings for all scales and study passages, was Bideau. In accord with Bréval's sentiments, Bideau stated that "this instrument is without doubt one of the most difficult to finger since one is continually forced to move, especially when one plays difficult passages."[4] Many of Bideau's fingerings are formed from sequential patterns like those for the chromatic scale (Ex. 4.28). However, in addressing the necessity of continuous shifting, Bideau advised economy of motion: recommending that "teachers must therefore teach their students those positions of the hand which change the least."[5] His preferred shifting patterns were those in which the same finger moved from one pitch to the next. The lower fingering for the D major scale illustrates this premise (Ex. 4.29).

Ex. 4.28 Bideau, *Grande et Nouvelle Méthode*, p. 97

Ex. 4.29 p. 6

A more complex example of shifting with the same finger is demonstrated with ascending and descending third spans (Ex. 4.30). In passages without slurs, Bideau's rule was that 1–1 fingerings were used for ascending lines and 4–4 fingerings for descending ones. The advantage of this type of fingering is that the shifts remain small. When slurs were incorporated, Bideau chose patterns which avoided placing a shift within the slur grouping, making 1–1 combinations sometimes necessary in a descending passage (Ex. 4.31).

4 Dominique Bideau, *Grande et nouvelle méthode raisonnée pour le violoncelle* (Paris: Nadermann, [1802]), p. 4.
5 Ibid.

Ex. 4.30 p. 95

Ex. 4.31 p. 96

The desire to avoid shifts within a slur also led Bideau to use finger replacement shifts, as shown in Ex. 4.32.

Ex. 4.32 p. 110

The execution of shifts using one finger was a popular convention. One further illustration is drawn from the method of Raoul (Ex. 4.33), who applied both 1–1 and 4–4 shifts to his upper fingering for the chromatic scale.

Ex. 4.33 Raoul, *Méthode*, pp. 14–15

The alternative point of view, which required fingerings to be organized into systematized patterns, was subscribed to by J. L. Duport, whose disapproval for Bréval's technique was a catalyst for the publication of his own method.[6] Duport credited Berteau with establishing the essentials of violoncello technique, ascribing continued emendations to the work of his older brother, J. P. Duport. He also remarked on the numerous interpretations of Berteau's strictures:

6 See Milliot, *Le violoncelle en France*, pp. 660–661.

As for BERTEAU, it is unfortunate that he did not leave us any of his principles other than by tradition; some of his students, it is true, have written methods for the instrument, but they are not satisfactory enough, the rules of fingering are only touched upon instead of being demonstrated; so that is why, to this day, there are almost as many methods of fingering as there are professors.[7]

Unlike many other players, Duport did not consider violoncello fingering to be problematic, nor did he believe in alternative fingerings for a given passage in the neck positions. His core tenet was that all fingerings should use successive digits, necessary extensions being taken between the first and second fingers. As seen in his fingering for the D♭ major scale (Ex. 4.34), this principle avoids shifts taken between notes with the same finger. Explaining his reasoning, he wrote:

One will find it perhaps extraordinary that in scales I have taken the greatest care to avoid playing two notes with the same finger, as one finds in all the rule books which have been published up until now. My opinion is that this way is incorrect, in that it leads to a wrong effect. Everyone knows that the delicacy of touch of the fingers is what makes a pearl, and it is certain that one does not have this touch when one slides one finger from one semi-tone to another, because if the timing of the bow has not caught the moment when the finger has slid to attack the string, a disagreeable sound follows.[8]

Ex. 4.34 Duport, *Essai*, p. 36

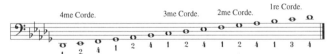

Duport allowed for limited exceptions to his stringent application of this rule, one example being the fingerings for broken thirds . His aversion to shifts taken with the same finger occasionally resulted in other strictures being superseded, as in one passage of Etude 4: overriding the premise that extensions were placed only between the first and second fingers, an extension between the third and fourth fingers is applied to bars 41 and 43 (Ex. 4.35). In this instance, Duport placed the extension between the A♭ and B♮, thereby avoiding a 1–1 shift.

Ex. 4.35 Etude 4, bars 40–43

---

7 Duport, *Essai*, p. 146.
8 Ibid., p. 17.

Duport also allowed for extensions between the third and fourth fingers in select *arpeggio* patterns. His recommendations were reiterated with particular clarity by Baudiot (Ex. 4.36).

Ex. 4.36 Baudiot, *Méthode*, vol. II, p. 198

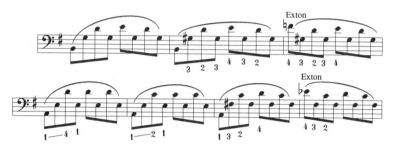

Having taught several prominent Parisian players before his forced departure from the French capital in 1790, Duport was the pre-eminent authority for many French violoncellists. His influence through Levasseur can be seen in the fingering methodology of the Conservatoire tutor: Duport's version of the chromatic scale, a sequential fingering of 1–2–3 patterns with open strings (Ex. 4.37), is duplicated in the Conservatoire tutor, with the addition of an alternate fingering which includes the fourth finger (Ex. 4.38).

Ex. 4.37 Duport, *Essai*, p. 41

Ex. 4.38 Baillot, *Méthode*, p. 107 (tc1)

Duport continually stressed the importance of clean playing combined with evenness of sound production. Like Alexander and many other violoncellists of his generation, Duport disliked shifting within slur groupings. While this limited slur length, Duport advised that bowings and fingerings must frequently be organized as a unit. Ex. 4.39 provides one illustration of this precept.

Ex. 4.39 Duport, *Essai*, p. 88

The systematization of violoncello technique as disseminated by the methods of Duport and the Conservatoire significantly influenced violoncellists of many nationalities. Baudiot, Dotzauer, and Lindley particularly acknowledged their debt to Duport, all being instrumental themselves in furthering his doctrines. Duport's illustrated fingerings thus became conventional among a majority of players and, at this juncture, fundamental facets of fingering technique ceased to be at issue. The division of the lower fingerboard into four positions with internal subdivisions occurs in all subsequent teaching methods, as does the placement of whole-tone extensions between the first and second fingers.

However, complete unanimity among nineteenth-century violoncellists did not exist and one who continued to display independent ideas about fingerings was Romberg. While agreeing with many of the principles held by his French colleagues, Romberg used certain select fingering methods more common among previous generations, as his oblique hand position would, in fact, suggest. Among his prescriptions for the first four positions, his methods of shifting are of special interest.

Unlike Duport, Romberg had no aversion to the execution of shifts with the same finger. The use of 1–1 and 2–2 shifts is seen in his illustrations for correct fingerings (Ex. 4.40). He preferred, like Alexander, to shift the minimal distance necessary to execute the given note patterns.

Ex. 4.40 Romberg, *School*, p. 51

A more extended example of three semi-tone shifts, all executed with the first finger, is found in an etude (Ex. 4.41). The avoidance of shifts within a slur grouping was not a matter of concern for Romberg, as it had been for Duport and Alexander, for the longer slurs intrinsic to his style of playing made this an impossibility.

Ex. 4.41 p. 47

Despite the considerable influence of the French school, shifting remained (and continues to remain) an issue among players. As important as the French contribution was to the codification of violoncello fingerings, the use of increasingly lengthy slur groupings, as well as the changes in style which accompanied the Romantic movement, expanded concepts of how, when, and where to shift. Duport's strong convictions regarding clean, uniform motions were not always adhered to, as the concept of "expressive" shifting took hold. In addition, the desire to demonstrate flamboyant virtuosity challenged violoncellists to conceptualize fingerings for tonal and even visual effects.

"Expressive" shifting had several manifestations. *Portamento*, still viewed in the first half of the nineteenth century as a special effect (see Chapter 6), became increasingly relied upon as a means to represent emotion; traversing the interval between notes with a same-finger shift was a common method of implementation. Both Franchomme and Dotzauer employed *portamento*; examples of conjunct third-finger shifts are illustrated in Ex. 4.42.

Ex. 4.42
(a) Dotzauer, Concerto op. 27, *Allegro*, bars 106–109

(b) Chopin and Franchomme, *Grand Duo Concertant ... sur des Thêmes de Robert le Diable*

bars 68–69

bars 163–164

Dotzauer was especially fond of *portamento* and incorporated it into the lower positions of the violoncello, using such fingerings to exploit the sonority of a given string (Ex. 4.43).

Ex. 4.43 Dotzauer, Concerto op. 100, *Allegro*, bars 85–88

Another form of expressive fingering was demonstrated by Baudiot. He wrote of a fingering technique complementary to articulated slur groupings (Chapter 5, p. 154), a method of bowing that came into use with the Tourte-design bow and was "much used on the Violoncello" for expressive passages.[9] Baudiot demonstrated finger-replacement shifts, the shift concurrent with the bow's hesitation within the long slur grouping (Ex. 4.44).

Ex. 4.44 Baudiot, *Méthode*, vol. I, p. 21 (tc1)

Placing an extended passage on one string became a popular device of Romantic composers. As Dotzauer's opening to his eighth concerto demonstrates (Ex. 4.43), this might be done to exploit the emotional qualities inherent in a particular timbre. In this instance, the composer chose to maintain the deep sonority of the violoncello's C string. In other instances, placing a series of ascending or descending notes on one string was visibly a virtuoso effect, the player purposely disregarding an easier fingering. Such fingerings are found in passages using the neck positions of the instrument (Ex. 4.45), as well as those using the entire range of one string (Ex. 4.46). This latter technique was a special attribute of Bohrer's performance style and, as demonstrated in his variation, incorporation of harmonics was a natural complement to such display.

Ex. 4.45 Lamare, Concerto I, *Allegro Vivace*, bars 285–293 (tc1)

9 Baudiot, *Méthode*, vol. I, p. 21.

Ex. 4.46 M. Bohrer, *Steyrer Volkslied*, var. 3, bars 1–17

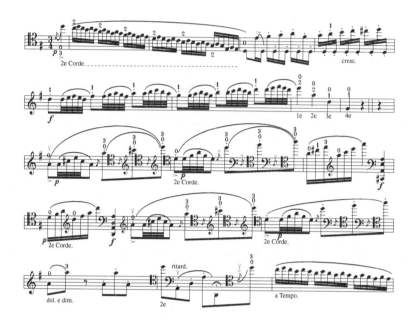

THUMB POSITION: ESTABLISHING THE FOUNDATION

The tessitura of solo works for the violoncello suggests that use of the
thumb became an established virtuoso technique during the 1730s. Implying that such fingerings were common by 1741, Corrette specified where
and how the thumb was to be included in fingering patterns. In keeping
with the inclination of his teaching towards violinists and gambists,
Corrette reasoned that the purpose of thumb fingerings was to facilitate the
transcription of violin music for the violoncello. He instructed that thumb
fingerings began in fourth position, because if the thumb was placed on the
E of the A string, "the thumb at this position puts the 4 strings of the Violoncello at the octave below the four strings of the Violin."[10] The thumb
could be moved forward, always maintaining its position a fourth below
the highest desired note. This gave the player the ability to play violin sonatas, "the thumb taking the place of the nut; this gives complete freedom
to the following three fingers."[11]

A fundamental attribute of thumb-position technique in the mid-part of

10 Corrette, *Méthode*, p. 41.
11 Ibid.

the eighteenth century was use of the fourth finger. It was Corrette's experience that thumb-position fingerings uniquely allowed for its use even in
fourth position. This was an advantage not possible with regular fingerings,
where "one prefers the index finger to the thumb," because the little finger
"becomes useless, as we have already said, after the 1st, 2nd, and 3rd position, being too short."[12] With the thumb in fourth position, the fourth finger
could play notes above the half-string harmonic, as Corrette explained:

One may however use the little finger without disturbing the thumb from the 4th
position [for] the B♮ and the B♭ on the 1st string, as on the same string [chanterelle]
of the violin – in like manner the E♭ on the 2nd string, the A♭ on the 3rd and the D♭
on the 4th string – all these without disturbing the thumb in the 4th position as I
have already said.[13]

Lanzetti's fingerings demonstrate frequent incorporation of the fourth finger above the half-string harmonic. While the tessitura of his exercises ex-
ceeds that mentioned by Corrette, extending to f^2, the technical concepts
illustrated concur with Corrette's teachings. In the excerpt shown in Ex.
4.47, Lanzetti first placed the thumb on G, moving it to fourth-position E
the following bar. Within this fourth-position hand setting, the B♭ is then
taken with the fourth finger.

Ex. 4.47 Lanzetti, *Principes*, p. 15 (C = thumb)

While use of the fourth finger was initially common, use, or non-use, of this
digit came to represent a point of division among violoncellists as thumb-
position fingerings evolved into increasingly complex patterns. French
violoncellists of Berteau's school did not consider use of the fourth finger to
be appropriate in upper-position fingerings; according to the professors of
the Conservatoire, "the use of the little finger with the various positions of
the thumb was unknown by the older teachers of the violoncello in
France."[14] In their opinion, use of the fourth finger came to be associated
with thumb-position fingerings only at the beginning of the nineteenth
century. Raoul and Baudiot both stated unequivocally that, in fact, it was
Romberg who introduced such playing techniques to Parisian players.[15]

12 Ibid.
13 Ibid.
14 Baillot, *Méthode*, p. 80.
15 Raoul, *Méthode*, p. 16; Baudiot, *Méthode*, vol. II, p. 104.

Romberg's exceptional proficiency in thumb position was based on a composite of two simple ideas: (1) that stationary, block hand positions are formed by the thumb acting as a movable nut, from which all ensuing notes extend, and (2) that both the fourth finger and the C string may be incorporated to enlarge the range of notes within a given hand position. The technical possibilities inherent within these two ideas were pushed to the instrument's limits by Romberg, but his playing style was the culmination, rather than the beginning, of this conception of violoncello technique. While the fingerings of Lanzetti suggest that this manner of playing has Italian origins, Romberg's school of performance, ultimately to be centered in Dresden, can be traced back to Mannheim.

The Mannheim court of the 1750s was home to two prominent violoncellists, Innocenz Danzi and Anton Filtz. Players known to have studied under one or both include Schetky, Tricklir, Ritter, and Franz Danzi. While the compositions of the Danzis and Ritter imply to various degrees the fingering techniques under discussion, it is from the notated compositions of Filtz, Schetky, and Tricklir that the path to Romberg is most easily drawn. Like Romberg, all three made a point of marking thumb fingerings. This fact is of itself suggestive of a technique uncommon to the majority of contemporaries, the notation of fingerings being the exception rather than the rule throughout the eighteenth century. Schetky, whose fingering patterns transferred to the Scottish school of the Reinagle brothers and Gunn, summarized Mannheim methodology:

The thumb is placed upon the first and second String in such a manner that the 3d or even the 4th String may be reached and covered. whenever [sic] the Thumb is put upon the Strings it should be press'd hard so that it does not move untill the position is changed.

Some eminent Professors do not allow the little Finger a share in the position of the Thumb. I have found it very useful and often necessary, as the shifting one finger for 2 or 3 notes running must be inconvenient...[16]

The key to the successful application of fingerings within this format is bow leverage. The capacity for increasing leverage against the string was focal to many bow designs of the period, and players associated with the court of Mannheim, such as Cramer and Fränzl, contributed to this element of the design process. Leverage is especially important when notes are played in the upper register of the C string, owing to the challenge of producing an adequate response and good sound from the thicker string. German musicians came to consider the sonority of the solo violoncello's lowest string a distinct attribute, with the result that, at least in Schetky's and Romberg's

---

16 Johann Schetky, *Practical and Progressive Lessons for the Violoncello* (London, 1811), p 30. (No. h1122; quotations are reproduced by permission of The British Library.)

case, they used a bow grip distinctive from that of other contemporaries. As discussed further in Chapter 9, this was a conception of the instrument not shared by players of other regions, French violoncellists, in particular, avoiding inclusion of the C string in solo works before 1815.

Four concertos by Filtz exist in manuscript, with fingerings notated in the B♭ major concerto. Placement of the thumb is consistently designated with the same "C" sign found in Lanzetti's *Principes*. The complexity and tessitura of the note patterns place it as a late work (Filtz died in 1760) and mark the violoncellist as a superb technician. However, the underlying fingering concepts, as noted above, are simple. Filtz put his thumb down, thus establishing his hand position, and took off.

The advantage of maintaining a fixed hand position using horizontal rather than vertical fingerings, is speed and greater reliability in the execution of widely spaced intervals. The thumb notations in Filtz's B♭ major concerto delineate when movement of the hand is necessary, with the melodic patterns within the concerto written to stay within one hand position over the course of extended interludes. These features are apparent in the final twelve bars of the first solo episode (Ex. 4.48). Once the thumb is set in bar 51, the hand setting is moved only in bars 55 and 57.

Ex. 4.48 Filtz, Concerto in B♭ major, *Allegro moderato*, bars 49–60 (tc1, C = thumb)

Use of the fourth finger to augment the range within a set hand position is not clearly implied in the preceding passage, but is strongly suggested in the following excerpt (Ex. 4.49).

Ex. 4.49 *Allegro moderato*, bars 99–106 (tc1, C = thumb)

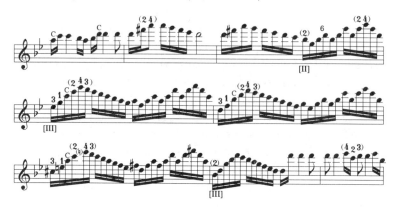

The fourth finger in thumb position is precisely marked in Tricklir's compositions, as are the block hand positions within which his melodic material and passage work are placed. Representative of these technical skills is a lengthy passage from his E major concerto (Ex. 4.50). The thumb is first placed on the F♯ of bar 84, moving to the B♮ in bar 87. Tricklir maintained the hand position set in bar 87 through the following twenty-three bars, before moving back one whole tone. The fourth finger is notated in bar 98.

Ex. 4.50 Tricklir, op. 1, Concerto III, *Allegro Moderato Risoluto*, bars 84–110 (*8va* at pitch, 0 = thumb)

Use of the fourth finger above the half-string harmonics was also adopted by Tricklir's student Bideau (see Ex. 4.28). The relationship between Tricklir and Romberg presents more of a puzzle, as there is little evidence to suggest a personal relationship except for the unconventional characteristics common to their writing for the violoncello. Two distinctive traits of

Tricklir's F♯ minor and A minor *Nouveaux Concertos* intimate that these works are predecessors to the concertos Romberg began composing the following decade. The first of these, notation at pitch (see Chapter 2), is unrelated to the technical aspects within the works, but was nonetheless contrary to the norm for the period. The second trait is the placement of upper-position passage work on the G and C strings, as seen in Example 4.51. In this phrase, the thumb is placed on the G of the G string in bar 63.

Ex. 4.51 Tricklir, Concerto in A minor, *Alla Breve*, bars 63–68

Sopra la 3d e la 4d corda

Although thumb-position fingerings became a German speciality, virtuosity in the upper registers of the violoncello was not exclusive to this group of players. Similar ambitions are inherent in the works of Austrian and Bohemian violoncellists. Many traits similar to those found in German writing are evident in the solos of Jan Stiastny and the violoncello concertos composed by Haydn for Joseph Weigl and Anton Kraft (although none of these specifically prescribes the fourth finger). Stiastny and Kraft did not make fourth finger usage an issue, but did use the upper positions of the lower strings in conjunction with stationary, block hand positions. Stiastny, to great effect, devised whole melodies to fit within a single hand position maintained by the thumb. Variations suited this scheme especially well and such writing is found in the op. 8 duets. The excerpt cited in Ex 4.52 illustrates only the first phrase, but the entire variation was designed for the thumb to remain stationary on the C and F of the A and D strings. Whether or not Stiastny executed the high G with a fourth finger remains open to conjecture.

Ex. 4.52 J. Stiastny, op. 8, duet 2, *Andantino con variationi*, var. IV, bars 1–8

Haydn's concertos exhibit many of the same characteristics, although their melodic invention betrays his unique talents. These works likewise exploit the sonorities of the lower strings, calling for a leveraged bow stroke. While many such passages are not written in thumb position, this being especially true of the C major concerto, one phrase of the D major concerto has challenged generations of violoncellists by the necessity of playing stopped octaves in thumb position on the G and C strings (Ex. 4.53).

Ex. 4.53 Haydn, Concerto in D major, *Allegro*, bars 119–126 (*8va* at pitch)

The fingering requirements of this excerpt are remarkably similar to passages in Beethoven's Sonata op. 5, no. 1 (Ex. 4.54) and the op. 56 Triple Concerto (Ex. 4.55).

Ex. 4.54 Beethoven, Sonata op. 5, no. 1, *Rondo Allegro Vivace*, bars 239–246

Ex. 4.55 Beethoven, Concerto op. 56, *Allegro*, bars 367–370

Appreciation for the sonority of octaves placed on the lower strings is also exhibited in Stiastny's Sonata op. 2, no. 2 (Ex. 4.56), written in the same period as Beethoven's Triple Concerto. The thumb-position demands of this composition are even more extensive than those placed on Kraft in the works by Haydn and Beethoven.

Ex. 4.56 J. Stiastny, op. 2, no. 2, *Andante con variazioni*, var. VI, bars 1–7

While the development of German, Austrian, and Bohemian thumb-position fingerings is traced through solo compositions, French practices are discerned from published methods, fingerings or string designation being a scarce commodity in French solo works before the nineteenth century. Tillière was the first of Berteau's school to address the issue of thumb-position fingerings, and his instructions demonstrate the clearly defined concepts which formed the basis of French technique. Predicated upon the universally accepted tenet that the thumb was used as a stationary nut, Tillière's exercises specify that upper-position fingerings are built around the octave formed between the thumb and the third finger on adjacent strings. As illustrated in Example 4.57, Tillière delineated the notes of the fifth upon which the thumb was to be placed, instructing that the thumb not be moved during the course of the ensuing exercise.

Ex. 4.57 Tillière, *Méthode*, p. 13 (tc1)

As the later Conservatoire professors noted, use of the fourth finger in thumb position was not included as a standard fingering technique. However, Tillière did make use of the little finger for occasional single-note additions on the A string, as illustrated in a passage of *arpeggios* (Ex. 4.58).

Ex. 4.58 Tillière, *Méthode*, p. 15 (tc1)

THUMB POSITION: EXTENDING THE LIMITS

Whereas numerous variations in methodology existed for lower-position fingerings during the entirety of the eighteenth century, patterns for upper-position fingerings were easily established among violoncellists. Virtuosos of the second half of the century uniformly adopted the practice of writing thumb-position passages to conform to block hand positions, with octaves established between the thumb and third finger. The only sources of notable disparity were the functions of the fourth finger and the C string.

Facility in thumb position was equated with virtuosity and numerous solo works composed during the 1750s and 1760s attest to the dexterity of violoncellists from all regions. In an era when technical limitations were viewed as challenges to be continually overcome, performers vied to add range, speed, and special effects to their compositions. The demands for ever-increasing virtuosity instigated changes to instrument and bow design, which in turn inspired performers to further development of technically difficult passage work. Nevertheless, increasing complexity could not alter the fundamental principles of thumb-position fingerings, the physical limitations of the violoncello naturally restricting the number of ways that fingers can be put down in its upper register. Violoncello technique was instead extended by virtuosos individually molding the principles of upper-position techniques to establish personal performance styles.

Among violoncellists of the late eighteenth and early nineteenth centuries, the three men viewed by contemporaries as especially progressive technicians were Boccherini, J. L. Duport, and Romberg. Boccherini was appreciated for his expansion of the violoncello's tessitura, the writing of lyrical melodies, and his integration of the violoncello into chamber ensembles. Duport's organization of fingering methodology imparted unprecedented cohesion to violoncello technique, while Romberg introduced new levels of technical complexity, similarly broadening concepts of how a violoncello should sound. It is probably not insignificant that all three spent part of their careers in Paris, experienced some degree of personal interaction, and were knowledgeable about each other's playing styles, although – notwithstanding that knowledge – they each had a significantly different style of playing.

With regard to fingering techniques, those of Boccherini are the most difficult to reconstruct, owing to a lack of notation in those works which remain. One key to inferring Boccherini's thumb fingerings was provided by Romberg, who wrote of Boccherini's use of block hand positions ("it is immediately perceived what position the thumb should occupy in playing the Thumb-passage"), explaining that in his early publications Boccherini

coordinated change of hand position with change of clef.[17] A concise example is provided by the *Allegro* of Boccherini's first concerto (Ex. 4.59).

The movement commences in alto clef, which, if one uses Romberg's
specifications, determines that the thumb is set across the G and C of the A
and D strings. With this placement, the first ten and a half bars fit into one
stationary hand position, the change to tenor clef indicating a return to
lower-position fingerings.

Ex. 4.59 Boccherini, Concerto no. 1, *Allegro*, bars 36–47

The second solo episode of this movement progresses through seven clef
changes, each signaling an alteration to the disposition of the thumb. In
the material which follows the restatement of the first theme, if the hand
settings suggested by Romberg are applied, the thumb is placed as illustrated in Ex. 4.60. Treble clef notes are executed at pitch.

Ex. 4.60 Boccherini, Concerto no. 1, *Allegro*, bars 111–142

17 Romberg, *School*, p. 65. See Chapter 2 for Romberg's explanation of Boccherini's clef usage.

The broadest range of upper-position fingerings was offered by J. L. Duport through the instructions of his *Essai*, his published concertos exhibiting minimal notation. In the exercises and etudes of his treatise, Duport illustrated varied methods of playing thumb-position note patterns, revealing a breadth of thinking not evident in the restrictive writing of his solo works. As with the patterns demonstrated for the lower positions, Duport's upper-position fingerings adhere to the central tenet of his methodology: systematic movement allows for clean, precise execution, the optimum goal being absolute equality of sound in all registers of the violoncello.

Consistent with the technical conventions of his era, several of Duport's studies address the subject of stationary, block hand positions. The second etude, for example, contains an explicit drill in bars 107–114 for horizontal fingerings (Ex. 4.61). Fourth finger usage in bar 109 extends the range of the hand position on the A string.

Ex. 4.61 Duport, *Essai*, Etude 2, bars 105–114 (*8va* at pitch, 0 = thumb)

Duport generally limited his inclusion of the fourth finger in thumb position to occasional notes which extend scale or *arpeggio* patterns on the A string. Fingerings marked in melodic passages suggest that he did not use the fourth finger in expressive phrases placed in the upper range of the instrument: in Etude 12 (Ex. 4.62) Duport inserts a third finger shift to the G in bar 118, rather than playing the note with a fourth finger.

Ex. 4.62 Etude 12, bars 117–120 (tc1, 0 = thumb)

The fingering of this melodic passage is designed to end with the thumb, a choice consistent with the practices of other contemporary violoncellists, but unfamiliar to most modern performers. In an era in which vibrato was primarily used as an ornament, it was not considered important to structure fingerings so that vibrato could easily be applied to notes of long duration or to phrase endings. The thumb was considered by virtuosos to be as suitable for expressive playing as the first, second, or third fingers.

Another exercise featuring stationary, block hand positions is Etude 11 (Ex. 4.63). Inclusion of the C string in these note patterns is one of the singular demands of this study. Duport's incorporation of the upper register of the C string is infrequent throughout the *Essai* and unapparent in his solo works. Nevertheless, this etude demonstrates familiarity with fingering techniques more readily exploited by other performers.

Ex. 4.63 Etude 11, bars 73–78 (tc1, 0 = thumb)

In addition to the block fingerings seen in bars 76–78, the 2–2 fingerings for the broken thirds of bars 73–75 illustrate Duport's one allowable exception for shifting with the same finger. It is the careful systematization of those fingerings used to reach upper-register hand positions which, in fact, especially set Duport apart from the majority of his contemporaries. The previous example of ascending thirds demonstrates only one stratagem. Scale patterns yielded more easily to Duport's preference for consecutive finger placement and much of his explanation for playing in the upper registers of the violoncello addresses this issue. Paramount to his methodology was Duport's formulation of a uniform fingering applicable to all scales irrespective of key signature. The key to his pattern was that the second degree of a scale was always taken with the first finger, the only exceptions being those keys such as B♭ and E♭ major, which Duport began in half position.[18]

Stressing the regularity of his procedure, Duport presented scales which ascend the A string in order to reach a stationary position inclusive of the thumb; the scale descends in thumb position (Ex. 4.64).

Ex. 4.64 p. 22 (tc1, 0 = thumb)

Duport included a brief demonstration of how to execute these same note patterns in a single, stationary hand position, remarking that some fellow

---

18 Duport, *Essai*, pp. 20–26.

violoncellists (i.e. Romberg) preferred this method, but expressed the opinion that his own ascending fingerings were more reliable for intonation because there was less chance of the thumb losing its position over multiple string crossings.[19]

Regularity was also Duport's key to other proffered methods of ascending and descending to and from thumb position. Because a majority of his solo writing was developed from scales or *arpeggios* executed on the A and D strings, Duport devised a formula for stepwise shifting which maintained note placement on these two strings. Preserving the octave created between the thumb and third finger, Duport moved the thumb in stepwise progressions, the encompassed notes being organized into various patterns. Series of broken thirds (Ex. 4.65) fell naturally into this system of fingering, as did harmonic motion through *arpeggios* and octaves (Ex. 4.66).

Ex. 4.65 p. 116 (tc1, 0 = thumb)

Ex. 4.66 Etude 13, bars 32–36 (tc1, 0 = thumb)

Thumb-position double-stops also fell within this fingering format. Using the natural fingerings inherent within the octave hand position, Duport executed thirds with the thumb and second or first and third fingers, sixths being taken with adjoining fingers. A demonstration of these fingerings is given in Etude 20 (Ex. 4.67).

19 Ibid., p. 26.

Ex. 4.67 Etude 20, bars 25–39 (tc1, 0 = thumb)

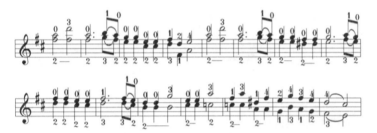

One of the more enticing avenues of conjecture for those interested in violoncello history is the relationship between J. L. Duport and Romberg during their joint tenure at the Prussian Kapelle in 1805–06. Many orchestral players have experienced the sharing of a desk with a partner who employs methods of playing substantially varied from one's own, but two more different players than Duport and Romberg cannot be imagined. While surviving evidence implies mutual respect, every physical aspect of their playing differed; bow grip, left hand position, and fingering methods.

Thumb position was Romberg's métier. Contemporaries considered his fingering methods to be innovative, but, in fact, his ingeniousness was to exploit the intrinsic possibilities of fingerings within stationary, block hand positions to the boundaries of their inherent limitations. Use of the fourth finger and the C string were formative to his playing, the newly designed Tourte bow contributing to his ease of execution. Romberg's notation was exacting; and the fact that he considered it necessary to state, in the preface to his first published concerto, that "it should also be observed that the author in taking the thumb position also uses the fourth finger"[20] suggests the exclusivity of his technique, especially among the French players with whom he was working when the concerto was published in Paris.

The constancy with which Romberg applied his fingerings is particularly demonstrated through the melodic figurations of his concertos, which were generally shaped to traverse a wide range of notes in the upper register of the violoncello. The melodies of these works were unquestionably devised to fit Romberg's fingering system, rather than the fingerings being chosen to accommodate melodic invention. Examples may be drawn from the soloist's opening statements in the third movement of the op. 3 concerto (Ex. 4.68) and the first movement of the op. 6 concerto (Ex. 4.69). All sixteen bars from the op. 3 citation are set within one thumb-position setting, while that from op. 6 encompasses fourteen bars.

20 Romberg, *Concerto*, op. 2.

Ex. 4.68 Romberg, Concerto op. 3, *Rondo, Tempo di menuetto*, bars 1–17

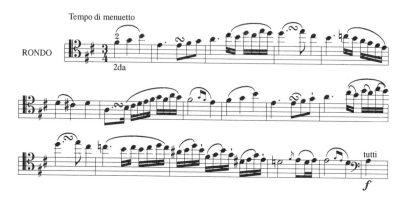

Ex. 4.69 Romberg, Concerto op. 6, *Allegro*, bars 63–76

Romberg's upper-position fingerings allowed for speed, precision, and clarity, attributes of his writing found even in the slow movements of his compositions. Many of these movements emulate operatic arias, and, as demonstrated by the *Adagio* of the seventh concerto (Ex. 4.70), stationary hand positions requiring minimal shifting allowed for ornate, yet meticulous playing in thumb position.

Ex. 4.70 Romberg, Concerto op. 44, *Adagio Cantabile*, bars 12–23

Characteristic to Romberg's vision of violoncello playing was consistent use of the entire four-octave range of the violoncello. With expanded possibilities in sonority resulting from alternative designs for bows and instruments, Romberg's trademark became use of the G and C strings for bravura passage work. Note patterns placed in the upper registers of those strings are incorporated into the majority of his compositions. In addition to including these strings in block hand positions, Romberg exploited natural harmonics, and wrote numerous passages displaying vertical fingerings that require speed and dexterity. As in the lower-positions, he made frequent use of same-finger shifting to ascend to and descend from the upper positions of the violoncello. C-string writing demonstrating note patterns inclusive of thumb and fourth finger, shifts being taken with the thumb, is illustrated in Ex. 4.71. Shifts using the second finger are shown in Ex. 4.72.

Ex. 4.71 Romberg, Concerto op. 3, *Fandango*, bars 201–207

Ex. 4.72 Romberg, Concerto op. 2, *Rondo*, bars 229–235

Much of Romberg's bravura writing also relied on the stepwise movement of octaves and double-stops. Romberg's leveraged stroke with the Tourte bow allowed him to set new precedents in the use of solid octaves and double-stops, consistent incorporation of slurs adding to the flamboyance of sound. The fingerings for this type of writing were traditional, based on the octave taken between the thumb and third finger and all shifts accomplished with the thumb (Ex. 4.73). The fingers employed for double-stops were those which naturally fell within the octave hand position. Additional to these traditional fingerings, however, was the incorporation of the fourth finger when convenient (Ex. 4.74), which minimized the number of necessary shifts.

Ex. 4.73 Romberg, Concerto op. 30, *Allegro non tanto*, bars 126–133

Ex. 4.74 bars 106–108

Romberg also used the fourth finger for the execution of tenths (Ex. 4.75).

Ex. 4.75 Romberg, Concerto op. 30, *Finale Allegretto*, bars 145–148

Romberg was one of the last virtuosos to use an oblique hand position in the neck positions of the instrument. While he sincerely believed that this method of playing allowed his fingers to press against the strings with greater weight, thereby benefiting his sound production, the angle of his fingers made exacting intonation more difficult to achieve in rapid, horizontal note patterns. Romberg overcame this limitation by using thumb-position fingerings in the lower positions of the neck (Ex. 4.76).

Ex. 4.76 Romberg, Concerto op. 6, *Allegro*, bars 115–122

The generation of violoncellists who followed J. L. Duport and Romberg were bequeathed a technical structure having little need of improvement. What followed was an amalgamation of playing techniques, players individually choosing those elements from the masters' playing style which appealed. Many violoncellists came to appreciate the logic of Duport's fingering systematization, but followed Romberg's lead in using the fourth finger in thumb position. Use of the upper range of the lower strings and thumb-position fingerings within the neck positions also became common. The most influential teachers to adopt this composite approach were Baudiot and Dotzauer; their legacy then passed to Norblin, Franchomme, and Kummer. However, specific elements from Duport's and Romberg's techniques are also found in the fingerings of N. Kraft, Merk, Bohrer, and Lindley.

The florid virtuosity which came to mark many of the violoncello compositions of the mid-nineteenth century in fact relied on the thumb-position techniques codified at the beginning of the century. There are several distinctive features of upper-position fingerings from performers of this era that are, however, of interest. Unlike Duport and Romberg, who were concerned to minimize shifting in configurations of double-stops,

Bohrer, Kummer, and Franchomme all executed numerous double-stop passages with consecutive fingerings based from the thumb (Ex. 4.77). Contradictorily, Franchomme's fingering of octaves was occasionally initiated with the first and fourth finger, lessening the number of necessary hand movements (Ex. 4.78).

Ex. 4.77
(a) Franchomme, *Thème varié*, bars 68–70 (0 = thumb)

(b) Kummer, Concertino op. 16, *Allegro molto moderato*, bars 69–76

(c) M. Bohrer, *Steyrer Volkslied, Allegro assai*, bars 107–113

Ex. 4.78 Chopin and Franchomme, *Grand Duo Concertant ... sur des Thèmes de Robert le Diable*, bars 326–327

Changing ideas of expression did alter players' perceptions of one idiomatic eighteenth-century skill: the reliance on stationary, block hand positions. While such fingering patterns necessarily remained one method of devising bravura passage work, composers were no longer content to settle in one hand position and limit their melodies to the encompassed notes. Frequent shifts within a melodic episode became customary, the performer in many instances moving in and out of thumb position. One aspect of thumb fingerings which did remain unchanged was acceptance of the thumb on an equal basis with other fingers in expressive writing. Examples 4.79 and 4.80 illustrate fingerings in which melodic material is begun and, in the writing of Franchomme, ended with the thumb.[21] Such conceptions would not change among players of any nationality until much later in the century, when stylistic demands required more continuous vibrato on all notes.

Ex. 4.79 Chopin and Franchomme, *Grand Duo Concertant ... sur des Thêmes de Robert le Diable*, bars 90–97

Ex. 4.80 N. Kraft, Concerto op. 4, *Adagio*, bars 7–14 (tc1, 0 = thumb)

21 No. IX 40102; quotations from N. Kraft's Concerto op. 4 are reproduced by permission of the Gesellschaft der Musikfreunde in Wien.

5

Bow strokes and their execution

Rules for bowing first evolved from the need for the bow to go back and forth in a manner suitable to the stress points within various rhythmic patterns. As playing techniques increased in sophistication, bow strokes additionally developed as a means to display virtuosity. Gradually, the method by which the bow was drawn also became a facet of musical style and, by the nineteenth century, facility and artistry were recognized as significant components of bowing technique. As preferences for bow models and the bow hold varied substantially over time and from region to region, so, too, the execution of bowing patterns and bow strokes suitable to the violoncello has been a diverse and ever-changing art.

THE RULE OF DOWN-BOW

The rule of down-bow is the oldest and most fundamental tenet of string playing. Simply stated, when using an overhand bow grip, the player executes the strong beats of the bar with a down-bow, i.e. on beats one and three in a 4/4 meter. The stroke is reversed for violoncellists using an underhand grip, the strong beats being taken with an up-bow. For French players of the late seventeenth and eighteenth centuries, this was an especially important concept because of the rhythmic stresses inherent in French dance music. While the rule of down-bow is easily accomplished when there are an even number of notes within a bar, the bowing becomes more complex when there are an uneven number of notes. The French solution to the problem was to retake a down-bow in order to keep the bowing pattern steady. Cupis illustrated this in his method, as shown in Ex. 5.1.

Ex. 5.1 Cupis, *Méthode*, p. 43 (ι = down-bow)

The pre-eminence of this rule for French performers also led to usage of *reprise d'archet.* Inculcated into French string playing by Lully, this method of retaking the down-bow on all strong beats in triple meter was carefully transcribed by Muffat in 1698. Muffat described the technique as exclusive to French dance music, remarking that Italian and German players did not bow in this manner.[1] Continued French use of *reprise d'archet* is seen in Corrette's method (Ex. 5.2), written forty years after Muffat. In this illustration of triple meter, it is the first beat of each bar which requires the down-bow.

Ex. 5.2 Corrette, *Méthode,* p. 26 (T = down-bow, P = up-bow)

The rhythmic impulse generated by *reprise d'archet* continued to be a stylistic nuance appreciated by French violoncellists at least through the 1760s. Although not specifically marked, *reprise d'archet* is implied in a dance movement from a set of J. P. Duport's sonatas (Ex. 5.3).

Ex. 5.3 J. P. Duport, *Six Sonates pour le Violoncelle ou Violon et Basse,* Sonata II, *Minuetto 2,* bars 1–6 (tc1)

Although the rule of down-bow provided the foundation for Italian and German bowing patterns of the eighteenth century, performers of these regions showed less concern with complete systematization. After completing his explanation of the French rules which governed when consecutive notes were to be executed with two up-bows or two down-bows, Corrette remarked that Italian players shared little concern for such matters. "I have heard some Italians who play as the bow strokes come," he wrote, "without being concerned about pulling and pushing twice according to the rules we have just given."[2] Corrette's observations are reinforced by the bowings notated in Italian performance literature. The following excerpt from a minuet by Lanzetti (Ex. 5.4) demonstrates by the application of slurs that in bars 5–8 alternate bars commenced with a down-bow.

---

1 Muffat, *Florilegium secundum,* p. 21.
2 Corrette, *Méthode,* p. 12.

Ex. 5.4 Lanzetti, op. 1, Sonata II, *Menuet Cantabile*, bars 1–8

In England, the eighteenth-century view of the importance of adhering to the rule of down-bow was summarized in the anonymous method published by Clementi & Co.:

The art of Bowing is rather difficult, & the marks that you find in Music in general are not very accurate…the number of Notes in each bar ought to be attended to for if you have 2,4,6,8, or any equal number, by playing the first down, the next up, & so on alternately down & up, you will of course finish with an up Bow, & be prepar'd to begin the next bar with a down bow, but when you find the number unequal, such as 3,5,7,9, &c. you should endeavour to play the two shortest notes with one stroke of the Bow, & in that case you will find yourself the same as if the number had been equal; sometime you will find a succession of bars with an unequal number of Notes, particularly in Triple Time, which frequently consists of three Notes in a Bar, in such a case you should bow alternately down & up, by which the first note of every second bar will come with a down bow…[3]

The rule of down-bow remained the foundation for all violoncellists during the nineteenth century, but longer and increasingly more complex bowings made for less dogmatic application. Attention was drawn instead to the importance of taking the upbeat with an up-bow, a feature given particular attention by Romberg and Kummer. Describing the importance of regulated bowings, Kummer wrote:

The different bowings originate from the various combinations of slurred and separate notes in down-bows and up-bows, and indisputably exercise an important influence on the character of the work to be performed. For that reason they are required to be placed by the composer with regularity, so that a special emphasis is always explicitly noted, as the following examples show. Where such a marking is missing, the student must become accustomed to arranging the stroke in such a manner that, wherever possible, the down stroke comes on the first note of every bar. For this reason, if a work begins with an upbeat, it will always start with an up-

bow, for example [4]

Romberg's comments take note of differences in attitude towards the application of bowings to solo music versus accompaniments. Discussing the up-bow for the upbeat, Romberg stated that "in Solo playing, an attention

3 *New and Complete Instructions*, p. 7.
4 Kummer, *Violoncell-Schule*, p. 22.

to this particular is highly important...[but] in accompanying, it is not considered of much consequence."[5]

DÉTACHÉ

Détaché, a term applied to separate bow strokes, was frequently notated, but rarely named before the beginning of the nineteenth century. Mid-eighteenth-century teachers provided simple instructions for playing with separate strokes. Corrette explained that one pulled and pushed the bow with large, firm strokes to obtain a clear, distinct sound and that "ordinarily one plays the notes by pulling and pushing alternately when the notes have the same value."[6] Concurring with Corrette, Tillière specified that the *détaché* stroke was notated with a wedge mark (Ex. 5.5) and that the first note of each bar received additional stress.[7]

Ex. 5.5 Tillière, *Méthode*, p. 5.

Composers and publishers were not always consistent with notation, however, frequently using a dot as well as a wedge to indicate the bow stroke. This can be seen in an English edition of Boccherini's A major sonata (Ex. 5.6).

Ex. 5.6 Boccherini, Sonata in A Major, *Allegro*, bars 12–13

Definitions, with attendant discrepancies, become more pronounced at the beginning of the nineteenth century. J. L. Duport remarked that the *détaché* stroke was of two kinds, "the first emphasized one, which one uses when one wants to draw sound, and the other a little bouncy, which one uses in passages which require lightness. This last is executed three quarters along the bow, towards the point."[8]

Demonstrating the greater variety of bow pressure points possible with the Tourte bow, the Conservatoire method gave precise playing instructions for *détaché* according to tempo. In passages of slow tempo, separate

5 Romberg, *School*, p. 35.   6 Corrette, *Méthode*, p. 9.

7 J. B. Tillière, *Méthode pour le violoncelle contenant tous les principes nécessaires pour bien jouer de cet instrument* (Paris: Imbault, [1764]), p. 5. (Quotations are reproduced by permission of The Music Library, University of California, Berkeley.)

8 Duport, *Essai*, p. 170.

strokes required the entire bow length, with the sound being sustained from one end to the other.[9] Passages of moderate tempo were to be played in the middle of the bow, with separation between each note, as demonstrated in Ex. 5.7.

Ex. 5.7 Baillot, *Méthode*, p. 128

Fast *détaché* passages were to be played between the middle and the upper third of the bow, but, according to the Conservatoire authors, "the point of the bow, being dry and hard and not sufficient to make the thick strings like those on the violoncello vibrate, should never be used."[10]

Later nineteenth-century French technique is addressed by Vaslin, a self-described acolyte of Baillot. Vaslin went into extensive detail in discussing the execution of separate bow strokes of all lengths. Striving for even and clean playing, he instructed that each stroke was to originate from a three-step process of push, pull, release:

The attacking movement, which appears to be only one, is composed of three phases which are quite distinct.
  (1) Pressing the stick with the first finger mainly with the intention of making it bend as well as the hair.
  (2) Whether in pulling or in pushing, the setting in motion of which only the immediate attack can be distinguished, the hair having acquired its bite from the pressure.
  (3) As soon as the clean and clear attack is obtained, the release of pressure or the care in supporting the bow leaves the string free from the constraint imposed at first, whilst enabling the hair to adhere to the strings especially when it is necessary to produce a long note.[11]

Extending the relationship between bow apportionment and tempo from that of the Conservatoire tutor, Vaslin produced a chart that specified the correct portion of the bow and the length of the stroke appropriate to separate notes of all note values. In addition, he gave directions for playing *détaché* strokes with and without attack. This chart is shown in Fig. 5.1.

The nineteenth-century French manner of playing *détaché* strokes was widely adopted by violoncellists who used a bow grip above the frog. Those who played with a lower bow grip differed in their perception of the *détaché* stroke. While Romberg, Dotzauer, and Kummer all acknowledged

9 Baillot, *Méthode*, p. 127.
10 Ibid., p. 128.
11 Vaslin, *L'art*, p. 9.

TABLEAU COMPARATIF DES DIVERSES SECTIONS D'ARCHET A EMPLOYER

INDENTITÉ DU PROCÉDÉ SUR TOUTES LES VALEURS

N.B. La figure toute linéaire suffisante pour la démonstration ne doit pas être prise comme modèle d'un bon archet qui bien que tendu doit conserver une certaine cambrure.

Avec attaque
ou Mordant, Pression sans perte aucune de respiration.

Sans attaque
Pression modérée ou prise de corde sans perte aucune de respiration.

Chaque ligne perpendiculaire indique le point de départ et d'arrivée; ou autrement l'intervalle compris entre ces deux lignes est la mesure de la portion de crin à employer selon la valeur de la note. S'il y avait deux rondes et même plus, liées; la division qu'il ne faut pas plus oublier que la tenue se ferait avec plus de modération.

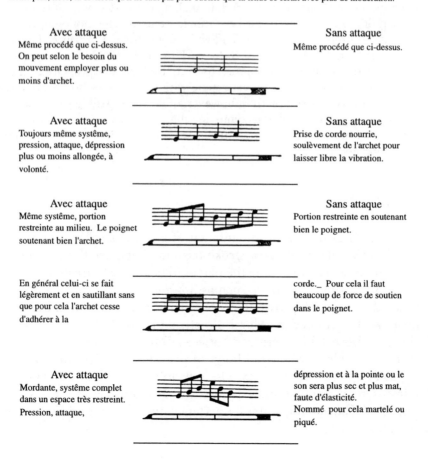

Avec attaque
Même procédé que ci-dessus. On peut selon le besoin du mouvement employer plus ou moins d'archet.

Sans attaque
Même procédé que ci-dessus.

Avec attaque
Toujours même système, pression, attaque, dépression plus ou moins allongée, à volonté.

Sans attaque
Prise de corde nourrie, soulèvement de l'archet pour laisser libre la vibration.

Avec attaque
Même système, portion restreinte au milieu. Le poignet soutenant bien l'archet.

Sans attaque
Portion restreinte en soutenant bien le poignet.

En général celui-ci se fait légèrement et en sautillant sans que pour cela l'archet cesse d'adhérer à la

corde._ Pour cela il faut beaucoup de force de soutien dans le poignet.

Avec attaque
Mordante, système complet dans un espace très restreint. Pression, attaque,

dépression et à la pointe ou le son sera plus sec et plus mat, faute d'élasticité. Nommé pour cela martelé ou piqué.

Fig 5.1 Vaslin, *L'art*, pp. 11-12

two differing types of separated bow strokes, these Germans, unlike the French, held the lighter *détaché* stroke somewhat in disdain. Romberg, in particular, considered the lighter *détaché* to be stylistically outdated, writing:

Of Detached Bowing

This mode of Bowing may be introduced in light, easy passages, and is peculiarly suited to those pieces which are written in a playful style, such as Rondos in 6/8 Time, or Solos for Chamber-Music. For Music of a higher order (i.e. concertos), it is not so well adapted, and should never be used except in quick movements...

In order to make the bow spring well upon the strings, it should be used in the middle. The bow should be held with the 1st finger and thumb, and the 3rd finger merely leaned against the nut, but not pressed firmly upon it; the 2nd and 4th fingers should not touch the nut; and, in making the stroke, not more than a finger's breadth of the length of the bow should be used. The motion of the bow is here made entirely with the hand, and with not too great a pressure. The arm, as usual, must be held free from all stiffness. This mode of Bowing cannot be employed in *forte* passages, since these latter require a greater pressure of the bow. This bowing was formerly in great repute with all Artists, who introduced it in passages of every description. It is, however, quite incompatible with a fine broad style of playing, which fully accounts for the inferiority of their compositions. Now-a-days Musical compositions are expected to contain more solidity, both in signification and expression.[12]

SLURS

While *détaché* is the most fundamental of all bow strokes, the linking of several notes within one bow stroke has long been used as a companion. Slurs were first used to enable the player to begin each stressed beat with a down-bow in time-signatures such as 3/4 and 6/8, but they came to be a stylistic device which provided contrast with *détaché*. The number of notes which may be grouped in a slur is directly tied to both bow design and bow hold, and appreciably increased between 1740 and 1840.

For violoncellists who used bows of pre-Tourte design, the majority of slur groupings encompassed two to four notes, with occasional groupings having as many as eight notes. Longer slur groupings were rare. A passage by Lanzetti (Ex. 5.8) illustrates his juxtaposition of four- and eight-note slur groupings.

12 Romberg, *School*, p. 109.

Ex. 5.8 Lanzetti, op. 1, Sonata X, *Allegro*, bars 20–23

Beginning in the 1770s, the judicious use of longer slur groupings is found
in the compositions of a few violoncellists. J. B. Janson, who was consistently at the forefront of innovative bowing techniques, wrote a passage of
twelve-note slur groupings in his op. 4 sonatas (*c.* 1774), shown in Ex. 5.9.
Such a lengthy passage of slurred, *legato* notes is unusual for violoncello
literature of the decade.

Ex. 5.9 Janson, op. 4, Sonata V, *Allegretto*, bars 52–55

The advent of the Tourte bow allowed for lengthy and consistent slurring.
A passage from the slow movement of Bohrer's third concerto illustrates
how nineteenth-century violoncellists expanded the number of notes
placed within slur groupings (Ex. 5.10).

Ex. 5.10 M. Bohrer, Concerto op. 10, *Adagio*, bars 26–28

J. L. Duport believed that select patterns of slurring evolved according to
fashion. According to him, one that became especially popular was employed in passages of strong expression.[13] Constructed from two-note slurs,
a pattern of syncopation was devised in which the slur began with the off-
beat note (Ex. 5.11).

13 Duport, *Essai*, p. 167.

Ex. 5.11 Duport, *Essai*, p. 167

Beethoven used a variation on this slurring pattern with dotted rhythms in the Sonata op. 5, no. 2 (Ex. 5.12).

Ex. 5.12 Beethoven, Sonata op. 5, no. 2, *Adagio sostenuto e espressivo*, bars 22–26

As seen in bar 28 of Ex. 5.10, another variety of slurring came to be used in conjunction with long slur groupings. Found in violoncello music composed only after the advent of the Tourte bow, articulated slurs were used by players of all schools. Dotzauer instructed that the second note of each pair should be shortened,  .[14] Raoul indicated that in his illustration (Ex. 5.13) the two-note slur groupings were played within the long slur without changing the bow.

Ex. 5.13 Raoul, *Méthode*, p. 27

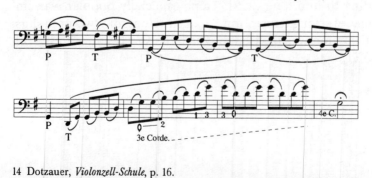

Baudiot also examined this type of slur, specifying by notation that such patterns were executed within one bow stroke (Ex. 5.14).

Ex. 5.14 Baudiot, *Méthode*, vol. II, p. 77 (T = down-bow, P = up-bow)

14 Dotzauer, *Violonzell-Schule*, p. 16.

There is one additional variation on the idea of articulated slurs that is found is the works of several violoncellists, including Lamare, Romberg, and Bernard Stiastny. Devised by Viotti, *effleurant la corde* is a bowing in which the bow skims lightly over the surface of the string, the bow maintaining one direction. Lamare used it to a greater degree than other violoncellists; an excerpt from Lamare's second concerto, composed by Auber (see p. 22 above), is illustrated in Ex. 5.15.

Ex. 5.15 Lamare, Concerto II, first movement, bars 95–98 (tc1)

SLUR/*DÉTACHÉ* COMBINATION

Conjoining *détaché* notes with slurs was an early method of providing contrast and such patterns are found in the earliest solo music for violoncello. Most eighteenth-century violoncellists were fairly haphazard in the application and uniformity of such bowing patterns. French players were the exception. Uncomfortable with irregularity, they applied these patterns as virtuoso displays and were especially diligent with organization and notation. An illustration by J. P. Duport (Ex. 5.16) demonstrates slur/*détaché* combinations in both duple and triplet figures.

Ex. 5.16 J. P. Duport, op. 2, Sonata VI, *Allegro*, bars 17–21

Eighteenth-century Austrian composers demonstrate a particularly high degree of non-uniformity in the application of slurs.[15] In the following example by Anton Kraft (Ex. 5.17), not one bar duplicates another in the pattern of slurs and *détaché* notes.

---

15 Dene Barnett is of the opinion that non-uniformity of slurring in Austro-German music, especially between orchestral parts, was not the result of carelessness or accident, but rather showed the desire for variety and contrast even within identical phrases. See Dene Barnett, "Non-uniform Slurring in 18th Century Music: Accident or Design?" *The Haydn Yearbook*, 10 (1978), 179–199.

Ex. 5.17 A. Kraft, op. 3, Duet I, *Allegro ma non tanto*, bars 20–25

In the latter part of the century, influenced by Tartini's *L'Arte del arco*, French violoncello teachers began formulating specific combinations of slurs and *détaché* notes. This sense of organization gradually permeated the playing of all violoncellists and the application of slurs during the nineteenth century is generally uniform. Romberg's notation of slur/*détaché* combinations is highly regimented; according to Baudiot, the German devised particular patterns of slur/*détaché* combinations which are frequently found in his works. Baudiot's illustration of these bowings is demonstrated in Ex. 5.18.

Ex. 5.18 Baudiot, *Méthode*, vol. II, p. 80, Romberg bowings (tc1)
(a)

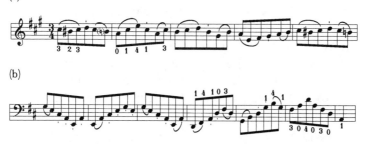

(b)

ARPEGGIOS

All violoncellists considered *arpeggios* as idiomatic to the instrument. Because chordal patterns were frequently used in solo compositions, chamber music, and orchestral and vocal accompaniments, violoncello tutors gave extensive attention to the execution of *arpeggio* figures. Corrette indicated that the notation for *arpeggios* was often abbreviated (Ex. 5.19).

Ex. 5.19 Corrette, *Méthode*, p. 39.

Modele.

This form of shorthand was widely used in the eighteenth century for patterns which incorporated repetitive bowing patterns (Ex. 5.20).

Ex. 5.20 Antoniotti, op. 1, Sonata II, *Prestissimo*, bars 23–31

Later in the century, as the use of multiple-string chords became more prevalent, some composers specified when *arpeggios* were to be played (Ex. 5.21). In this passage, Janson drew the distinction between *arpeggios* and multiple-string chords.

Ex. 5.21 Janson, op. 15, Concerto V, *Allegro Majestuoso*, bars 196–202 (tc1)

Varied bowing patterns became an interest for nineteenth-century teachers and abbreviated notation for *arpeggios* gradually disappeared. Cataloguing the number of possible bowing combinations became an intellectual exercise for some teachers, with Dotzauer illustrating eighty-one combinations and Stiastny eighty-five. Bréval, too, demonstrated varied combinations, a sample of which is shown in Ex. 5.22.

Ex. 5.22 Bréval, *Traité*, pp. 121–126
(a)

(b)

(c)

(d)

(e)

As the nineteenth century progressed, the use of longer and consistent slurs became more frequent, as did the addition of accents within a slur grouping. Merk, for instance, placed accents within slurred groupings of *arpeggios* (Ex. 5.23).

Ex. 5.23 Merk, *Introduction et Variations sur une Valse Favorite de François Schubert*, var. 4, bars 1–10

BATTERIES

Batteries – a term first applied to violoncello procedures by Corrette – are patterns in which notes are alternated between neighboring strings. Although they were long used in all forms of violoncello music, rules for their execution became carefully regulated only after the midpoint of the eighteenth century. These rules were the subject of special attention by Tillière, whose tutor is the first to provide precise illustrations for bow management. According to his instructions, if a note pattern commences with notes placed on an upper string and moves to those on a lower string, the pattern begins down-bow. The opposite occurs if the pattern goes from a lower string to an upper string (Ex. 5.24). When executed with separate bow strokes, these regulations were adhered to by violoncellists of all succeeding generations.

Ex. 5.24 Tillière, *Méthode*, p. 11

Rapid execution of *batteries* was a virtuoso device and regional differences existed in the choice of strings used. French performers were especially circumspect in their inclusion of the C string in solo music and *batteries* placed on the lower two strings are rare in French music before 1815. Composers from Germany and Austria had much greater appreciation for the lower strings of the violoncello and *batteries* on the G and C strings are commonly found in eighteenth-century music. As an example, Filtz exploited contrasting sonorities in his Concerto in F major, juxtaposing passages of *batteries* in the upper range of the D and A strings with those placed on the C and G strings (Ex. 5.25).

Ex. 5.25 Filtz, Concerto in F major, *Allegro*, bars 134–149 (tc1)

The use of alternating strings restricted variables in workable bowing patterns. To increase virtuoso display, violoncellists extended the tessitura and interval range in which *batteries* were placed. Instruction in this type of playing on the D and A strings was provided by Bréval (Ex. 5.26).

Ex. 5.26 Bréval, *Traité*, p. 205 (tc1)

Austrian and German composers exploited both the upper and the lower registers of the violoncello in *batteries*; Example 5.27 shows a passage on the lower strings by Beethoven.

Ex. 5.27 Beethoven, Concerto op. 56, *Allegro*, bars 191–194 (tc1)

Batteries played in the upper register of the lower strings were a technique featured by Romberg (Ex. 5.28). The wide vibrations of the strings engendered by his forceful style of playing were one reason he found it necessary to place a groove in the fingerboard beneath the C string (see pp. 62–63).

Ex. 5.28 Romberg, Concerto op. 6, *Allegro*, bars 278–283

BRISURE

Brisure is a technique similar to *batteries*, but the alternating notes are between non-adjacent rather than neighboring strings. Tillière instructed that these patterns were subject to the same bowing regulations as *batteries* (Ex. 5.29). His rules were generally adopted by subsequent violoncellists. An excerpt from a sonata by Canavas, in which he alternated the bowing pattern by bar, demonstrates, however, that not all violoncellists adhered to the strictures advocated by French teachers (Ex. 5.30).

Ex. 5.29 Tillière, *Méthode*, p. 11

Ex. 5.30 Canavas, op. 2, Sonata V, *Allegro comodo*, bars 47–58 (tc1)

French eighteenth-century performers used this stroke judiciously with the C string. Janson, who was familiar with Mannheim performance traits, used the lower register for solo works more frequently than other French violoncellists (Ex. 5.31).

Ex. 5.31 Janson, op. 6, Concerto IV, *Allegro*, bars 164–168

Austro-German composers enjoyed using *brisure* patterns as a method of exploiting the sonority of the lower strings. Haydn placed a passage of *brisure* using the open C string against double-stops in the final movement of the C major violoncello concerto (Ex. 5.32).

Ex. 5.32 Haydn, Concerto in C major, *Finale, Allegro molto*, bars 208–210

As with *batteries*, the nature of the string crossing precluded complex bowing patterns from being applied to *brisure*. *Brisure* was used with greater frequency in the eighteenth century, as it was not conducive to the *legato* style of playing favored by nineteenth-century players. Nevertheless, some nineteenth-century performers found *brisure* to be useful for virtuoso display. Works by Bohrer demonstrate two differing circumstances. The first excerpt (Ex. 5.33) demonstrates the influence of the Tourte bow. This is a variation in which Bohrer specified that the notes are to be played at the frog. Bars 1–8 are executed beginning down-bow and bars 9–18 are notated to begin up-bow. In the second example (Ex. 5.34), Bohrer contrasted widely spaced intervals in a *brisure* pattern to build a cadence.

Ex. 5.33 M. Bohrer, *Steyrer Volkslied*, var. 7, bars 1–18

Ex. 5.34 M. Bohrer, Concerto op. 10, *Allegro Maestoso*, bars 77–80

Nineteenth-century violoncellists developed another idiom featuring large intervals which is not true *brisure*, but gives a *brisure*-like effect. The player traverses the length of an individual string , alternating stopped notes with the same open string or a neighboring one. An example is drawn from Dotzauer (Ex. 5.35).

Ex. 5.35 Dotzauer, Concerto op. 100, *Allegretto*, bars 148–151

BARIOLAGE

Bariolage is a nineteenth-century term for another device favored more in the eighteenth century than in the nineteenth. This bowing technique exploits the distinct, individual timbres of the various strings by oscillating notes, one of which is usually an open string or reiterated pitch, between

two, three, or four strings. The technique is usually indicated by the reverse
stemming of the reiterated note. French violoncellists were especially organized in constructing bowing patterns for virtuoso display and were
adept at the use of *bariolage*. Bréval included an illustration on how to play
the pattern in his method (Ex. 5.36).

Ex. 5.36 Bréval, *Traité*, p. 172 (tc1, 0 = open)

Bariolage is found in the works of J. P. Duport (Ex. 5.37) and in highly virtuoso passages by Janson (Ex. 5.38).

Ex. 5.37 J. P. Duport, *Six Sonates*, Sonata IV, *Allegro*, bars 57–60 (tc1)

Ex. 5.38 Janson, op. 6, Concerto II, *Allegro Moderato*, bars 256–258 (treble clef at pitch)

Contrasting sonorities were an attribute of many Austro-German violoncello works. At Mannheim, Ritter employed scordatura (see pp. 206–207)
to give several of his concertos individual timbres and wrote *bariolage* figures to exploit these sonorities. Such figures are found in his concerto in B♭
major. The violoncello was tuned a semi-tone higher than the orchestra in
this work and the solo score is notated in A major (Ex. 5.39).

Ex. 5.39 Ritter, Concerto in B♭ major, *Moderato*, bars 172–180 (notated scordatura)

Bariolage is found infrequently in works by later Austro-German violoncellists. However, this bowing was featured in the solo part of an op. 2 sonata by Jan Stiastny. One passage of *bariolage* is executed with slurred bow strokes (Ex. 5.40a), while another is conjoined with *staccato* slurs (5.40b).

Ex. 5.40 J. Stiastny, op. 2, no. 1, *Allegro molto* (tc1)
(a) bars 154–155

(b) bars 194–196

ONDEGGIANDO

A slurred bowing, *ondeggiando* extends the concept of oscillating between strings. Cupis illustrated its use with *arpeggios*, demonstrating that bow direction was regulated similarly to that of *batteries* and *brisure*. *Arpeggio* patterns which begin on a lower string commence up-bow and vice versa for those starting on an upper string (Ex. 5.41).

Ex. 5.41 Cupis, *Méthode*, pp. 10–11

Bréval illustrated *ondeggiando* with a non-*arpeggio* grouping, to be played on three strings (Ex. 5.42).

Ex. 5.42 Bréval, *Traité*, p. 188 (tc1)

Baudiot also addressed this bowing in his violoncello method, illustrating *ondeggiando* on four strings (Ex. 5.43).

Ex. 5.43 Baudiot, *Méthode*, vol. II, p. 139 (tc1)

Among nineteenth-century players, *ondeggiando* was especially useful for accompaniment figures, as seen in a set of duos by Anton and Max Bohrer (Ex. 5.44). Lengthy passages of slurred *arpeggios* are common to nineteenth-century compositions because of their sustained quality of sound.

Ex. 5.44 Anton and Max Bohrer, *1r & 2d Duo Concertant*, Duetto 1, *Allegro Moderato*, bars 46–55

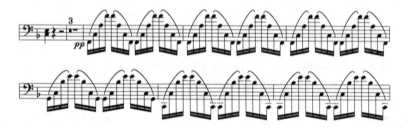

PIQUÉ

Piqué is the method by which dotted-rhythm patterns are played. Receiving little attention in eighteenth-century violoncello tutors, these figures were usually played with separate bow strokes, regardless of the tempo of the movement. Antoniotti frequently used dotted rhythms in slow introductory movements; he marked such movements *sostenuto*, but the bowings were to be executed without slurs (Ex. 5.45).

Ex. 5.45 Antoniotti, op. 1, Sonata XII, *Adagio, è Sostenuto*, bars 1–3

Adagio è Sostenuto

Graziani used separate *piqué* bowings at fast tempos (Ex. 5.46).

Ex. 5.46 Graziani, op. 2, Sonata VI, *spiritoso*, bars 1–10

Duport presented detailed instructions for *piqué* in his *Essai.* He stated that there were two bowings used, one of separate strokes and one in which two notes are hooked together in one bow stroke. Duport considered separate strokes to be the easiest to play: one simply pulled the first note firmly and caught the second note while pushing the bow back.[16] "The second manner is a little more difficult," he wrote, "but has the advantage of being executed with more vivacity and even more force."[17] Duport instructed that the bow is pulled almost to the tip, stopped, and then the second note given a separate attack before the bow is returned, where the same movements are duplicated at the frog. He believed this hooked bowing to be difficult to understand by means of explanation alone; the student had to play the bowing many times before he could feel the correct movements.[18]

Although most nineteenth-century violoncellists used *piqué* sparingly, one virtuoso acclaimed for it was Lamare, who was said to emulate Rode's style of playing and who featured dotted-rhythm figures in his solo works. He placed the instrument in a low position on his left foot, and is reported as having been adept at playing with the tip of his bow, a technique well suited to the Tourte design.[19] As illustrated in Ex. 5.47, Lamare performed rapid *piqué* with separate strokes.

16 Duport, *Essai,* pp. 170–171.
17 Ibid.
18 Ibid.
19 "Etwas über Lamare," 102.

Ex. 5.47 Lamare, Concerto I, *Allegro vivace*, bars 1–23(tc1)

While nineteenth-century French violoncellists continued to adhere to Duport's definition of *piqué*, Austro-German players not only used the above-mentioned bowings but also began to expand the length of slurs used in the execution of dotted rhythms. Bernard Stiastny demonstrated slurs of extreme duration in his method, also varying the rhythmic patterns (Ex. 5.48).

Ex. 5.48 B. Stiastny, *Violoncell-Schule*, vol. II, p. 7

Although any bowing which detracted from a sustained sound gained little appreciation from members of the Dresden school, these long slurs are also found in the compositions of Kummer (Ex. 5.49).

Ex. 5.49 Kummer, *Concertino* op. 16, *Andantino*, bar 47

PORTATO

Notes played *portato* are drawn in one bow stroke, the bow on the string, but executed with a gentle separation. This stroke is applied to passages of slow tempo. In solo repertoire, its use was more frequent before 1785 than afterwards. A passage from a sonata by Antoniotti serves as an illustration (Ex. 5.50).

Ex. 5.50 Antoniotti, op. 1, Sonata VII, *Adagio*, bars 13–15

Romberg was one of the few nineteenth-century performers to provide instruction, writing:

when, in a slow movement, notes occur, which are marked to be played together in one Bow, and also marked with dots above, each note must be separated from the other by a short cessation of the bow. In order to give more force to the expression, a slight pressure is also frequently made upon each note.[20]

STACCATO

Staccato is a bow stroke subject to numerous interpretations. As with many bowing skills, it originated among Italian players and several violoncello tutors define the term according to its Italian meaning of distinct or detached. Crome translated "stoccato" or "staccato" as played "in a plain and distinct manner," while Reinagle simply stated that "staccato" meant "distinct."[21] One application of the term is that of a separate bow stroke. It is so marked in a sonata by Boismortier (Ex 5.51).

20 Romberg, *School*, p. 98.
21 Crome, *Compleat Tutor*, p. 35; Joseph Reinagle, *A Concise Introduction to the Art of Playing the Violoncello* (London: Goulding, Phipps & D'Almaine, [1800]), p. 46.

Ex. 5.51 Boismortier, op. 26, Sonata V, *Giga*, bars 1–6

Graziani also applied the term in this manner in the accompaniment part of one sonata (Ex. 5.52).

Ex. 5.52 Graziani, op. 2, Sonata III, *Rondeau*, bars 37–38

Discrepancies in early nineteenth-century definitions and notation confuse a modern understanding of how separate *staccato* was performed during this period. In contemporary French tutors, *staccato* using separate bow strokes is not referred to by this term, but is illustrated as a variation of *détaché*, as is *martelé* (see p. 173). The Conservatoire method distinguished between the notation of wedge marks and dots. When wedges were placed above the notes, the bow was pulled with a faster stroke of greater bow length than was the case for plain *détaché*. However, the authors' example (Ex 5.53a) does not demonstrate the difference. When dots were notated (Ex. 5.53b), the bow stroke was to be shorter than that given to notes with wedges, but with the bow placed far enough away from the bridge for the sound to be round and sweet.

Ex. 5.53 Baillot, *Méthode*, p. 128

Cursory attention was given to separate *staccato* in the methods of other schools. Dotzauer referred to this bowing as an Italian technique, stating that Italian "professors" executed separate *staccato* strokes with a dry, detached sound.[22]

The more prevalent understanding of *staccato* for eighteenth- and nineteenth-century violoncellists was as a slurred bow stroke. According to Corrette, Lanzetti was especially adept at playing slurred *staccato*.[23] Corrette illustrated the Italian's method of execution in his method, remarking that the notes were equally articulated in the same bow stroke (Ex. 5.54).

Ex. 5.54 Corrette, *Méthode*, p. 37 (T = down-bow, P = up-bow)

notes égales et articulées d'un même coup d'archet.

Following the lead of Italian performers, French violoncellists rapidly integrated slurred *staccato* into their repertoire of virtuoso techniques, and the bowing is commonly found in passages of both moderate and fast tempos. Variations of slur groupings also extended the concept of virtuosity. One example taken from a sonata by Cupis illustrates that slurred *staccato* was played as a grouping in which the slur was executed up-bow (Ex. 5.55). In contrast, an excerpt from a sonata by J. P. Duport used slurred *staccato* in groups of two, the notes articulated with both down- and up-bows (Ex. 5.56).

Ex. 5.55 Cupis, op. 1, Sonata III, *Allegro*, bars 46–49

Ex. 5.56 J. P. Duport, *Six Sonates*, Sonata I, *Allegro*, bars 32–37

22 Dotzauer, *Violonzell-Schule*, p. 26.
23 Corrette, *Méthode*, p. 12.

English performers, too, integrated slurred *staccato* into their bowing practices. Crome described the stroke as "the Feather" or "Feathering the Bow"
and categorized it as a form of slur. His description of how to accomplish
the stroke reads:

the Slur is known by this semicircle put over the number of notes it contains,

thus ⌢ the same sign serves for the Feather, only dotted ⌢ the differ-

ence is this, for the Slur; the Bow is to keep on the String, and for the Feather; it is
just taken off the String, but with the same Bow.[24]

French performers continued to extend the possible variations on slurred
staccato by varying the lengths of slurs. Raoul, as part of his transcription of
Tartini's *L'Arte del arco*, included a complex variation of slurred *staccato* in
his violoncello method (Ex. 5.57).

Ex. 5.57 Raoul, *Méthode*, p. 92 (t: = down-bow, p: = up-bow)

Notwithstanding the consistent use of slurred *staccato* by eighteenth-century Italian and French performers, nineteenth-century violoncellists generally viewed slurred *staccato* as a difficult bowing. J. L. Duport, who
considered his grasp of slurred *staccato* to be one of his lesser attributes,
wrote:

I do not believe it necessary to explain how it is executed; it is entirely a matter of
delicacy and of skill; one achieves it with much practice; there are some people
who grasp it right away, others are never able to perfect it. I am of their number.[25]

The Conservatoire method was more informative about this bowing technique. Illustrating slurred *staccato* in up-bow patterns, they recommended
the performer not to use more bow than was necessary for the number of
notes in the *staccato* group and to play the first and the last note of the group
forte, the other notes *piano* (Ex. 5.58).

24 Crome, *Compleat Tutor*, p. 14.
25 Duport, *Essai*, p. 171.

Ex. 5.58 Baillot, *Méthode*, p. 128

Baudiot later added further elucidation in his own tutor. Referring to his consultation with the violinist Rode, he observed that slurred *staccato* came naturally to only a few performers, but could be learned by anyone if practiced slowly and carefully. Then, quoting Norblin, he recommended playing the stroke with the bow straight on the string, without inclining the stick towards the fingerboard.[26]

German violoncellists were distinctly averse to the use of slurred *staccato*. Although Schetky is reported to have successfully executed this stroke with his underhand bow grip, slurred *staccato* is a bowing rarely found in eighteenth-century German violoncello compositions. Romberg, whose lower bow grip contrasted with that of Italian and French violoncellists, strongly advised against slurred *staccato*, considering it to be a violin bowing and unnatural to the violoncello because of the vertical position of the instrument:

This mode of Bowing, when used for several notes or passages consecutively, is more peculiarly adapted to the Violin; since in playing this Instrument, the bow rests upon the strings, and requires but a slight motion of the hand to produce the staccato. It is required of the Violin-player, that he be able to execute this sort of Bowing. But this is not the case with the Violoncello, where the bow does not rest with its own weight on the strings, and where the staccato cannot be produced with merely a gentle pressure, so that it must either be made with the arm held stiff, or the bow must be drawn up so tight as to spring upon the strings by its own tension, and even then, the Player can never be sure of success. Indeed, as the Violoncellist is so seldom called upon to employ the staccato, it would be a great pity that he should spoil his Bow-hand by practicing it to any extent; and I would rather advise him to abstain from it wholly and entirely.[27]

Notwithstanding Romberg's dislike of slurred *staccato*, he did include instruction for this stroke. He remarked that each note marked with a slur and a dot was played with gentle pressure, and slightly longer than notes marked with a wedge and a slur.[28]

The execution of slurred *staccato* was addressed by Dotzauer, who employed the stroke with reasonable frequency in works composed before his studies with Romberg. His time with the older violoncellist likely resulted in a change of bow grip and therefore a differing view of this bowing tech-

26 Baudiot, *Méthode*, vol. II, p. 72.
27 Romberg, *School*, pp. 109–110.
28 Ibid., p. 98.

nique. Dotzauer states that slurred *staccato* is played with a rigid hand and wrist, the *staccato* notes being articulated in the slur by a slight pressure on each. "It is also incorrect," he instructed, "as sometimes occurs, to raise the little finger of the right hand in executing staccato."[29]

Austrian and Bohemian contemporaries did not share Romberg's aversion to slurred *staccato*. Although not commonly used by eighteenth-century players, slurred *staccato* was a favored virtuoso device of the Stiastny brothers and is found with regularity in the compositions of Merk. The difference in approach may be attributed to differences in bow grip.

MARTELÉ

Martelé is a bowing technique whose use began towards the end of the eighteenth century in tandem with bows of a Tourte-type design. Violoncellists who wrote of this stroke at the beginning of the nineteenth century viewed *martelé* as a variation of *détaché* or *staccato* bowing. As discussed above in Ex. 5.53a, the Conservatoire method illustrated *martelé* as a separate stroke, played with a faster, longer bow stroke than *détaché*.[30] J. L. Duport discussed *martelé* in the context of both a separate and a slurred *staccato* bowing for *arpeggios*, but gave no precise directions for the execution of the stroke. Two illustrations in which the notes with dots are directed to be played *martelé* are shown below (Ex. 5.59).

Ex. 5.59 Duport, *Essai*, p. 81
(a)

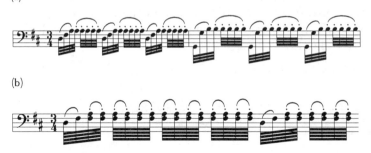

(b)

Romberg referred to a slurred *martelé* stroke as a variant of *portato* and slurred *staccato*. Contrary to Conservatoire practice, he explained that slur groupings with wedge strokes are played shorter and more detached than those marked with dots. However, he also remarked that many composers were careless with the precision of their notation.[31]

29 Dotzauer, *Violonzell-Schule*, p. 28.
30 Baillot, *Méthode*, p. 128.
31 Romberg, *School*, p. 98.

The concept of *martelé* as a thrown, or hammered, off-the-string stroke does not appear in violoncello methods written before 1840. However, this type of stroke is implied in several compositions from post-1815 French solo literature. Hus-Desforges made use of the technique in several passages in the third movement of his op. 23 concerto. One example is shown in Ex. 5.60a. Another, which Hus-Desforges instructed was to be played at the frog, is illustrated in Ex. 5.60b.

Ex. 5.60 Hus-Desforges, Concerto op. 23, *Rondeau* (tc1)
(a) bars 72–75 (tc1)

(b) bars 179–181

SAUTILLÉ

Bowings executed off the string are rare in violoncello literature before 1840. Baudiot was one of the first violoncellists to mention off-the-string playing. Illustrating *sautillé* by example, he stated that, with the pattern shown, the performer plays two notes down-bow and one up-bow, letting the bow "jump" (Ex. 5.61).

Ex. 5.61 Baudiot, *Méthode*, vol. II, p. 71 (tc1)

Writing later in the century, Vaslin gave more specific instructions for the execution of *sautillé*. He considered the technique to be charming for *arpeggios*, demonstrating its use for patterns slurred in groups of two (Ex. 5.62). According to his teaching, *sautillé* was executed by keeping the thumb relaxed outwardly and the wrist rounded, but rigid. The middle of the bow was used, the player being careful to articulate the first note of each group equally. Comparing himself to the violinist de Beriot, who executed this stroke with ease on all four strings, Vaslin expressed the opinion that *sautillé* was only successfully played on the violoncello's upper three strings.

Ex. 5.62 Vaslin, *L'art*, p. 20

In keeping with their views of slurred *staccato*, musicians of the Dresden school had little appreciation for the *sautillé* stroke. Dotzauer, perceiving difficulties in executing *staccato* bowings with a bow grip at the frog, wrote of a *staccato* stroke that some performers played with "a springing bow." He was of the opinion that this stroke "is seldom employed and therefore not recommended."[32] Romberg, like Vaslin, taught *sautillé* as an *arpeggio* bowing, with slurs grouped in two-note units. For bowing patterns beginning on a lower string, Romberg used reversed bowing patterns (Ex. 5.63).

Ex. 5.63 Romberg, *School*, p. 63

As with slurred *staccato* bowings, Romberg warned against the use of *sautillé* by inexperienced players, believing that bowings of this type fostered the development of a stiff arm. Recommending the substitution of a slurred *staccato* stroke in the upper third of the stick, his instructions read:

> The arpeggios with the detached-bow, must be made only with the middle of the bow, and very little of it used for the up-bow. This sort of arpeggio however, can be made only in a quick movement, because the bow itself must partly produce the spring…It has a much better effect when played in detached notes with the up-bow, where each note occupies but a small portion of the bow, used at about a hand's breadth from the end of it.[33]

SLURRED TREMOLO

According to the editors of Bréval's method, slurred tremolo was a bowing used in "old music."[34] This footnote was included despite the fact that Bréval illustrated this technique. A variation of *staccato*, slurred tremolo repeats notes of one pitch in a single bow stroke, each note being slightly articulated. It was a bowing generally used by players using pre-Tourte bows. An example from the earlier part of the eighteenth century is found in the fourth book of sonatas by Barrière (Ex. 5.64).

---

32 Dotzauer, *Violonzell-Schule*, p. 28.
33 Romberg, *School*, p. 63.
34 Bréval, *Traité*, p. 132.

Ex. 5.64 Barrière, *Sonates, Livre IV*, Sonata VI, *Allegro*, bars 65–68

J. P. Duport frequently employed this stroke with double-stops in sets of variations, Ex. 5.65 demonstrating one passage slurred in groups of two.

Ex. 5.65 J. P. Duport, *Six Sonates*, Sonata I, *Minuetto*, var. 3e

Bréval also used this bowing with double-stops, but included an example using a longer slur grouping (Ex. 5.66).

Ex. 5.66 Bréval, *Traité*, p. 132

DOUBLE-STOPS

For eighteenth-century violoncellists, the playing of double-stops was a technique closely related to the execution of *batteries* and *arpeggios*. In method books, these skills are explained as a unit in order to teach fingering patterns. Eighteenth-century tutors provide little explanation for the bowing of double-stops, but solo repertoire contains many examples of their employment. As demonstrated in the sonatas of Lanzetti (Ex. 5.67), early eighteenth-century literature features the predominant use of separate bow strokes, the exception being slurred tremolo figures, wherein pitches remained stable.

Ex. 5.67 Lanzetti, op. 1, Sonata XI, *Rondeau Andante*, bars 1–10 (a♭ in bar 2 = *sic*)

Bowing techniques for double-stops expanded concurrently with bow designs formulated to increase leverage against the strings. The addition of a
pedal tone to moving notes became a popular device after the mid-part of
the century. The sustaining quality of the held note was complementary to
legato playing. The pedal tone could be created by the addition of an open
string (Ex 5.68), or by playing stopped notes (Ex. 5.69).

Ex. 5.68 Lanzetti, *Six Solos After an Easy and Elegant Taste,* Sonata V, *Allegro Pastorale,* bars 1–4

Ex. 5.69 Graziani, op. 2, Sonata V, *Rondeau comodo,* bars 1–8

The desire for *legato* playing and the capabilities of bows with a concave
stick ultimately led to double-stops being commonly played within slur
groupings. Players created several variations on this concept. One type of
legato double-stop juxtaposes a sustained voice against a second voice of
shorter accompaniment notes, creating a composite stroke. This bowing
was featured in an etude by J. P. Duport, published as Etude 8 in his brother's treatise (Ex. 5.70).

Ex. 5.70 Duport, *Essai,* Etude 8, bars 1–9 (tc1)

By the turn of the nineteenth century, violoncellists were playing complex
passages of double-stops and solid octaves within slur groupings as a display of virtuosity. One example of such techniques is drawn from a concerto performed by Lamare (Ex. 5.71).

Ex. 5.71 Lamare, Concerto III, *Allegro Maestoso*, bars 162–173 (tc1)

Regional variations are discernible in the choice of register for double-stop passages. In keeping with the Austro-German regard for the lower sonorities of the violoncello, double-stops and pedal tones using the lower strings are a feature of numerous works from these countries. This trait is especially apparent when Austro-German solo works are compared with those of French violoncellists writing before 1815 (although the tessitura of the French repertoire is due, at least in part, to the lower French pitch standard). Musicians with Mannheim associations had a special fondness for the sonorities of the lower strings, including the upper registers of the G and C string. It is not clear if such techniques were influenced by the level of pitch or the choice of bow or bow grip, but leverage is a key element to the execution of such passages. Such writing is found in the concertos of Filtz and Tricklir, and, although the nature of any relationship is unknown, very close similarities exist between the compositions of Tricklir and Romberg. Viennese composers who exploited the lower strings include Haydn, A. Kraft, and Beethoven. Following Romberg's lead, violoncellists of succeeding generations were uniformly adept at playing on the lower strings of the violoncello.

Filtz's employment of double-stops is seen in an example from his F major concerto (Ex. 5.72). Owing to the width of the intervals, the configuration of this passage strongly suggests the placement of the notes across the four strings of the instrument.

Ex. 5.72 Filtz, Concerto in F major, *Adagio*, bars 45–46 (tc1)

As demonstrated in Ex. 5.73, Tricklir favored pedal tones as a means of creating sonority. This passage uses a G-string pedal against notes climbing the C string.

Ex. 5.73 Tricklir, op. 1, Concerto I, *Allegro*, bars 216–222

Romberg used a pattern of reversed design in his sixth concerto, a C-string pedal juxtaposed with notes climbing the G string (Ex. 5.74). The length of Romberg's slurs demonstrates the change in bowing style which occurred over the twenty-five-year span between Tricklir's concerto and that of Romberg.

Ex. 5.74 Romberg, *Concerto Militaire* op. 31, *Allegro*, bars 193–197

MULTIPLE-STRING CHORDS

Multiple-string chords are note groupings which were viewed as closely related to *arpeggios*. Although the frequency of use increased in tandem with changes to bow design, the manner of execution remained consistent from 1740 to 1840. The most succinct description regarding the perform-ance of multiple-string chords is provided by the Conservatoire method. They instructed that this form of *arpeggio* was to be played with dynamic nuances: the lower note of the chord was stressed, with the succeeding notes softer and shorter in duration (Ex. 5.75).

Ex. 5.75 Baillot, *Méthode*, p. 132

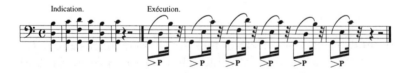

The manner in which multiple-string chords were used by differing gen-erations of violoncellists provides interesting insight into how certain per-forming techniques were expanded as bow leverage increased with design modifications. For violoncellists of the early and mid-part of the eighteenth century, multiple-string chords were used to reinforce the harmonic structure of a phrase and were predominantly found at cadence points (Ex. 5.76). (See Chapter 8, pp. 257–269, for a discussion of figured bass chords.)

Ex. 5.76 Antoniotti, op. 1, Sonata I, *Allegro*, final cadence

In occasional instances, composers integrated chords into the midst of a passage to enlarge the harmonic impact (Ex. 5.77).

Ex. 5.77 Lanzetti, op. 1, Sonata IX, *Allegro*, bars 19–21

Towards the beginning of the nineteenth century, the execution of multiple-string chords developed into a bowing device distinct from *arpeggios*, as playing sequential chords became a way of achieving a large, prolonged sound. This is graphically illustrated in the op. 15 concertos of Janson, who notated chords as shown in Ex. 5.78.

Ex. 5.78 Janson, op. 15, Concerto VI, *Allegro Moderato*, bars 186–189

As Ex. 5.21 demonstrates, Janson sometimes juxtaposed chords and *arpeggios*, but clearly distinguished one from the other. The chords of Ex. 5.21, similar in scope to those of Ex. 5.78, project a large volume of sound.

The desire for power and virtuoso drama is seen again in a passage from a concerto written for Lamare and dedicated to Rode: Ex. 5.79 shows the final bars. This is one of the earliest works for violoncello to use multiple-string chords for such duration. The passage exemplifies the changed concepts of style and sound which resulted from the introduction of the Tourte-design bow.

Ex. 5.79 Lamare, Concerto I, *Allegro Vivace*, bars 370–375 (tc1)

6

Special effects

In addition to those fundamental skills explicitly devised for fingering or bowing, stringed instruments of the violin family are susceptible to varied techniques and devices whose purpose is to produce supplementary tonal colors. Non-essential in nature, the majority of these effects were conceived for solo literature, violoncellists integrating favored choices into performance material as an additional means of communicating with their audience. Some techniques, such as vibrato or *portamento*, were applied in order to elevate the emotional impact of a musical phrase, while harmonics or the use of a mute provided an element of surprise, heightening the audience's awareness of virtuosity. Use of special effects was a very personal matter and, especially in the eighteenth century, subject to remarkable individuality and regional distinctions.

DYNAMICS

The disposition of loud and soft shades in music varied among composers and was often a contentious subject. Different approaches to dynamics were an important part of the various national peforming styles; French playing in particular diverged from that of other regions. While the Italians and their adherents were of the opinion that contrasting dynamics lent depth and excitement to emotional nuances, the French traditionally considered such variation to be extreme and even offensive. The battle lines were initially drawn between the advocates of Italian and French opera, but stylistic preferences were soon extended to instrumental works.

The tenor of this debate was set at the beginning of the eighteenth century in the writings of François Raguenet and Jean Laurent Le Cerf de La Viéville. Raguenet, a proponent of Italian opera after a sojourn in that country, observed:

It is not to be wondered that the Italians think our music dull and stupefying, that according to their taste it appears flat and insipid, if we consider the nature of the French airs compared to those of the Italian. The French, in their airs, aim at the soft, the easy, the flowing and coherent; the whole air is of the same tone...

The more hardy Italian changes the tone and the mode without any awe or hesitation; he makes double or treble cadences of seven or eight bars together upon tones we should think incapable of the least division. He'll make a swelling (*messa di voce*) of so prodigious a length that they who are unacquainted with it can't choose but be offended at first to see him so adventurous, but before he has done they'll think they can't sufficiently admire him...The Italians venture at everything that is harsh and out of the way, but then they do it like people that have a right to venture and are sure of success.[1]

La Viéville responded:

A piece of music should be natural, expressive, harmonious. In the first place, natural, or rather, simple, for simplicity is the first part, the first sign of the natural, which is almost equally an ingredient in these three qualities. In the second place, expressive. In the third place, harmonious, melodious, pleasing – take your choice...

A last rule, which must be added to the little rules and the three great rules, and which clarifies and fortifies both groups, is always to abhor excess. Let us make it a habit and a merit to have contempt, distaste, and aversion without quarter for all that contains anything superfluous. Let us hate even an expression which is of the right character but which goes beyond the appropriate degree of force.[2]

The contrary attitudes expressed by these two writers are correspondingly perceptible in violoncello literature of the eighteenth century. Although composers of the early and mid-eighteenth century were less didactic in their notating of dynamics than those who worked later in the century, Italian violoncellists did use abrupt changes in dynamic levels to surprise and stimulate their audience. Lanzetti, in particular, distinguished his sonatas by the consistent inclusion of *piano* and *forte*. A first example (Ex. 6.1) is that of a slow, introductory recitative. Lanzetti separated the voices within the solo line by designating the notes of the recitative *piano*, the solo violoncello joining the accompaniment at the bars notated *forte*.

1 François Raguenet, "A Comparison Between the French and Italian Music," trans. Oliver Strunk, *The Musical Quarterly*, 32, no. 3 (July 1946), 417–418.
2 Le Cerf de La Viéville, Seigneur de Fréneuse, "From the 'Comparaison de la musique italienne et de la musique française,'" in Oliver Strunk, *Source Readings in Music History: The Baroque Era* (New York: W. W. Norton & Co., Inc., 1965), p. 133.

Ex. 6.1 Lanzetti, op. 1, Sonata XI, *Adagio*, bars 1–5

More conventional was Lanzetti's incorporation of dynamic contrast to create an echo effect (Ex. 6.2) and as a method of voicing the melody line (Ex. 6.3).

Ex. 6.2 Sonata III, *Menuet Allegro*, bars 9–20

Ex. 6.3 Sonata VI, *Gavotta Allegro ma non presto*, bars 1–4

The Italian violoncellist also employed *forte* as an accent (Ex. 6.4).

Ex. 6.4 Sonata III, *Allegro*, bars 21–28

Varied and abrupt dynamic changes became a salient feature of Austro-German composition and such characteristics are evident in the music composed at Mannheim during the mid-part of the century. Contrasts between *forte* and *piano*, accents, and *crescendos* were all a well-used part of the musical language.[3] In violoncello concertos, these shadings were generally specified in the orchestral accompaniments, rather than in the concertante part. Filtz's orchestral parts to the B♭ major concerto are so notated, with the dynamic contrasts of the first violin and tutti violoncello part correspondingly marked (Ex. 6.5). While the cited example does not include *crescendos*, such notation is found in other passages within the concerto.

Ex. 6.5 Filtz: Concerto in B♭ major, *Allegro molto*, bars 1–25

The A minor violoncello concerto of C. P. E. Bach provides a further example of the German approach to sudden contrasts in dynamic levels (Ex. 6.6); such abrupt changes are a customary feature of his compositional style. Bach did not integrate marked *crescendos* into this work, but carefully notated varied degrees of soft and loud.

---

3 For a modern view of the music performed at Mannheim, see Eugene K. Wolf, *The Symphonies of Johann Stamitz: A Study in the Formation of the Classic Style* (Utrecht: Bohn, Scheltema & Holkema, 1981).

Ex. 6.6 C. P. E. Bach, Concerto in A minor, *Andante*, bars 13–21

The violoncello method of Cupis was the first to teach how to vary the force of sound. This instruction is based on a precept affirmed by all subsequent players: if one desires a large sound, the bow is moved towards the bridge and, on the contrary, if a *diminuendo* or softer sound is needed, the bow pressure is lightened and the bow is moved towards the fingerboard.[4] Cupis, however, was sparing with his use of notated dynamics both in the violoncello method and in his solo works. The same tendency may be observed in the compositions of Berteau, Bréval, J. P. Duport, and J. L. Duport. J. L. Duport, who excluded virtually all dynamic markings from the exercises of his *Essai*, provided the summation for this school of thought. He considered that stylistic nuances and musical expression were best conveyed through varieties of bow strokes, rather than through dissimilar levels of sound or timbre, and that beauty and equality of sound throughout all ranges of the violoncello was a superior attainment:

One might tell me that when speaking of nuance and expression, I recommend monotony. I answer that everything has a center, and that the center of beautiful playing, if I may use that expression, is the great equality of sound. This great equality of sound, from the most low to the most high, is not to be neglected, since it is the opinion of all the professors that it is the most difficult and most rare thing.[5]

Not all French violoncellists were restrained in the use of dynamic variation. Tricklir, who studied for three years at Mannheim, skillfully integrated dynamic contrasts and accents into his compositions. This is evident in the *Romance* from the second sonata (Ex. 6.7), published *c.* 1783.

---

4 Cupis, *Méthode*, p. 2.
5 Duport, *Essai*, p. 162. (One presumes that Duport uses the word "monotony" here in its strictest sense, meaning a single homogeneous sound.)

Ex. 6.7 Tricklir, op. 3, Sonata II, *Romance*, bars 1–17

Janson, who spent considerable time studying in both Italy and Germany, also featured incisive dynamic gradations in his solo works. His op. 6 concertos (1779) present a variety of shadings from *pianissimo* to *forte*, accents, *crescendos*, and swells. In these early concertos, the notation for *crescendos* and swells is of particular interest owing to the infrequency of such notation in violoncello music of the period. Ex. 6.8 demonstrates several examples of Janson's use of *crescendo* and Ex. 6.9 illustrates a swell conjoined with a *crescendo*. Swells were most frequently used to enhance sustained notes, especially as a cadence was approached.

Ex. 6.8 Janson, op. 6 (tc1)
(a) Concerto III, *Rondeau*, bars 182–184

(b) Concerto IV, *Adagio* bars 10–12

(c) bars 29–30

Ex. 6.9 Concerto V, *Allegro Moderato*, bars 67–70 (tc1)

Janson's dynamic markings are even more dramatic in the op. 15 concertos, composed during the early 1790s as teaching material for Conservatoire students. The range extends from *pianissimo* to *fortissimo*, but it is the multiplicity of accents which invites attention. Accents are notated in several ways. The term *rinforzando* (Ex. 6.10) is one method, but Janson also used *forte* (Ex. 6.11).

Ex. 6.10 Janson, op. 15, Concerto V, *Allegro Majestuoso*, bars 103–110 (tc1)

Ex. 6.11 Janson, op. 15 (tc1)
(a) Concerto V, *Rondo Allegretto*, bars 39–46

(b) Concerto V, *Allegro Majestuoso*, bars 219–221

Janson's influence upon the Conservatoire evaporated following his political disagreement with Sarrette. The Conservatoire tutor's commentary on dynamics suggests none of the forceful playing inherent in Janson's works, but, rather, echoes the sentiments of J. L. Duport. When compared to Duport's *Essai*, however, the Conservatoire method does contain more cogent explanation of how to execute variations in dynamic levels, and it focuses on practice techniques.

The first concern of the Conservatoire professors was that the student develop the ability to achieve a sustained sound, played at a continuous level of *forte* or *piano*. Their instructions for a "seamless" bow change reflect the influence of Tourte's bow design. In the execution of this exercise,

it was recommended that the bow maintain a position absolutely parallel
to the bridge; instructions for playing *forte* read:

It is necessary to begin by playing very loudly, by gripping the bow with all the
fingers and pressing strongly enough on the string to set it in full vibration. One
keeps the sound equally strong from one end of the bow to the other, and one
avoids doing anything to allow the perception of a change of bowing when it takes
place, whether at the point or at the heel (frog) of the bow, and which one quickly
facilitates by minimizing the interval between the pulled sound and that of the
pushed sound.[6]

The achievement of a soft sound was included in the discussion of the *crescendo* and *diminuendo*, topics which engendered greater interest among
many writers than other dynamic effects. The ability to control precisely a
gradual increase or decrease in sound within one bow stroke was considered of paramount importance to most violoncellists, a reflection on the
fact that the quality of sound was rarely enhanced through use of vibrato.
To create a *crescendo*, the professors of the Conservatoire implied that one
should begin up-bow:

To increase the sound, begin piano far from the bridge; one gradually approaches
it and little by little one augments the force of sound as one pushes the bow towards the frog.[7]

To create a *decrescendo*, the bow stroke was reversed:

The sound is diminished by placing the bow at the usual distance from the bridge,
pressing with force, and diminishing the force of sound by degree and in an imperceptible manner. As one approaches the tip of the bow it must move away
from the bridge so that the sound finishes by absolutely dying away.[8]

The Conservatoire method also addressed the subject of swells (*le son filé*),
which are illustrated on notes of long duration analogous to those notated
in Janson's concertos. The explanation for this technique reads:

The swell is made by beginning piano, and forcing the sound little by little as far
as the middle of the bow, and by imperceptibly diminishing it until the end,
whether in pushing or in pulling.
    The swell is indicated by this sign ◇[9]

6 Baillot, *Méthode*, p. 133.
7 Ibid.
8 Ibid., p. 134.
9 Ibid.

French violoncello methods were circumspect in their treatment of accents. The Conservatoire's method illustrated the following effects (Ex. 6.12), including *piqué* strokes, but provided no written explanation as to execution.

Ex. 6.12 Baillot, *Méthode*, pp. 129–130, accents

(a)

(b)

(c)

(d)

(e)

Also included in this list of bow strokes is the Viotti bowing, a stroke that is a composite of accents and slurred *staccato* (Ex. 6.13). Although it is attributed to the French violinist, it is found in works by Hus-Desforges, Lamare (Ex. 6.14), and Bohrer (Ex. 6.15), albeit without notated *forte* marks. Bohrer's fondness for *staccato* strokes was one of the reasons why his playing was criticized as "too French" by German reviewers.

Ex. 6.13 Baillot, *Méthode*, p. 129

Ex. 6.14 Lamare, Concerto II, first movement, bars 160–163 (tc1)

Ex. 6.15 Anton and Max Bohrer, *1r & 2d Duo Concertant,* Duetto 1, *Allegro Moderato,* bars 31–34

Careful attention to dynamic shadings became an important component of violoncello works from all other schools of performance and, indeed, of French works composed after the end of the Napoleonic Wars. However, while regional variations in the use of dynamics became less distinctive over time, similarity of markings did not necessarily result in similarity of sound production among players from different countries. One familiar example open to contemplation is the opening of the first op. 5 sonata of Beethoven (Ex. 6.16).

Ex. 6.16 Beethoven, Sonata op. 5, no. 1, *Adagio sostenuto*

As a procession of continuous contrasts, this introductory movement includes a majority of the dynamic shadings and accents available to late eighteenth-century violoncellists. The work was first performed by one of the Duport brothers and Beethoven in Berlin in 1796, but received a second performance in Vienna shortly thereafter, by Romberg and Beethoven.[10] While contemporary testimony provides little information about the two performances, the playing style of the French and German violoncellists was antithetical, especially so when bow attack and volume of sound was at issue. Despite Beethoven's precise notation, the two renditions likely sounded very different. Quality of sound was the objective of the Duports, robustness that of Romberg. The execution of dynamics would have conformed to the overall sound ideals of each man, Romberg's contrasts being the more extreme, especially on the lower strings. The Duport "French" sound, however, apparently did not displease Beethoven in performance. Despite his friendship with Romberg, Beethoven was quoted as saying that among all instrumentalists, Duport gave him the greatest enjoyment.[11]

The execution of dynamics was given comprehensive treatment by Austro-German violoncellists, an indication of the importance which the inclusion of "light and shade" held for these players. According to Romberg, dynamic nuances "infuse life and spirit into music" and he provided thorough instructions and a list of definitions (Fig. 6.1).[12] Of special interest is Romberg's translation of *sforzato*, which is not designated as an accent, but rather as a term indicating a continual increase in the volume of sound.

In addition to explaining *crescendo* and *diminuendo* signs, Romberg continued his survey of dynamics by describing the notation for accents. According to him "most of these signs are of modern invention": $>$ designated that "a slight increase is intended to be made on the beginning of the note; and $<$, when applied to the end of the note."[13] Romberg then provided instruction for the swell, stating:

When two signs are combined thus: $<>$ it indicates that first an increase and then a diminution of tone should be made. The middle of the sign shows the place at which the tone should be at its highest degree of loudness.[14]

The following *Adagio* (Ex. 6.17) is, according to Romberg, "accurately marked with all the expressions of light and shade necessary to indicate the

10 Historians have long considered that J. P. Duport was the original executant of this sonata. However, recent studies cast doubt on this assumption, evidence indicating that it may have been J. L. Duport who debuted the sonata with Beethoven. See John Moran, "Fingering in Beethoven's Cello Music: An Evaluation of Historical Sources" (Diplomarbeit, Schola Cantorum Basiliensis, 1994).
11 *BMZ*, no. 45 (1805), 178.
12 Romberg, *School*, p. 96.
13 Ibid.
14 Ibid.

f	. . . .	forte	. . . .	loud.
ff	. . . .	fortissimo	. . . .	very loud.
P or P°	· · · · · · · · · · · · · · ·	piano	. . . .	soft.
PP	. . . .	pianissimo	. . . .	very soft.
PPP	· · · · · · · · · · · ·	piano pianissimo	. . . . .	as soft as possible.
Pf	. . . .	poco forte	. . . .	not very loud.
fP	. . . .	forte piano	. . . .	loud, and directly after, soft.
mf or mez.f	· · · · · · · · ·	mezzo forte	. . . . . .	moderately loud.
rf or rinf:	· · · · · · · · · ·	rinforzando	. . . .	with additional tone.
fz	. . . .	forzando	. . . .	suddenly emphatic.
sfz	. . . .	sforzato	. . . .	continually increasing in tone.
sempre forte	· ·			always loud.
sempre piano	· ·			always soft.
a mezza voce	· ·			moderately loud, neither too loud nor too soft.
sotto voce	· ·			with a soft tone.
dolce	· ·			soft and sweet.
cresc:	· · · · · · · · · · · · · · ·	crescendo	. . . .	with increasing loudness.
decrescendo calando ⎫				These expressions when found together, signify
diminuendo · · · · ⎬ · · · · · · · · · · · · · · · · · · ·				that the music should become gradually softer.
morendo ·				dying away.

Fig. 6.1 Romberg, "Of Light and Shade in Music"

feeling with which the piece should be played."[15] Romberg's specifications require a facile bow stroke for both down- and up-bows, the placement of swells and accents not necessarily conforming to convenience. *Crescendos* are demanded from the down- as well as the up-bow. Accents are placed within the middle of down- and up-bows, in addition to those played at the beginning of a down-bow.

Ex. 6.17 Romberg, *School*, p. 98, *Adagio* ♩ = 60

15 Ibid.

HARMONICS

Rousseau defined harmonics, or "Sons de Flutés", as

A singular type of sound which one draws from certain instruments, such as the
violin and violoncello, with a particular movement of the bow, which one draws
nearer to the bridge, and in placing the finger gently on certain divisions of the
string.[16]

The use of natural harmonics as an idiomatic playing technique was a
feature of the violin family known to early eighteenth-century musicians.
Corrette's illustration of the notes and shifting positions on the violoncello
fingerboard (Fig. 6.2) succinctly outlines the natural divisions of the strings,
and familiarity with such notes is intimated by disparaging remarks made
by Hubert Le Blanc, who, disliking all aspects of the violoncello, pointedly
compared the sound of its harmonics with that of the *trompette marine*.[17]
Specific designations for harmonics, however, are found in published violoncello music only at the midpoint of the century; according to Rousseau,
Berteau was the first to integrate such sounds into violoncello repertoire.[18]

Few of Berteau's compositions are extant. However, the final movements from Sonatas II and III of his first opus demonstrate that he used
harmonics as a virtuoso device.[19] Variations 3 and 6 from the *Aria* of Sonata
II serve as an illustration (Ex. 6.18).

16 Rousseau, *Dictionnaire de musique*, p. 449.
17 Hubert Le Blanc, *Défense de la basse de viole contre les enterprises du violon et les prétensions du violoncelle*
    (Amsterdam: Pierre Mortier, 1740/R 1975), p. 85.
18 Rousseau stated that J. J. Mondonville was the first violinist to integrate harmonic tones into per-
    formance literature, in his op. 4, *Les sons harmoniques* (1738). Notwithstanding the use of such
    sounds by Mondonville, de Lusse, L'Abbé le fils, and Domenico Ferrari, Robin Stowell states that
    violinists of the French and German schools were slow to accept harmonics into their technical
    vocabulary. See Robin Stowell, *Violin Technique and Performance Practice in the Late Eighteenth and
    Early Nineteenth Centuries* (Cambridge University Press, 1985), pp. 211–212.
19 A copy of these sonatas was recently found by Jane Adas in the British Library. The set includes
    the famous G major sonata previously attributed to Sammartini. See Adas, "Le célèbre Berteau,"
    368–380.

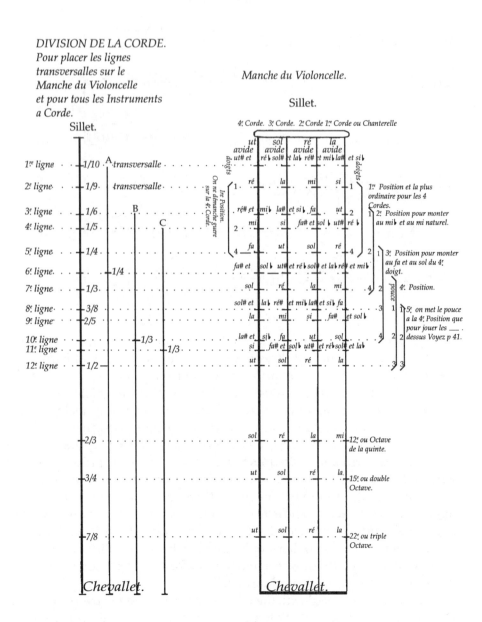

Fig. 6.2 Corrette's divisions of the violoncello fingerboard

Ex. 6.18 Berteau, op. 1, Sonata II, *Aria* (0 = thumb, Λ = natural harmonic)

Natural harmonics were much used by French performers following Berteau. According to both Bréval and J. L. Duport, the use of harmonics was actually more popular in the years preceding the beginning of the nineteenth century, than in 1804 and 1806, the years in which their methods appeared. Bréval, whose verbal discussion of playing techniques is brief throughout, intimated that instruction for the performance of harmonics was unnecessary because everyone knew how to play them, for "in earlier times harmonics were much used, they caused surprise."[20] Duport wrote, "It is perfectly possible to play the violoncello and not make any harmonic sounds; nowadays one meets them more rarely than in the past, but as one who likes to know his instrument well, who does not want to neglect anything, I felt I could not avoid presenting this article."[21] Further endorsement of the use of harmonics by French violoncellists is lent by the Conservatoire's method, whose instruction for their execution duplicates that of Duport in a condensed format.[22]

Apparently fascinated with the theoretical aspects of the overtone series, Duport presented a detailed discussion of natural and artificial harmonics. He first explained the natural divisions of the strings (Fig. 6.3), both above and below the half-string harmonic.

20 Bréval, *Traité*, p. 134.
21 Duport, *Essai*, p. 54.
22 Baillot, *Méthode*, pp. 136–137.

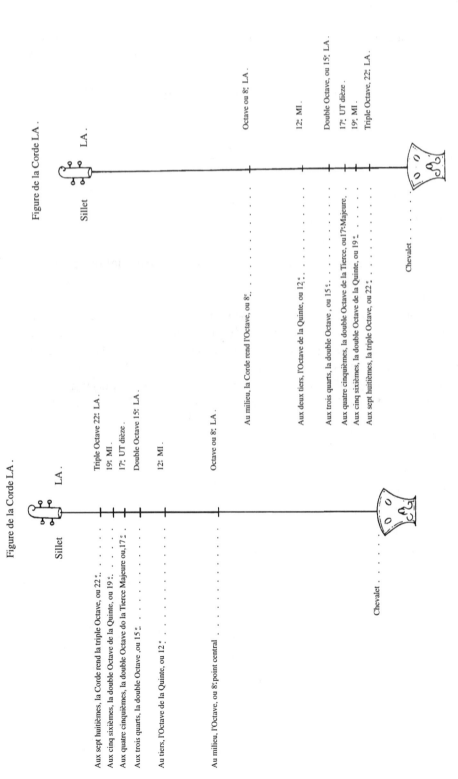

Fig. 6.3 J. L. Duport's illustrations for the natural subdivisions of the string

His instructions then specify that the most convenient part of the instrument from which to choose natural harmonics for performance is from neck fingerings in the third position, with the flatly positioned finger touching the string lightly. His text includes the example shown in Ex. 6.19.

Ex. 6.19 Duport, *Essai*, p. 49 (tc1)

Duport's discussion then moves to the execution of artificial harmonics, a technique he considered necessary for the performance of diatonic scales using harmonics. Fingering artificial harmonics in the neck positions by stopping the fundamental note with the first finger and touching the above interval of the fourth with his fourth finger in an extended position, he reasoned that the first finger operated as a movable bridge.[23] His examples demonstrate that scales could be played either by integrating artificial harmonics into patterns of natural harmonics (Ex. 6.20), or by playing a series of artificial harmonics (Ex. 6.21). The treble clef pitches in these examples are notated one octave higher than they sound.

Ex. 6.20 Duport, *Essai*, p. 51 (tc1)

23 Ibid., pp. 49–50.

Ex. 6.21 p. 52 (tc1)

In addition to common harmonic sounds, according to Romberg, J. L. Duport developed a variant not described in his treatise. Romberg wrote:

Louis Duport, who combined in his playing the greatest taste and execution with the purest and most beautiful tone, particularly excelled in blending Harmonics with other notes. He not only used them alternately, but introduced a third species of tone, something between a firm note and an Harmonic. This tone he produced, not by pressing the finger tightly against the Finger-board, but by bending the string sideways from right to left, by which means he produced a species of Harmonic. In this tone, he executed whole passages, and with the most delightful effect.[24]

Although many of the passages in eighteenth-century performance literature restrict natural harmonics to the third position, at least one performer pushed the boundaries of harmonic tones beyond such limitations. Likewise intrigued with the integration of harmonic sounds into performance literature, Jean Tricklir explored their use in his last two concertos, published *c.* 1788–89. Of the six movements contained in the two works, only the *Adagio* of the F♯ minor concerto omits the use of harmonics. The other five movements feature natural harmonics in passages of single notes (Ex. 6.22) and double-stops (Ex. 6.23), and as trills (Ex. 6.24).

Ex. 6.22 Tricklir, Concerto in A minor, *Allegro Moderato*, bars 181–191 (notated at pitch)

---

24 Romberg, *School*, p. 73.

Ex. 6.23 Tricklir, Concerto in F♯ minor, *Allego Moderato*, bars 130–137 (notated at pitch)

Ex. 6.24 Tricklir, Concerto in A minor, *Andantino*, bars 48–51 (notated at pitch; the third note in bar 48 should probably be *g*[1])

Although harmonics were perhaps less fashionable at the beginning of the nineteenth century, Romberg, following Tricklir's and Duport's lead, employed them as virtuoso devices in two concertos composed in the first decade of the new century. The op. 3 concerto, his first to be composed in Paris and a work displaying many radical bravura techniques, used both natural and artificial harmonics.[25] The passage of artificial harmonics placed on the D string (Ex. 6.25) is of particular interest owing to the rarity of such passages in stringed-instrument literature from this decade.

Ex. 6.25 Romberg, Concerto op. 3, *Fandango*, bars 189–197 (Flagroletto = *sic*)

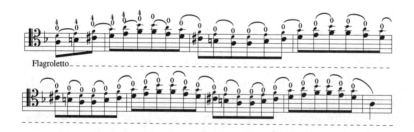

The second of Romberg's concertos to exploit harmonics was the op. 44, subtitled "a picture of Switzerland." Composed in Moscow in 1811, the work portrays pastoral elements popular during this era. He used natural harmonics to emulate the sound of Swiss cow bells (Ex. 6.26); in keeping with his style of virtuosity, the notes were placed in the upper register of the G and C strings.

---

25 Although published as Romberg's second concerto, this work was the third to be composed. The op. 6 concerto was composed in Bonn in 1791, but not published until 1802. For a dating of Romberg's works, see Fuchs, *Allgemeine Wiener Musik-Zeitung*, no. 109 (September 11, 1841), 453–454.

Ex. 6.26 Romberg, Concerto op. 44, *Rondo pastorale*, bars 20–51

Later, reacting to the fame engendered by Paganini's use of harmonics, Romberg expressed the opinion that such notes should not be overused. "By many Artists, Harmonics are made a prominent feature of the Instrument," he wrote, "it certainly cannot be denied, that they possess a peculiar charm where tastefully managed, but they should be considered as musical *Bonbons*, and used sparingly, or the ear will soon tire of them."[26]

For violoncellists following Romberg, harmonics were a standard artifice. Baudiot included extensive discussion regarding the natural subdivisions of the string, reiterating much of Duport's instruction and remarking upon Romberg's incorporation of rarely used notes. Baudiot differed from Duport and the earlier Conservatoire method in the fingering of artificial harmonics, preferring that the thumb and third finger be used, rather than the first and fourth fingers.[27] Dotzauer's instruction for harmonics is similar, but extends to the execution of harmonic trills (Ex. 6.27). According to Dotzauer, this particular example was included because "a trill with flageolet sounds is possible on two strings, and is also considered at the same time as a useful exercise for the suppleness of the right hand."[28]

Ex. 6.27 Dotzauer, *Violonzell-Schule*, p. 50

26 Romberg, *School*, p. 73.
27 Baudiot, *Méthode*, vol. II, p. 218.
28 Dotzauer, *Violonzell-Schule*, p. 50.

PIZZICATO

Although it was overlooked by most eighteenth-century violoncello tutors, *pizzicato* occurred as a type of accompaniment device throughout this period. It was discussed as such by the flutist Quantz: treating the four members of the violin family as one unit, he stated that most performers plucked the string by the end of the fingerboard with the thumb. Multiple-string chords were arpeggiated with the thumb, starting with the lowest note, in quick succession. While Quantz was of the opinion that, at least for single notes on the violin, *pizzicato* should be played with the forefinger, he did not mention this preference for the violoncello.[29] Use of the forefinger is, however, indicated by Gunn. The English violoncellist taught *pizzicato* to beginning students, having them pluck notes before use of the bow was learned.[30]

The integration of *pizzicato* into solo literature becomes evident towards the end of the eighteenth century. An early example is found in the opening of the third sonata in Nochez's op. 1 collection (Ex. 6.28), published in 1765.[31] As Milliot remarks, "the resonance of the open strings gives much majesty to the opening of this movement."[32]

Ex. 6.28 Nochez, op. 1, Sonata III, first movement

Pizzicato is also found in the writing of Tricklir, who included a *pizzicato* motif in the slow movement of his F♯ minor concerto (Ex. 6.29). This is the one movement of his final two concertos which does not use any form of natural harmonics.

---

29 Quantz, *On Playing the Flute*, p. 234.
30 Gunn, *Theory and Practice*, second ed., p. 9. (Quotations from the second edition are reproduced by permission of The Music Library, University of California, Berkeley.)
31 J. J. Nochez (1722–1801) was a student of G. B. Cervetto and Abaco and spent some years in Italy. While very little is known about his life, he was a member of the orchestras of the Opéra-comique and the Concert Spirituel. He was also appointed as teacher to the second class of violoncellos of the Conservatoire upon the school's foundation in 1795. See Milliot, *Le violoncelle en France*, pp. 162–171.
32 Ibid., pp. 170–171.

Ex. 6.29 Tricklir, Concerto in F♯ minor, *Andantino*, bars 14–27

Pizzicato was also a left hand technique, the interjected notes used as a form of self-accompaniment. This is demonstrated in Bréval's violoncello method, albeit without any specific instructions (Ex. 6.30).

Ex. 6.30 Bréval, *Traité*, p. 201 (tc1)

A similar manner of playing is ascribed to J. P. Duport, who spent an after-noon with Ludwig Gerber as accompanist. At the end of this session, the historian was allowed "to hear a solo in the true sense of the word, in which he played the most beautiful and tasteful melody with the bow on the A and D strings and simultaneously, with all possible nonchalance, added a neat bass pizzicato on the lower strings, in which nothing was left out."[33]

Instructions for *pizzicato* became more specific towards the fourth decade of the nineteenth century. Baudiot gave a concise description for French players in the second volume of his own method. He stated that *pizzicato* created a good effect on the violoncello and was frequently used by "modern" composers. He instructed that to achieve a round, soft sound, the string should be plucked with the fleshy part of the finger.[34]

Baudiot illustrated varied examples of *pizzicato* techniques, the first being the playing of single notes (Ex. 6.31). In this instance, the choice of which finger to use against the string was left to the performer.

Ex. 6.31 Baudiot, *Méthode*, vol. II, p. 226 (tc1)

33 Gerber, *Lexikon*, vol. II, cols. 955–956.
34 Baudiot, *Méthode*, vol. II, p. 226.

His next example addresses the execution of double-stops (Ex. 6.32). For this technique, he recommended plucking the string simultaneously with the thumb and index finger.

Ex. 6.32 p. 226 (tc1)

The third illustration presents multiple-string chords, two varied techniques being demonstrated. Baudiot's first method (Ex. 6.33) was to use one finger for each note, placing the fourth finger first, pulling the notes simultaneously. This passage has notes of longer rhythmic values, giving the performer time to reset the fingers.

Ex. 6.33 p. 227 (tc1)

The second example of multiple-string chords displays notes of consistently shorter time values (Ex. 6.34) and here Baudiot chose to strum the strings. His method for this effect was to begin with the upper C, pulling downward with the fleshy inside part of the index finger and then striking the string upward on the return with the nail of the same finger.

Ex. 6.34 p. 227 (tc1)

Following the explanation of chords, Baudiot illustrated a passage of alternating strings (Ex. 6.35). To play this passage, the performer places his
third finger against the A-string side of the fingerboard and alternates
plucking notes with the thumb and index finger.

Ex. 6.35 p. 228 (tc1)

The final example is left-hand *pizzicato*; it resembles Bréval's illustration.
Baudiot recommended using the second or third finger of the left hand to
facilitate plucking the string.

Ex. 6.36 p. 228 (tc1)

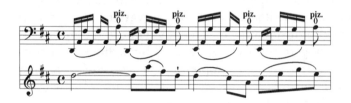

The violoncellists of the Dresden school presented uniform instructions for
pizzicato. Single notes were plucked with the first or second finger of the left
hand, with the thumb placed against the C-string side of the fingerboard to
act as a base.[35] Three-string chords were plucked simultaneously, not
strummed. Romberg gave instructions for these:

If chords occur such as ![notation], the B should be pulled with the 2d [*sic*], and the

D with the 1st finger, and the G should be pulled with the thumb, in a contrary
direction to the two fingers.[36]

Dotzauer used the same technique, but illustrated an alterative chord pattern, writing:

![notation]

---

35 Romberg, *School*, p. 82; Dotzauer, *Violonzell-Schule*, p. 51; Kummer, *Violoncell-Schule*, p. 44.
36 Romberg, *School*, p. 82.

In contemporary music one now finds such passages as the following: One takes the G with the thumb so that it is pulled in the direction of the A string, and the d and b double-stops are taken with the first and second finger.[37]

For four-string chords, Romberg instructed that the A string was to be played with the second finger, the D string with the first finger, and the G and C strings with the thumb, all notes being pulled together.[38] Dotzauer and Kummer likewise advocated this technique, but also allowed four-string chords to be arpeggiated starting with the lowest note, using the thumb.[39]

SCORDATURA

Scordatura is the term used when instruments of the violin family are tuned to pitches varying from those normally used. Re-tuning the instrument allowed for varied tone color and otherwise unavailable chords, and – providing the new tuning remained in fifths – made automatic transposition possible. Scordatura was employed on the violin with regularity from the beginning of the seventeenth century.[40] While variant tunings were applied to the violoncello during the seventeenth century, tuning pitches differing from C–G–d–a were so rarely designated by eighteenth-century composers, that those few surviving examples may be considered anomalous. This intimation is further reinforced by an absence of discussion about scordatura in violoncello teaching literature.

The most well-known work to have been written scordatura is J. S. Bach's fifth unaccompanied suite for violoncello, composed in the early 1720s. In this instance, the top A string is tuned down one full tone to a G. Bach's re-tuning of the violoncello was unconventional for the decade in which it was written and it appears that it was not until the end of the century that a violoncellist used this technique again. Demonstrating a distinct flair for integrating unusual sonorities into his violoncello compositions, and possibly exploiting a procedure that may not have been uncommon to Mannheim soloists, Peter Ritter employed scordatura in five of his thirteen concertos.[41] His tuning for the B♭ major concerto raises all strings of the violoncello a semi-tone higher than the orchestra – a device which Mozart also applied to the viola in the Sinfonia concertante (KV364) for violin and viola, a work written following his visit to Mannheim in 1778. The higher tunings allowed for use of thinner strings, thereby adding brilliance and

37 Dotzauer, *Violonzell-Schule*, p. 51.
38 Romberg, *School*, p. 82.
39 Dotzauer, *Violonzell-Schule*, p. 51; Kummer, *Violoncell-Schule*, p. 44.
40 See Stowell, *Violin Technique*, pp. 232–239.
41 Elsen, "Instrumental Works of Peter Ritter," p. 173.

clarity to the instrument's tone, and facilitated the execution of double-stops and *bariolage* passages within the given key signature. The violoncello part to Ritter's B♭ major concerto is notated in A major, the open A string sounding as a B♭. The resulting effect on a passage of double-stops is demonstrated in Ex. 6.37.

Ex. 6.37 Ritter, Concerto in B♭ major, *Moderato*, bars 262–270 (tc1)

CON SORDINO

Con sordino indicates that a mute is to be placed on the bridge of a stringed instrument. The most comprehensive information regarding the use of mutes is provided by Quantz, who appreciated varied sonorities:

In some pieces it is customary to place mutes or *sordini* on the violin, viola, and violoncello to express more vividly sentiments of love, tenderness, flattery, and melancholy, and also – if the composer knows how to adapt his piece accordingly – more violent emotions such as recklessness, madness, and despair … Mutes are made of various materials, such as wood, lead, brass, tin, and steel. Those of wood and brass are worthless, since they produce a growling tone. Those of steel are the best, provided their weight is proportioned to the instruments. The size of the mutes for the viola and violoncello must be in correct ratio with the size of these instruments, and hence must always be larger for the latter instrument than for the former.

It should be noted that when you play slow pieces with mutes, the greatest force of the bow should not be used, and you must avoid the open strings as much as possible. In slurred notes the bow may be pressed rather firmly against the strings. But if the melody requires frequent repetition of strokes, a short, light stroke, animated by a kind of inner stress, produces a better effect than a long, drawn out, or dragging one. Above all, however, you must regulate yourself in accordance with the ideas that you have to express.[42]

42 Quantz, *On Playing the Flute*, pp. 233–234.

Plates 9a–b: Wooden mutes (The Shrine to Music Museum, Vermillion, South Dakota)

Although Quantz was dismissive of wooden mutes, wood, being easy to shape, was commonly used. Two varied styles of carved violoncello mutes are illustrated in Plate 9. The three-pronged mute is made from ebony, the single-pronged one from a lighter, undetermined wood.

Mutes are little remarked upon by violoncellists of the eighteenth and nineteenth centuries. However, in the context of solo performances, Ritter is reported to have frequently used a mute to contrast the sonorities of slow and fast movements. A review of Ritter reads:

Konzertmeister Ritter played a violoncello concerto of his own composition …When he played the Adagio, I noticed that he restrained his instrument by the use of a strong mute which, I have been assured, is customary for him to do. I heard a few connoisseurs in the audience remark during the applause that when Ritter plays an Adagio, he has a completely different sound than in the Allegro.[43]

SUL PONTICELLO

Sul ponticello is a technique whereby the bow is drawn as close as possible to the bridge in order to achieve a whistling, dry sound, created by an over-abundance of harmonics. While the majority of violoncellists used "sul

43 *AMZ* (November 1803), cols. 86–87.

ponticello" to designate this manner of playing, Romberg preferred the expression "alla gamba."

The French school specified that *sul ponticello* was used as a special effect for accompaniment. They considered the technique as applicable only to rapidly played notes, stating that it had no effect on notes played in a slow tempo (Ex. 6.38).

Ex. 6.38 Baillot, *Méthode*, p. 135

Austro-German players, in keeping with their regard for diverse sonorities, also employed *sul ponticello* in solo contexts. Romberg remarked that this technique was especially effective in variations, or compositions of a similar genre.[44] Anton Kraft used the technique in the final bars of the first op. 3 duo for violin and violoncello (Ex. 6.39). This passage combines *sul ponticello* with extreme dynamic contrasts.

Ex. 6.39 A. Kraft, op. 3, Duet I, *Allegretto*, bars 240–258

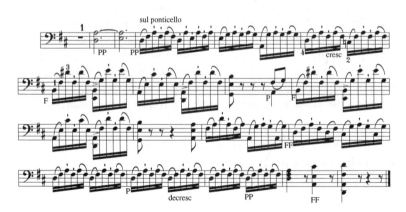

Romberg incorporated *sul ponticello* in the *avant-garde* op. 3 concerto (Ex. 6.40).

Ex. 6.40 Romberg, Concerto op. 3, *Fandango*, bars 170–179 (a la gamba = *sic*)

44 Romberg, *School*, p. 97.

ONDULÉ

Ondulé is a bowing technique in which an undulation, or swell of sound, is created by fluctuations in bow pressure. It was viewed as a form of vibrato by some players,[45] and treated as a separate issue by others. The method of the Conservatoire describes the technique thus:

The bowing which is called *Ondulé* and which is indicated with this other sign ‑‑‑‑‑‑ is one composed of many swelled notes, every one of which should have its loudest part at the beginning of each beat or of each half beat.

The same gradations which one makes on each single note are also produced on a succession of several notes, and even on whole passages. Without these gradations which the player should endeavor to observe, or to put in at the right moment if they have not been indicated, the music lacks effect, clarity, and consequently attraction; one cannot observe them with too much attention, whether in a piece where the Violoncello is a solo part, or in those where it is only an accompanist; but in the latter case above all, consideration must be given to the type of music which one plays, proportioning the gradations to the forces involved, and consequently making a great difference between a *forte* placed in a symphony, or a *forte* placed in a quartet, or in the accompaniment of a voice. An author may not indicate on paper all the small gradations which are found in the nuances themselves.[46]

Ondulé was notated very infrequently in printed music. One example is found in a sonata by Graziani, shown in Ex. 6.41.

Ex. 6.41 Graziani, op. 2, Sonata III, *Adagio*, bars 1–4

45 Stowell quotes Baillot in this regard. Baillot included undulations of the bow in his explanation of violin vibrato. See Stowell, *Violin Technique*, p. 207. Dotzauer also discussed a tremolo created by the bow. The present discussion addresses bowed tremolo as a form of vibrato.
46 Baillot, *Méthode*, pp. 134–135.

VIBRATO

While *ondulé* generates a sound sometimes described as vibrato, violoncellists treated vibrato primarily as a left hand technique. It was added to notes as an ornament during the eighteenth century, and from that time onwards its employment and style of execution varied greatly according to period, region, and individual taste.

Information regarding the use of vibrato by eighteenth-century violoncellists is sparse. One of the few writers to direct instructions in ornamentation towards violoncellists was the violinist Geminiani, who published *A Treatise of Good Taste in the Art of Musick* in London about 1740. A great advocate of vibrato as a means of emphasizing the affect within each genre of composition, Geminiani wrote:

Of the Close Shake

This cannot possibly be described by Notes as in former Examples. To perform it, you must press the Finger strongly upon the String of the Instrument, and move the Wrist in and out slowly and equally, when it is long continued swelling the Sound by Degrees, drawing the Bow nearer to the Bridge, and ending it very strong it may express Majesty, Dignity, etc. But making it shorter, lower and softer, it may denote Affliction, Fear, etc. and when it is made on short Notes, it only contributes to make their Sound more agreable [*sic*]; and for this Reason it should be made use of as often as possible.[47]

That vibrato was incorporated unsparingly by some eighteenth-century players is attested to by Romberg, who believed it should be judiciously applied only to the beginning of select notes. Recommending that vibrato be used as a method of enhancing a strong bow stroke, he instructed:

The close shake, or Tremolo is produced by a rapid lateral motion of the finger when pressed on the string. When used with moderation, and executed with great power of bow, it gives fire and animation to the Tone, but it should be made only at the beginning of the note, and ought not to be continued throughout its whole duration.

Formerly, the close shake was in such repute, that it was applied indiscriminately to every note of whatever duration. This produced a most disagreeable and whining effect, and we cannot be too thankful that an improved taste has at length exploded the abuse of this embellishment.[48]

He added:

The 2nd finger will be found the best in making the close-shake... The close-shake must never be held on through the whole duration of the note, otherwise it will fail

---

47 Francesco Geminiani, *A Treatise of Good Taste in the Art of Musick* (New York: Da Capo Press, 1969), p. 3.
48 Romberg, *School,* p. 87.

in its object, which is, to add power to the tone; and should never exceed in time the third part of the value of the note.[49]

Vibrato received minimal attention from French teachers. However, one statement by Vaslin intimates that, for early nineteenth-century performers, clarity and simplicity of execution were of paramount importance:

Style does not exclude variety; variety is inherent in the multiple techniques which one strives to acquire, nevertheless knowing how to be sparing in the means for special effect, because their too frequent use becomes a tiring monotony, as with the constant vibration of the left hand, exaggerated glissandos, and even too much staccato.[50]

As Vaslin suggests, at the time in which his method was written (1884), vibrato was again in vogue. The trend towards the more frequent use of vibrato is reflected in the methods of Dotzauer and Kummer, who, although still reserved by later standards, were more positive in their attitudes towards the technique than Romberg. For this later generation of violoncellists, vibrato was an addition suitable for long, sustained notes. Remarking that it was used by Italian performers, Dotzauer described both left hand vibrato technique and *ondulé* created with the bow:

With sustained sounds many solo players have the custom of performing them with tremolo, that is with the finger rocking back and forth; and many seek to bring this about through the bow which would be approximately marked so:

51

Kummer remained conservative in his approach, warning the student against the frequent use of vibrato:

One can give a tone occasionally more expression and distinction through a certain shake, that is produced if one sets the finger firmly on the string and makes a designated movement where one, in order to facilitate the same free performance, places the thumb completely loosely against the neck. This shake is expressed through the marking ⁓ , for example:

52

PORTAMENTO

Portamento, an effect whose popularity coincided with Romanticism, is accomplished by expressively sliding the finger from one note to another.

49 Ibid., p. 90.
50 Vaslin, *L'art*, p. 18.
51 Dotzauer, *Violonzell-Schule*, p. 47.
52 Kummer, *Violoncell-Schule*, p. 45.

Discussed by Romberg, Dotzauer, and Kummer, the technique was considered an emotional enhancement similar to vibrato. Romberg categorized it as an ornament:

The expression *Portamento di Voce* (the sustaining and combining of notes) is applicable in the same manner to Instrumental, as to Vocal Music, and signifies the gliding from one note to another, by which means, the most strongly accented notes of the air are blended together with those which precede them, and an agreeable effect produced.[53]

Dotzauer explained *portamento* as a fingering technique dependent upon the correct use of the bow. It was to be accomplished with a slurred bowing: "each note receives a gentle attack with the bow, executed for the most part by the forefinger, without which the hair entirely leaves the string."[54] He provided the following examples (Ex. 6.42) to demonstrate the combined fingering and bowing techniques. His illustrations show the notes encompassing the *portamento* shift played with the same finger.

Ex. 6.42 Dotzauer, *Violonzell-Schule*, p. 46

Kummer's discussion of *portamento*, which he termed *glissando*, suggests that this technique was becoming increasingly popular among mid-nineteenth-century players. He noted that the up-or-down sliding of the finger could be applied to intervals of thirds, fourths, etc. and that when incorporated sparingly, *portamento* could produce a pleasant effect. However, if employed too frequently, such exaggerated playing could become generally accepted, while tasteful, unspoiled playing would seem offensive to the listener.[55] A different view of *portamento* was expressed by Vaslin. As is evident in his statement regarding vibrato (p. 212), Vaslin had little regard for *portamento*, bemoaning what he considered to be the exaggerated use of both techniques.

While vibrato was generally added at the whim of the performer and not notated, *portamento* indications abound among violoncello compositions, especially in those composed after 1820. Max Bohrer flamboyantly displayed the technique in his third concerto. In one instance (Ex. 6.43a), Bohrer slid up an *arpeggio* on the D string with a second finger. In another passage from the same movement, he coordinated a *portamento* fingering with the "Viotti" bowing (Ex. 6.43b).

53 Romberg, *School*, p. 87.
54 Dotzauer, *Violonzell-Schule*, p. 16.
55 Kummer, *Violoncell-Schule*, p. 46.

Ex. 6.43 M. Bohrer, Concerto op. 10, *Rondo*
(a) bars 67–69

(b) bars 119–121

Portamento was not exclusive to German violoncellists. The Conservatoire method illustrates the notation of this technique as it pertains to appoggiaturas, instructing that such "petites notes" may be employed to express *portamento* or *port-de-voix* (Ex. 6.44).

Ex. 6.44 Baillot, *Méthode*, p. 124

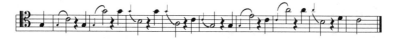

However, "expressive" shifting was employed sparingly by those players who followed J. L. Duport's methodology, such as Baudiot, Hus-Desforges, and Vaslin. As Vaslin intimated, later French violoncellists were not as restrained. Franchomme was one who liberally applied *portamento* fingerings, examples of which are illustrated in Chapter 4 (Ex. 4.42, p. 124) and in Ex. 6.45.

Ex. 6.45 Franchomme, *Thême varié*, var. 4, cadenza

7

Rules of ornamentation

The elusive quality of good taste was the chief consideration for most performers who were required to apply ornaments to written music. Quoting
Rousseau, the Conservatoire method defined the subject thus: "ornaments
or embellishments are several notes of taste which one adds to performance to vary a melody frequently repeated, or to decorate passages too
'simple' which the author himself often composes with the intention of
leaving the exercise to the taste of the performer."[1] The authors continued
their discourse by reasserting Tartini's conviction that "the imagination
invents ornaments but good taste restrains them, giving them the proper
form and expression and likewise excluding them entirely from all pieces
where the subject of the composition and its parts present an object or a
particular sentiment which cannot be altered in any manner and which
should be expressed just as it is."[2]

As with other aspects of violoncello performance, opinions varied as to
what constituted good taste. The French violoncello school, especially conservative under Baillot's influence, counseled restraint. Borrowing an ex-
tract from the violin method, the professors of the Conservatoire stated:

> It is not enough to have consideration for the place where ornaments are to be
> added, one must also avoid multiplying them. Many ornaments do damage to real
> expression, disfigure the melody and in the end become monotonous. They are
> often used to make up for sensitivity, or with the intention of adding charm to the
> execution, but this is an error: nothing but the simple is beautiful and touching:
> expression should be embellished by these graces, but not eclipsed by them.
> Good taste requires that ornaments be used with moderation, and especially that
> they be drawn from the natural expression of the melody.[3]

---

1 Baillot, *Méthode*, p. 141.
2 Ibid.
3 Ibid.

215

Finally, they warned that "it should be observed besides that the character of the violoncello will not allow so many ornaments as another instrument offering greater variety."[4]

Brevity of instruction for ornamentation is indeed a characteristic of many violoncello tutors. Notwithstanding the fact that violoncellists were not called upon to expand the beauties of a solo line with the same frequency as those instrumentalists whose tessitura was the soprano register, knowledge of correct execution for the most common ornaments was considered indispensable by most players. Additionally, a few violoncellists transcended the artificial limitations placed on their instrument and were fluent with a full range of embellishments. However, it must be noted that, while violoncellists of varying nationalities might execute ornaments in much the same way, the description and terminology for these embellishments were as individual as the performers who used them, inconsistency abounding. J. L. Duport's remark that, as decorations, ornaments were subject to ever-changing fashion is a truism.[5]

THE TRILL

The trill, or shake, was the most commonly recognized ornament and, as such, was discussed by most teachers. Notation for the ornament differed between the Italian and French styles. According to Corrette, in the mid-part of the eighteenth century the Italians used "t," the French "+."[6] Geminiani, whose treatise presents the Italian viewpoint for "those who are Lovers of Musick,"[7] differentiated between trills without terminations, marking them "tr," and trills with terminations, notated "⌁."[8] Variations in notation continued into the nineteenth century without the distinction made by Geminiani. Raoul commented that both "tr" and "+" were used by composers of France and Italy,[9] but the Conservatoire method used the sign "⌣" exclusively, while Baudiot stated that either "⌁" or "tr" was used.[10] Baudiot's op. 5 concerto uses the former sign, while his later works adopted the Italian notation.

The majority of writers on violoncello performance considered the trill to be inexorably linked to cadences, French terminology, in fact, referring to it as a cadence, rather than as an ornament. According to Corrette, the

---

4 Ibid.
5 Duport, *Essai*, p. 129.
6 Corrette, *Méthode*, p. 36.
7 Geminiani, *A Treatise of Good Taste*, p. 2.
8 Ibid.
9 Raoul, *Méthode*, p. 23.
10 Baudiot, *Méthode*, vol. II, p. 36.

"cadence" consisted of two notes struck alternately, always executed beginning with the upper note (Ex. 7.1).[11] In Corrette's examples, use of the
open string was considered an acceptable fingering and the trill was not
terminated with a turn.

Ex. 7.1 Corrette, *Méthode*, p. 36

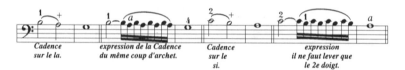

Geminiani carefully drew the distinction between the "plain shake" and
the "turned shake." His plain shake was executed as described by Corrette
and was to be used only in quick movements. The turned shake, with termination (Ex. 7.2), "being made quick and long is fit to express Gaiety; but
if you make it short, and continue the Length of the Note plain and soft, it
may then express some of (the) more tender Passions."[12]

Ex. 7.2 Geminiani, *A Treatise of Good Taste*, p. 4 (tc1)

The use of open strings as shown by Corrette was no longer acceptable by
the beginning of the nineteenth century. Raoul specified that such
fingerings were never to be used for cadences except for those incorporating double-stops.[13] His example of recommended fingerings is shown in
Ex. 7.3.

Ex. 7.3 Raoul, *Méthode*, p. 25

Raoul presented a detailed explanation of cadences and trills, stating that
there were many types of cadences or "tremblements." Observing that the
general purpose of the trill was to terminate a melody which was returning

11 Corrette, *Méthode*, p. 36.
12 Geminiani, *A Treatise of Good Taste*, p. 2.
13 Raoul, *Méthode*, p. 25.

to the tonic or dominant, Raoul in his first example (Ex. 7.4) reiterates the information given by Corrette.[14] Beginning the cadence from the note above the designated trill note remained consistent practice, as did the absence of terminating notes.

Ex. 7.4 p. 23

Raoul next stated that good effect could be had if the performer held the note of preparation for one or two beats before commencing the ornament (Ex. 7.5).

Ex. 7.5 p. 24 (tc1)

Raoul considered the trilled cadence to be abrupt if the anacrusis was not included as part of the preparation to the final note (Ex. 7.6) and demonstrated his method of obtaining a smooth termination (Ex. 7.7).

Ex. 7.6 p. 24

Ex. 7.7 p. 24

After discussing plain cadences, a more ornate version was demonstrated, additional trilling being applied to the anacrusis of the final note (Ex. 7.8).

Ex. 7.8 p. 24

14 Ibid.

Still more intricate was the illustrated execution for a passage of trilled notes (Ex. 7.9). Each trill begins from the note above and has a termination. This passage differs from the "continued shake", described further on, in the use of terminations and in the fact that the ornamented notes are not restricted to stepwise movement. A cadence of this type from contemporary French concerto literature is shown in Ex. 7.48 (p. 239).

Ex. 7.9 p. 24

The previous example integrated the termination with the trill and such additions are shown similarly in Raoul's instructions for executing trills in thumb position (Ex. 7.10). He stated that the thumb was never used for the fundamental note of the trill.

Ex. 7.10 p. 25 (tc1, 0 = thumb))

In slow movements, Raoul's instructions show that the trill might begin slowly and softly, increasing in speed and dynamic level as the trill was completed (Ex. 7.11). The opinion was also expressed that the notes of the trill must be evenly struck and were generally executed faster on the thinner, upper strings than on the thicker, lower ones.[15]

Ex. 7.11 p. 25

Raoul's final example for single-note trills introduced the possibility of changing the octave in which the cadence was completed, allowing for further applied ornamentation. He indicated that if the trilled note was the second step of the key signature, the player could ascend to the seventh step before completing the cadence (Ex. 7.12).

15 Ibid., p. 26.

Ex. 7.12 p. 26

Also provided was instruction for trills played in passages of double-stops. The rules for execution remained the same, except for changes in fingering methods. Allowing the use of open strings in passages of thirds and sixths, Raoul's example is illustrated in Ex. 7.13.

Ex. 7.13 p. 39
(a) thirds

(b) thirds

(c) sixths

Included in the discussion of cadences using double-stops were two examples of composite passages in which the trilled notes acted as accompaniment figures (Ex. 7.14). It was remarked that the second example was rarely used in the keys of E and B major and that the performance had to have enough vivacity to camouflage the changes of fingering.

Ex. 7.14 p. 40
(a)

(b)

J. L. Duport, likewise, discussed the execution of trills at cadence points, particularly the differences in fingerings for major and minor cadences. His discourse relating good taste to the performance of trills makes two points. Firstly, the speed of trilling differed between slow and fast movements. According to Duport, the trill was always faster during a quick movement, but it was charlatanism to think that it should ever be performed with extreme speed and force. Secondly, the fingers playing the trill must always be relaxed, the notes executed evenly and with moderate pressure.[16]

Duport's examples show trills commencing from the note above and concluding with terminations. He carefully differentiated major from minor cadences, taking to task the numerous professional violoncellists who, in his opinion, did not. The problem, as he saw the matter, was two-fold. Some players performed inaccurate cadences because the hand position (i.e. the oblique hand position of Janson and Romberg) placed the fourth finger in an elongated disposition, while others suffered distress when the trill had to be accomplished by the weaker third and fourth fingers.[17] Duport considered the cadences of E major and E minor (Ex. 7.15) to be among the most difficult, owing to the position of the hand around the neck joint.

Ex. 7.15 Duport, *Essai*, p. 128 (tc1)

Cadence in E major (first string)

Cadence in E minor (first string)

The method of the Conservatoire was less dogmatic about the beginnings of trills. The authors stated that there were several methods of preparing and terminating a cadence, demonstrating three examples of each (Ex. 7.16).

Ex. 7.16 Baillot, *Méthode*, pp. 124–125
(a) preparation

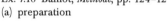

16 Duport, *Essai*, p. 127.
17 Ibid., pp. 126–128.

(b) termination

The last example of a termination demonstrates the addition of an extra note. This addition was allowable in a descending passage, but never in one that ascends.[18]

The Conservatoire method also demonstrated examples of trilled double-stops. In addition to the variants discussed by Raoul, trills of thirds and sixths could be executed with only one note of the double-stop being trilled (Ex. 7.17).

Ex. 7.17 p. 126
(a) thirds

(b) sixths

German practice for the beginning of the nineteenth century is illustrated in detail by Alexander and Kauer. Alexander defined three species of trill, all of which were required to be completed with terminating notes. The common trill (Ex. 7.18), commencing from above the principal note, was the first to be defined.

Ex. 7.18 Alexander, *Anleitung zum Violoncellspiel,* p. 34

Two additional methods of preparation were then demonstrated, that from above (Ex. 7.19a), and that from below (Ex. 7.19b).

18 Baillot, *Méthode,* p. 125.

Ex. 7.19: p. 34
(a)

(b) (the third note of the explanation should probably be omitted)

Kauer illustrated distinct differences between trills with and without termination, the trill with *Nachschläge* having specified notation (Ex. 7.20).

Ex. 7.20 Kauer, *Kurzgefasste Anweisung*, p. 10
(a) trill without termination

(b) trill with termination

Alexander and Kauer were among the few violoncellists to explain the half-trill, or *Pralltriller* (Ex. 7.21), an ornament termed *Schneller* by some eighteenth- and early nineteenth-century musicians (see p. 234 for discussion of inverted mordent). Echoing conventional wisdom, Alexander instructed that this short trill must be executed sharply and as rapidly as possible.

Ex. 7.21 Alexander, *Anleitung zum Violoncellspiel*, p. 34

Kauer's example (Ex. 7.22) examines the length of the *Pralltriller* by note value, that placed on the eighth note – this illustration in fact matches Alexander's description of a *Schneller* on p. 234 – is shorter than when the ornament is applied to a quarter note.

Ex. 7.22 Kauer, *Kurzgefasste Anweisung*, p. 10

Performance practice for trills and cadences in music composed between 1820 and 1840 is delineated by Baudiot, Dotzauer, and Romberg. Dotzauer's instructions on this subject drew on French practice: his text included documented quotes from the method of the Conservatoire and Duport's *Essai*.[19] Both Baudiot and Dotzauer began the trill from the note above, accelerating gradually (Ex. 7.23a and b). Baudiot's example, which is illustrated as a fingering exercise, separates the first note of the trill in order to prepare the fingering pattern. The line underneath the 3 indicates that the upper pitch is struck with the third and fourth fingers together, while the first and second hold down the main note.

Ex. 7.23
(a) Baudiot, *Méthode*, vol. II, p. 36

(b) Dotzauer, *Violonzell-Schule*, p. 41

Romberg, who considered the trill to be the most beautiful of all ornaments, recommended a steady trill, likewise prepared from the note above. Differentiating between violin and violoncello performance practice and

19 Dotzauer, *Violonzell-Schule*, p. 43.

register, he – contrary to French taste – recommended that no license be taken with the rhythm or tempo of the trill itself:

As the shake is the most beautiful, so it is the most important of the Graces. When ever the sign *tr* (contracted for trill) is placed over a note, it signifies that the note immediately above the former, should be struck alternately with it several times, and that this should continue during that time which is due to the value of the note over which the sign stands. Thus the following expression, [music] if the time be Allegro, should be executed as if written thus [music] which represents the degree of rapidity with which the shake should be made. If the time of the movement should be slower, the shake must not partake of its slowness but must always be played with equal rapidity, or it will otherwise produce a bad effect. On the Violin, however, some difference in the rapidity is allowed, as, in the Allegro movement, the Violinist can shake faster than the Violoncellist. This is caused by the pitch being so much lower on the Violoncello than on the Violin, and the Violoncellist must also lift the finger which makes the shake, higher from the string than is necessary for the Violin player. The lower down upon the string the shake is required to be made, the more slowly must the note be struck. On the upper part of the Instrument, the shake may be made almost as rapidly as upon the Violin.[20]

Dotzauer offered a number of methods by which the trill could be prepared and completed within a cadence (Ex. 7.24).

Ex. 7.24 Dotzauer, *Violonzell-Schule*, p. 44

Romberg spoke of the preparation only in instances where the trill is approached from above:

If the upper note (with which the shake is made) should stand before the shaken note, the player, by way of preparing the shake, must first sound the preceding note, thus: [music] .[21]

Romberg also included specific instructions for completing a cadence. Echoing the rule given by Alexander, Romberg implied that terminations were always included with the trill. Romberg additionally specified bow direction, an aspect of playing that was apparently not clear to all players:

20 Romberg, *School*, p. 82.
21 Ibid., p. 83.

The resolving notes of a shake are two small notes, one below, and the other on the same degree with the note shaken, as: 𝄢 . If the movement be Adagio (a slow time) and the first note of the following bar should descend; in order that the shake may not finish too abruptly, another note is placed between the two above-mentioned, thus: 𝄢 and this shake, when it concludes the phrase, should be always played with an up-bow, and should include the resolving notes in the same bow. Many who are unacquainted with what they are playing, and who, consequently, do not know how it should be played, frequently make the shake with a down-bow, which should never be done except where the phrase is incomplete.[22]

THE CONTINUED SHAKE

The continued shake, so called in the English translation of Romberg's method, is a variant of trilling. The ornament name refers to a step-wise passage of trilled notes. French teachers, who recommended using the same fingering and sliding from note to note, offered various means of execution. As illustrated in the Conservatoire method, one could play the series beginning from the note above (Ex. 7.25a), or on the trilled note itself (Ex. 7.25b). According to French practice, a "chain" of trills could also include a termination (Ex. 7.25c).

Ex. 7.25 Baillot, *Méthode*, pp. 125–126
(a)

[written]

(b)

22 Ibid., pp. 82–83.

(c)

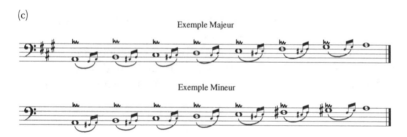

These authors also demonstrated a variant in which the sixteenth note acted as a link (Ex. 7.26): beginning the trill from above or on the note was equally acceptable and no terminations were included. The Conservatoire designation for such ornamentation was *brisé* or *mordant* (see p. 233); the former term was also chosen by Dotzauer, who quoted the Conservatoire's first illustration in his tutor.

Ex. 7.26 Baillot, *Méthode*, p. 125

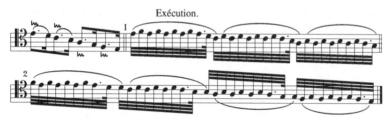

Romberg's teaching did not allow for options. Being of a different opinion with regard to fingering than the professors of the Conservatoire, he believed that performance of the continued shake had greater restrictions when played on the violoncello than on the violin, owing to the nature of shifting and thumb position on the larger instrument. His instructions specify that the "Continued Shake" is trilled from the note above, with the whole pattern concluded by one termination; his advice for bowing, however, conflicts little with the instructions of the Conservatoire method:

The Continued Shake, is a shake held on for several consecutive notes, of which the last only requires resolving notes, and the others must be played as if slurred together. This is difficult to perform in the common position (neck positions) on the Violoncello, since, in that position, all the notes cannot be shaken with the same finger, but the finger must be changed according as the Interval may be a Major or a Minor Second.

This is not necessary on the shift, and consequently it is here less difficult to execute. A passage of this description written thus: should be

executed in moderate time thus:

Even if no Bowing be marked above such a passage, the notes must be always played in one Bow, and without any pressure of the bow on the string in the change from one note to another. If the phrase be not complete, the resolving notes may, for the sake of ornament, be made a Minor second, but where the shake finishes the phrase the resolvents must form a Major second. On the shift

 they must conclude with a Major second, because the thumb

must here remain in its position.[23]

APPOGGIATURAS

Violoncellists of the eighteenth century wrote little regarding the execution of appoggiaturas. Corrette's method incorporated no examples of the ornament, and while Tillière and Cupis placed appoggiaturas in their studies, no practical explanations were given for performance. Cupis, whose etudes take the student to a higher level of accomplishment than those of Tillière, included the following types of appoggiaturas (Ex. 7.27).

Ex. 7.27 Cupis, *Méthode*
(a) appoggiaturas from above, p. 26

(b) appoggiaturas from below, p. 29

(c) short appoggiaturas, p. 40

(d) double appoggiaturas, p. 20

23 Ibid., p. 85.

(e) triple appoggiaturas, p. 29

Earlier Italian practice was described by Geminiani, who, generically applying his rules to those who play and sing, discussed appoggiaturas coming from above and below the main note. The first he designated as the "Superior Apogiatura" (Ex. 7.28) and recommended that it be held longer than the note which the appoggiatura embellished:

The Superior Apogiatura is supposed to express Love, Affection, Pleasure, etc. It should be made pretty long, giving it more than half the Length or Time of the Note it belongs to, observing to swell the Sound by Degrees, and towards the End to force the Bow a little: If it be made short, it will lose much of the aforesaid Qualities; but will always have a pleasing Effect, and it may be added to any Note you will.[24]

Ex. 7.28: Geminiani *A Treatise of Good Taste*, p. 4 (tc1)

"The 'Inferior Apogiatura,'" according to Geminiani, "has the same Qualities with the preceding, except that it is much more confin'd, as it can only be made when the Melody rises the Interval of a second or third, observing to make a Beat [see p. 234 below] on the following Note." His illustration of the "Inferior Apogiatura" with the "swell," "beat," "trill," and "turned shake" is given in Ex. 7.29.

Ex. 7.29 p. 4 (tc1)

English violoncellists were apparently comfortable with Geminiani's prescriptions, although Crome considered that notating appoggiaturas as ornament signs added unnecessary complexity to a work. The trill and the written-out appoggiatura were the only embellishments he considered necessary to violoncellists. Including ornaments with instructions for bow management, Crome discussed the necessity of playing appoggiaturas with a slurred bowing, and considered their execution from above and below to be the same:

24 Geminiani, *A Treatise of Good Taste*, p. 2.

The Apoggiatura is a kind of Slur, sometimes from the sound above, and sometimes from the sound below, and takes half the Time of the Note it stands before;
which if it does, wou'd it not be the same without? I mean to set it plain…for
suppose it is a Minim with an Apoggiatura, is not two Crotchets with a Slur the
same? most certain. for we look upon the Apoggiatura as unnecessary and Answer no end except puzzling the cause, the Apoggiatura generally is a retardation
of some Discord, and may be done as well with the plain Notes.[25]

French instruction for appoggiaturas became more explicit at the beginning of the nineteenth century. The Conservatoire method distinguished
appoggiaturas from above and below by the requisite interval of pitch.
Appoggiaturas written above the note could be either a whole tone or a
semi-tone from the embellished note (Ex. 7.30a), but those written below
were restricted to the interval of a semi-tone (Ex. 7.30b). It was stated that
appoggiaturas ordinarily took half the value of the note which followed.
The professors allowed that the appoggiatura could be "leaned on" in execution, but doing so required care, for if stressed too much or too little, the
ornament lost its effect.[26]

Ex. 7.30 Baillot, *Méthode*, p. 123
(a) appoggiaturas from above

(b) appoggiaturas from below

The Conservatoire tutor furnished two methods of notating double
appoggiaturas. The first (Ex. 7.31), which does not conform to usual
descriptions of the double appoggiatura, was described as never being
marked. The authors stipulated that the placement was left to the taste of
the player.

Ex. 7.31 p. 123

25 Crome, *Compleat Tutor*, p. 16.
26 Baillot, *Méthode*, p. 123.

With the second type of double appoggiatura, the two notes were to be articulated equally, the appoggiaturas then being played more lightly than the principal note (Ex. 7.32).

Ex. 7.32 p. 123

The professors of the Conservatoire also identified appoggiaturas of three notes, designated a *petit grouppe*, or *gruppetto* (also spelled *grupetto* on the same page) (Ex. 7.33). This ornament was required to be formed with the notes of a minor or diminished third, the first note being played more strongly and with greater length than those that followed.[27]

Ex. 7.33 p. 127

German violoncellists varied in their assessment of appoggiaturas. Kauer illustrated long (Ex. 7.34a) and short appoggiaturas (Ex. 7.34b): in executing the long appoggiatura the ornament took the emphasis, while in the short appoggiatura the main note was played more strongly.[28]

Ex. 7.34 Kauer, *Kurzgefasste Anweisung*, p. 10
(a) long appoggiatura

(b) short appoggiatura

27 Ibid., p. 127.
28 Kauer, *Kurzgefasste Anweisung*, p. 10.

The most detailed explanation was presented by Dotzauer, whose illustra-tions address the question of duration, but not pitch relationships. Dotzauer separated appoggiaturas into two categories; long appoggiaturas, in which duration is determined by the time value of the main note, and short appoggiaturas, in which the length is played as notated. Dotzauer made no distinction between the ascending and descending forms, giving three examples of long appoggiaturas. His rule for duration, which reiter-ates that of C. P. E. Bach and other German writers, stated that if the principal note was capable of being equally divided, the appoggiatura took half the time value (Ex. 7.35); if not (as in the case of dotted notes), the

appoggiatura took two-thirds of the value, i.e.  .29

Ex. 7.35 Dotzauer, *Violonzell-Schule*, p. 40

Dotzauer's rule in this regard was also adhered to by Alexander, but not by Romberg.[30] The latter was of the opinion that the appoggiatura took half the value of an equally divisible principal note, but only one-third of a dotted one: "If an appoggiatura stand(s) before a dotted note, the dot does not affect the appoggiatura, which must occupy no more time than if the note were not dotted."[31]

Short appoggiaturas, according to Dotzauer, were not affected by the value of the principal note, but were simply marked as eighth, sixteenth, or thirty-second notes (Ex. 7.36).

Ex. 7.36 p. 40

Dotzauer also illustrated double appoggiaturas (Ex. 7.37a) and triple appoggiaturas; like the Conservatoire professors, he applied the Italian term *gruppetto* to the latter (Ex. 7.37b).

29 Dotzauer, *Violonzell-Schule*, p. 41.
30 Alexander, *Anleitung zum Violoncellspiel*, p. 34.
31 Romberg, *School*, p. 43.

Ex. 7.37 p. 41
(a) (the note values of the fourth explanation are thus in the original, but should probably be two semiquavers and a quaver)

(b)

Dotzauer's illustrations demonstrate that the appoggiatura was always slurred to the principal note. Romberg agreed: "[the appoggiatura] must always be slurred with the note before which it stands."[32]

MORDENTS

Much confusion surrounds this term, as numerous performers employed the word "mordent" to refer to ornaments which are trill variants. The definition provided by Robert Donington clarifies the issue for the purposes of this discussion:

The mordent, known earlier as the open shake or beat, in its standard form consists in the very rapid alternation of the main note with a subsidiary note a step below. In this form it is also known as a lower mordent.[33]

The mordent is one of the two ornaments discussed by Corrette, the other being the trill. Corrette stated that *le Pincé* was one or two reiterations of a principal note with one a semi-tone lower. The number of reiterations depended upon the value of the principal note. He instructed that this ornament could be made on notes of long duration (Ex. 7.38), but that it was never marked in violoncello music.[34] Corrette illustrated the mordent slurred to the principal note.

32 Ibid.
33 Robert Donington, "Ornaments," *NG*, vol. XIII, p. 846.
34 Corrette, *Méthode*, p. 36.

Ex. 7.38 Corrette, *Méthode*, p. 36

Geminiani was more expansive in his description of Italian taste, considering "the beat" (Ex. 7.39) to be a useful ornament of variable length and volume:

This is proper to express several Passions; as for Example, if it be perform'd with Strength, and continued long, it expresses Fury, Anger, Resolution, etc. If it be play'd less strong and shorter, it expresses Mirth, Satisfaction, etc. But if you play it quite soft, and swell the Note, it may then denote Horror, Fear, Grief, Lamentation, etc. By making it short and swelling the Note gently, it may express Affection and Pleasure.[35]

Ex. 7.39 Geminiani, *A Treatise of Good Taste*, p. 4 (tc1)

Discussion regarding the use of mordents becomes scarce among French and English violoncellists after the mid-part of the eighteenth century, but these ornaments continued to be taught by German teachers. Alexander identified the proper mordent, which he termed *Mordent*, as well as the inverted mordent (also known as an upper mordent), to which he applied the designation *Schneller*. He instructed that the *Schneller* was notated with small notes and played as fast as possible (Ex. 7.40).

Ex. 7.40 Alexander, *Anleitung zum Violoncellspiel*, p. 35

As with his illustration of the *Pralltriller*, Kauer defined the mordent in relation to the time value of the ornamented note: longer notes received more repercussions than shorter ones (Ex. 7.41). His representation of the *Pralltriller* (see p. 224 above) is laid out in the same way; this suggests that he viewed it as an inverted mordent.

---

35 Geminiani, *A Treatise of Good Taste*, p. 3.

Ex. 7.41 Kauer, *Kurzgefasste Anweisung,* p. 10

Dotzauer and Romberg also provided guidance on this issue, although they were not in complete agreement. Dotzauer simply stated that lower and upper mordents, which he grouped together under the general term *Mordent,* existed, illustrating them as shown in Ex. 7.42. Dotzauer specified that lower mordents were comprised of notes a semi-tone apart.

Ex. 7.42 Dotzauer, *Violonzell-Schule,* p. 42

Romberg, writing towards the end of the 1830s and in contrast to Dotzauer, stated that "the beat" (i.e. the lower mordent) (Ex. 7.43) had become obsolete as it implied "too much stiffness and pedantry"; the ornament "is no longer found in its original form, but whenever the Composer wishes to express it in his Music, he writes it down in small notes."[36] Romberg did not, however, deem the inverted mordent (designated *Schneller* in his German edition and "passing shake" or "jerk" in the English translation) to be antiquated, but represented it in a manner compatible with Alexander's earlier description. Considering the inverted mordent to be especially effective in fast movements, Romberg was partial to placing the ornament in descending passages, as shown in Ex. 7.44. The instructions specify that although the embellishments must sound with a break between every two notes, no change of bow was to be made.

Ex. 7.43 Romberg, *School,* p. 85

36 Romberg, *School,* p. 86.

Ex. 7.44 pp. 85–86

the passing shake or jerk   illustration   execution

The professors of the Conservatoire did not discuss the mordent proper as conventionally understood. Portraying an inverted mordent (Ex. 7.45), they remarked that this ornament could act as a mordent or a turn (*gruppetto*). Vague in their definition of a mordent, the authors also employed the term *mordant* as an alternative to *brisé* (see p. 227 above).

Ex. 7.45 Baillot, *Méthode*, p. 127

TURNS

The majority of violoncellists treated turning ornaments as related to the *gruppetto*, albeit using differing names for designation. This form of embellishment was either placed on the principal note, or had the effect of linking it with the next note. It existed in two forms, one moving above the principal note, the other below it. Although there existed individual preferences for timing, the execution of turns gave little cause for contention. The most explicit description of turned embellishments was given by Romberg, whose description of these ornaments follows below. Noting one change from earlier practice, Romberg observed that the quick turn was no longer played in the form which he illustrated, but rather, instead of dotting the last note, its length was given to the first note.[37]

the turn   the turn

the quick turn

The turn is made in two ways, either from above or below. When written thus (1) 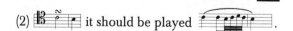 it should be executed thus: ; if on the other hand, thus,

(2) it should be played .

37 Ibid.

There are however, some Composers, (among whom I include myself) who write in such haste, that they do not take the trouble to mark this grace in such a way as to show whether they intend it to be executed from above or from below. They invariably either use but one sign, and leave the player to discover how the grace is to be executed, or else they write the sign so illegibly that it is next to impossible to guess its real meaning. I shall therefore here lay down a more certain rule for this case, and one upon which the player may always depend. If the note which follows, be higher than the one marked with the sign, the turn must be made from above, if lower, the turn must be taken from below.

From above, (1) [musical notation] From below, (2) [musical notation] If a note be dotted, and a turn be placed above the dot, the turn must be made on the dot, but if the sign stand over the note itself, the note must be separated into two parts, thus: [musical notation] When a note used in the turn is required to be raised or depressed a semitone, and is not so marked in the signature, a sign either of a sharp, flat, or natural, is placed above or under the sign of the turn: thus: with a sharp, [musical notation] with a flat, [musical notation] with a natural, [musical notation]

This also is often not marked; and it is frequently left to the Player's ear to decide upon what Interval he should use in making the turn. Those who are naturally endowed with musical feeling can seldom err in such a case, though it may be proper to mention, that, whenever possible, it is advisable to make the turn with a minor Third: But when the grace consists of 3 semitones [it] is absolutely necessary that it should be so marked. On the shift, the turn is always more difficult to execute than in the common position, and the length of time employed in making it must always be regulated by the relative value of the note over which the turn is placed.[38]

One additional point of taste was prescribed by Baudiot, whose instructions address tempo of execution in addition to note configurations. Illustrating the turn as a "*groupetto*" of three or four notes (Ex. 7.46) which act as a link, he stated that turns placed in *adagio* movements were always executed much more slowly than those in faster movements.[39]

Ex. 7.46 Baudiot, *Méthode*, vol. II, p. 50 (tc1)

38 Ibid., pp. 86–87.
39 Baudiot, *Méthode*, vol. II, p. 49.

IMPROVISATION

The ability to embellish a melody line or extend a cadence *ad libitum* was considered a requisite skill among eighteenth- and early nineteenth-century soloists.

Baudiot included instructions illustrating the embellishment of a melodic line (Ex. 7.47). He remarked that the execution of embellished phrases was more tastefully accomplished if the soloist kept a strict meter, allowing the accompaniment to maintain a steady rhythm, the two voices completing the phrase simultaneously. Also illustrated was a second version of the final cadence demonstrating additional embellishment, which served to prolong the approach to the final note.

Ex. 7.47 Baudiot, *Méthode*, vol. II, pp. 50–51 (tc1)

Improvising a cadence was an art little discussed by eighteenth-century violoncellists. A more restricted form of virtuoso extravagance than the extended Classical cadenza, such embellishments were indicated by a fermata (Ex. 7.48). They occurred in both slow and fast movements and were not relegated to final cadences, at which point a longer cadenza could be displayed.

Ex. 7.48 J. L. Duport, Concerto no. 4, *Romance*, bars 29–38 (tc1)

While J. L. Duport left the improvisation of the cadence to the discretion of the performer, Baudiot and Romberg were specific in their directions, frequently writing out the embellishments. Romberg provided instructions in his method, including a detailed description of the long trill with termination with which each cadence should end:

The Pupil will find the practice of the long shake extremely useful; especially when a Pause occurs, and a cadence is required to be made, that is, on the Pause, which is marked with a curve and dot ⌢ placed over a note, and which note must then be held out beyond its usual time. When arrived at the pause, and before he comes to the shake, the performer executes a short passage *ad libitum*, the shake is then held on beyond its usual time, and its resolving notes are played slower than usual, in order that those who are accompanying may fall into the following bar at the same time with the Player.

   To give the Pupil an idea of the nature of a Cadence, I annex the following example, remarking at the same time, that by many players they are extended to a much greater length.[40]

Romberg included written cadences in several of his concertos; the length, in fact, corresponds to that shown in his method. By way of example, one of the cadences from the slow movement of the op. 31 concerto is illustrated in Ex. 7.49.

Ex. 7.49 Romberg, Concerto op. 31, *Lento*, bars 15–16

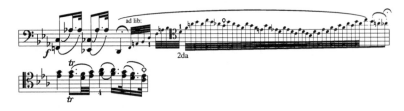

40 Romberg, *School*, p. 83.

Baudiot included an embellished cadence in the first movement of his op. 5 concerto (Ex. 7.50). Like that of Romberg, Baudiot's cadence is used to link two differing thematic ideas. The sign '⚹' specifies a trill.

Ex. 7.50 Baudiot, Concerto op. 5 , *Allegro moderato*, bars 106–107 (tc1)

8

The art of accompaniment

Accompanyment should be the first Object of a Violoncellist, the Instrument being principally invented and intended for that purpose.[1]

The violoncello has historically acted as the consort of solo instrumentalists and singers. While eighteenth-century violoncello solo repertoire testifies to the successful efforts of those players who sought to transcend such musical confines, the development of such solo skills did not obviate the necessity of being a proficient and perceptive accompanist. As a composer, solo player, and teacher, Quantz wrote authoritatively and persuasively on the importance of accompanimental expertise to a professional violoncellist:

Anyone who practises the violoncello as an amateur is justly free to do whatever gives him the greatest pleasure, but somebody who intends to make it his profession will do well to apply himself above all else to becoming a good accompanist, for in this way he will make himself more useful and of greater service in ensembles. If, on the contrary, he rushes immediately into solo playing, before knowing how to perform a ripieno bass well, and in consequence perhaps strings his instrument so feebly [with thin strings] that he cannot be heard in the accompaniment, he will be of little use in the ensemble. He might well be put to shame by some amateur who excels both in playing solos and in accompanying. Good accompaniment is the chief quality demanded from this instrument. And even if accompanying and solo playing do not represent the same degree of excellence, a good accompanist is of greater service in an orchestra than a mediocre soloist.[2]

---

1 J. G. C. Schetky, *Twelve Duetts for Two Violoncellos, with some Observations & Rules for playing that Instrument,* op. 7 (London: Preston & Son), p. 1.
2 Quantz, *On Playing the Flute,* p. 246.

DEFINING THE TRADITION OF ACCOMPANIMENT

Eighteenth-century violoncellists had a clear understanding that the development of their instrument was directly tied to its use as an accompaniment for the violin. As Gunn explained:

> For some time after the introduction of the Violin into concerts, the under parts were performed on the Tenor Viol and Bass Viol; it was after discovering the insufficiency of these, especially of the latter, that instruments of its own species, the Tenor Violin and Violoncello, were made of the same shape, but increasing in size in proportion to the additional length and thickness of the strings they were to carry. The Violins were conceived to be so powerful in tone, as to require Basses of a considerably greater size and length of string than those now in use.[3]

Gunn correctly ascertained that violoncellos used for accompanying were not the same as those used for solo playing, but the larger "church basses" described in Chapter 2. It is indeed in the orchestras of Italian churches that violoncello-type instruments are first found consistently. Viols had distinctive secular associations and were generally excluded from performances of Italian religious music by the seventeenth century.[4] However, those qualities of the violoncello most appreciated in reverberant churches – sonority, volume of sound, and pitch accuracy regardless of key signature or chromaticism – also began to be valued by composers for secular music. In discussing the qualities of the violin family, Marin Mersenne, writing in 1636, observed:

> It must still be noted that the Violin is capable of all the genres and all the species of music, and that one can play the enharmonic, and each species of the diatonic and chromatic upon it, because it carries no frets, and contains all the intervals imaginable...[5]

Claudio Monteverdi, born in the violin-making center of Cremona, employed the *basso viola da braccio* in *L'Orfeo* (1607) and in Books VII (1619) and VIII (1638) of his madrigals.[6] The "bass" voice of the violin family was also designated as the accompanimental instrument in the violin sonatas of G. B. Buonamente (Book 6, 1636) and Giovanni Legrenzi (op. 8, 1663).[7]

By the final decades of the seventeenth century, when solo sonatas for the violoncello began to be composed, violoncello-type instruments were already well established in Italy as suitable for accompaniments in all musical genres. The capabilities of Italian players led composers to write in-

---

3 Gunn, *Theory and Practice,* first ed., p. 19.
4 Bonta, "Terminology for the Bass Violin," 11.
5 *Marin Mersenne, Harmonie Universelle: The Books on Instruments* trans. Roger E. Chapman (The Hague: Martinus Nijhoff, 1957), p. 239.
6 Bonta, "From Violone to Violoncello," 69.
7 Ibid., 69–70.

creasingly intricate and demanding passage work, the bass parts of Corelli's violin sonatas, for instance, being used as study material for violoncellists for the ensuing century after their composition.[8] Italian musicians were also responsible for introducing violoncello accompaniments into musical establishments throughout the rest of Europe. Corette suggested that the violoncello's strength of sound, precision of pitch, and clarity of articulation made it especially suitable for opera orchestras because singers found it easier to determine their own pitches when listening to the violoncello.[9] A five-string *basse de violon* tuned C–G–d–a–d¹ was added to Lully's opera orchestra as early as 1676, the Italian player Theobaldo di Gatti being welcomed upon his arrival in Paris. His duties in the *petit chœur* included the accompaniment of recitatives and *airs*. Lully is also known to have used larger instruments, tuned B♭₁–F–c–g, in the *grand chœur*.[10]

Despite the expediency of "bass" violins to continuo playing, well into the 1730s violoncellists were frequently members of an eclectic grouping of bass instruments within opera orchestras. This seems to have been especially true at the French opera, where at least one work specifies bass viols, five-string violoncellos, four-string violoncellos, violones, and bassoons.[11] This same eclecticism is also apparent in English productions: for instance, the continuo section for Handel's opera *Giulio Cesare* (1724) combined viola da gamba, violoncello, contrabass, bassoon, theorbo, harp, and harpsichord.

Nevertheless, this same period saw a move towards more standardized orchestral forces. Italian opera composers such as Leonardo Vinci (1690–1730), G. B. Pergolesi (1710–36), and Leonardo Leo (1694–1744) were inclined to simplify musical texture, especially in the overture, and homogeneous instrumental sections were a noticeable by-product. String sections were increasingly restricted to the voices of the violin, viola, and violoncello/bass and from about 1730 onward, the preferred medium for the orchestral bass line was violoncello and contrabass. This preference was soon established internationally, as seen in the scores of Rameau at the French opera,[12] the later works of Handel in England, and at Mannheim within an additional orchestral form developed from the Italian opera overture – the symphony.[13] The distinctive colors from a multiplicity of stringed instruments were soon to be irrelevant to the symphonists of the

---

8 Gunn, in particular, used Corelli's bass parts as elementary teaching material.
9 Corrette, *Méthode*, Preface. See also Dimitry Markevitch, "A New Sound for Familiar Music: The Cello as an Accompanying Instrument in the 18th-Century," *Strings*, 6, no. 3 (November/December 1991), 18–21.
10 Mary Cyr, "*Basses and basse continue* in the Orchestra of the Paris Opéra 1700–1764," *Early Music*, 10, no. 2 (April 1982), 158.
11 Dr. Cyr quotes the orchestration for Matho's opera *Arion* (1714) to make this point. Ibid., 160.
12 Ibid., 161.
13 Wolf, *Symphonies of Johann Stamitz*, pp. 354–355.

eighteenth century, the violoncello and contrabass being sufficient for the purposes required.

The same tendencies witnessed in orchestration are also apparent in compositions for chamber ensembles, with one distinction. While composers retreated from eclectic groups of bass instruments in orchestras after the 1730s, the violoncello remained but one choice – albeit the usual one – for a tenor/bass string voice in chamber music even into the nineteenth century: such compositions as Peter Ritter's *Drei Stücke für Flöte, Viola da Gamba und Horn* (after 1800) attest to composers' abiding interest in unusual combinations of instruments.

The importance of accompanying skills was well recognized by violoncellists of the eighteenth and nineteenth centuries, for it was these skills which consistently put food on the table. Even Romberg, who earned as much for his solo performances as the famed singers and violinists of his era, was employed for a major part of his career as a member of a Kapelle. The more conventional career was that of Robert Lindley, who successfully served as accompanist to all of London's principal music groups for forty-eight years.

In discussing the merits of an accomplished accompanist, teachers of the violoncello were not addressing those skills needed to execute the increasingly intricate concertante parts included by many composers in both orchestral and chamber music, for these differed little from solos in their demands on the player. Rather, writers of the period make clear that a good accompanist required training additional to mere technical proficiency. "A well played Solo on the Violoncello is doubtless agreeable and delightful," wrote Schetky, "but let the Solo player be ever so eminent, as such, he will fall considerably in the estimation of all real Connoisseurs when they find that he is not a good Accompanyer."[14] To become an able accompanist, according to the professors of the Conservatoire, "requires an entirely special study and above all great experience in accompanying the voice and executing ensemble music."[15]

REGULATION OF RHYTHM, METER, AND TEMPO

Of all the duties of violoncello accompanists, that considered the most fundamental, yet requisite of the greatest experience and sensitivity, was the ability to differentiate between when to follow and when to lead the melody line, whether vocal or instrumental. Violoncellists were expected to know how to regulate rhythm, meter, and tempo appropriately. This

14 Schetky, *Observations*, p. 1.
15 Baillot, *Méthode*, p. 137.

subject was of major import for Corrette, who framed the earliest guidelines for violoncello accompanists in the final page of his method. Corrette, an organist by training, stipulated that within a performance group "the violoncello holds the reins at a concert."[16]

He recommended that those reins be held gently. Vocalists generally had to be followed, rhythmic license being expected in both recitatives and quick movements. Instrumentalists executing the melody in a sonata or concerto also presumed that the violoncellist would follow the melody line, as, according to Corrette, the soloist usually desired expressive freedom and was frequently required to execute difficulties which did not yield to rhythmic stability. However, if the solo voice began to speed, the violoncellist had to "play with force and beat out the tempo for a measure or two," firmly preventing the soloist from playing any faster.[17] Corrette likewise held that in slow instrumental movements, the violoncellist was responsible for maintaining a steady pulse, whether with bow or foot, although "skillful violinists play the Adagios and Largos without beating the tempo."[18] He remarked that Italian players were especially accurate in their execution of slow movements, the beating of time occurring only in music performed by large choruses.

Rhythmic consistency in the violoncello part was of similar concern to Quantz. Evincing a preference for assertive violoncello accompaniments, he linked rhythmic accuracy to correct use of the bow. His concern for this aspect of violoncello technique extended to the recommendation that an overhand Italian bow grip be used. In his experience, this hold allowed for more emphasis to be placed on the strong beats of the bar (i.e. beats one and three in a quadruple meter), which were to be played down-bow at the lower part of the stick.[19]

Meter, bow stroke, note duration, and emotional affect were interrelated in Quantz's view, meter being the determining factor for correct articulation. Providing examples to demonstrate how the violoncellist must vary his bow stroke to meet the requirements of various tempos and meters, he wrote:

In a melancholy Adagio, the slow notes, that is, the quavers in common time and the crotchets in alla breve, must be played with a quiet bowstroke. The bow must not be drawn hastily or hurriedly to its tip, since this would impede the expression of the sentiment of melancholy, and would offend the ear. In the Allegro the crotchets must be played in a sustained or *nourissant* manner, and the quavers very short. The same is true in an Allegretto written in alla breve time. But should the

---

16 Corrette, *Méthode*, p. 46.
17 Ibid.
18 Ibid.
19 Quantz, *On Playing the Flute*, p. 241.

Allegretto be written in common time, the quavers are sustained, and the semi-quavers played short. The short notes must be played not with the whole arm, but with only the hand, by moving the wrist.[20]

In the same vein was the remark that:

If in a Presto that must be played in a very lively fashion several quavers or other short notes appear upon the same pitch, the first in each measure may be stressed by pressure on the bow.[21]

Further instruction for proper articulation addressed the execution of figures in dotted rhythm ◼▝▭ . Quantz required that his violoncellists stress the long note and quickly articulate the short note:

Dotted notes must always be bowed more earnestly and heavily than the violinist would play them, but the semiquavers that follow must be executed very briefly and sharply, whether in a quick or slow tempo.[22]

The violoncellist must preserve the correct tempo and proper degree of liveliness by the execution of a steady tempo, neither rushing nor dragging the beat, and – further to facilitate the performance of the solo voice – was expected to pay attention. Quantz's acerbic statement that the accompanist "must direct his thoughts with constant attentiveness both to the rests and to the notes, so that it is unnecessary to remind him to begin again after a rest"[23] certainly implies occasional attention lapses.

Many of the same points addressed by Corrette and Quantz were covered by Baumgartner, whose entire violoncello method was directed towards teaching inexperienced players the foundations of accompanimental skills. Rhythmic assurance was considered by Baumgartner to be one of the great difficulties:

since you are not able to learn the time beating with the hand while playing, as do those who learn to sing: you should use the foot in the following manner: to know, in a sustained and slow tempo, for example, to accompany or play an Adagio, you should practice in the tempo, beating all the eighth notes with the foot, and paying attention to the value of each note. In brisk tempos or in the Allegro, you strike the foot on all of the quarter notes. If you follow my advice, you will be secure with tempo.[24]

Beating time with the hand or foot was also a discipline given extensive coverage by Crome, who stated that "all Musical Performances must be

20 Ibid., p. 243.
21 Ibid., p. 245.
22 Ibid.
23 Ibid., p. 244.
24 Jean Baumgartner, *Instructions de musique, theorique et pratique, a l'usage du violoncello* (The Hague: Daniel Monnier, [1774]), pp. 6–7.

done by the Rule of Time keeping either with the Hand or Foot, but on an Instrument with the Foot."[25] Coordinating foot action with rhythm and bow direction, Crome choreographed precise motions for four types of meters. The foot was always brought down with the first beat of each bar; the upwards movement varied according to meter. In Ex. 8.1, b. and f. are abbreviations for backward and forward bow strokes and d. and u. stand for down and up movements of the foot.

Ex. 8.1 Crome, *Compleat Tutor*, pp. 12–13

Baumgartner advised his readers that it was not possible "to accompany a solo, a trio, or a quartet" without being rhythmically secure. He added that possessing a good instrument strung with well-proportioned strings contributed towards the ease of enunciating a defined beat. Being the optimistic teacher, he remarked that, in any case, one could first learn to "accompany" symphonies because there were multiple violoncellos to cover mistakes (one must assume that mistakes were not a major issue among professional players who followed Quantz's dictum and paid attention to the solo part).[26]

25 Crome, *Compleat Tutor*, p. 12. Tapping a foot to maintain the beat was not a performance trait restricted to violoncellists. Viennese violinist Ignaz Schuppanizigh is said to have been an inveterate foot tapper. See Morrow, *Concert Life in Haydn's Vienna*, p. 170.
26 Baumgartner, *Instructions*, p. 30. The word "symphony" was frequently used during this period to refer to any orchestral work using a large group of players and it is in the general context that Baumgartner makes his designation.

While stressing the importance of rhythmic precision, Baumgartner held that the violoncellist was required to follow the vicissitudes of the upper voice, especially if one was playing with amateurs.[27] Of the opposite opinion were the professors of the Conservatoire, who considered accompanists of instrumental music to be dogmatic conservators of consistent tempo:

> The one who executes the principal part may indulge himself in his inspiration and occasionally use great freedom in his playing, but the bass accompaniment, whose function it is to determine the progression of the chords, ought to allow itself nothing equivocal, nothing irregular, no distinctive expression by which it might take leave of its character and render the music diffuse by depriving it of the fundamental part. The bass in its grave and simple movement should always be articulated clearly and should not only keep steady but also play tastefully. The accompanist should remain undisturbed in the midst of those slight changes of tempo which are allowed for the sake of expression, and in that seeming disorder which the Italians call *Tempo disturbato*, the bass should serve as the regulator in ensemble pieces in the same manner as the left hand should maintain steadiness in the execution of a sonata for piano.[28]

The advent of Maelzel's metronome during the first decade of the nineteenth century made the study of rhythmic accuracy and tempo consistency less of an issue, although rhythm remained the foundation of an accompanist's art. A comment by Romberg addresses one other situation encountered by touring professionals when playing with ensembles – the fact that concepts of tempo varied substantially among regions: "the Allegro is played faster in Paris than in Vienna, and in Vienna, again, faster than in the north of Germany."[29] A proponent of the metronome, Romberg articulated his concepts of tempo in the following chart. The metronome markings are given for common time.

LARGO	very slow, and lengthened	♩ = 50
GRAVE	not much faster, but with dignity	♩ = 54
LARGHETTO	less slow than Largo and Grave	♩ = 56
ADAGIO	rather faster than Larghetto	♩ = 60
LENTO	rather faster than Adagio	♩ = 69
ANDANTINO	proceeding quietly and slower than Andante	♩ = 76

(This time is frequently misunderstood, and many play it faster than the Andante)

27 Ibid.   28 Baillot, *Méthode*, p. 140.

29 Romberg, *School*, p. 110. The tempos taken by London musicians were also reported as being faster than those in Germany. According to comments made in reply to Fétis' criticisms of English music, "It is generally thought that instrumental music is played much too quick in London. M. Salomon, who knew the time of Haydn's grand symphonies better than any other person, always declared that they, latterly, were much too rapidly performed. And it appears, from the life of Mozart just published at Leipzig, that this great composer complained of the hurried manner in which all his compositions were executed." See *The Harmonicon*, 7, no. 8 (September 1829), 217.

ANDANTE	going gently	♩ = 80
ALLEGRETTO	somewhat cheerful	♩ = 100
ALLEGRO	with vivacity	♩ = 116
PRESTO	quick	♩ = 138
PRESTISSIMO	as quick as possible	♩ = 160

ACHIEVING THE PROPER SOUND

Just as they were expected to know when to follow and when to lead, violoncellists when accompanying also had to be sensitive to tone, volume of sound, and articulation. Gunn affirmed the importance of these practices, recommending that the student

observe the manner in which the best performers accompany, and more particularly to attend to the effects produced from the different degrees of force given to the passages, and the very exact degree of sound, and time, that is requisite to observe in every part, to produce a good effect from the joint performance. He will then observe how much it is in the power of the Violoncello, by inattention to the other parts, to destroy their finest effects, and to counteract the most beautiful expression; and, on the other hand, by a judicious management of it, how much fullness, mellowness, and spirit, it can give to the whole, without injuring the softest passages, or most delicate expression, in any of the other parts. Hence it follows, that to accompany well comprehends the best use of the instrument, and constitutes the greatest praise of a performer.[30]

Romberg stipulated:

the Violoncellist must always regulate his tone by that of the instrument he is accompanying. If his tone be too powerful, it will drown that of the other instrument; if it be too weak, it will check the expression of the player he is accompanying.[31]

Earlier, Quantz had appreciated a full-sounding accompaniment: he was of the opinion that an orchestral violoncellist must play with a larger, heavier-strung violoncello and orchestral bow (see Chapter 2, pp. 50 and 70)[32] and stressed the important relationship between sound and bow management:

In general the violoncellist must strive to draw a full, round, and virile tone from his instrument; in this regard the manner in which he guides the bow is of great

---

30 Gunn, *Theory and Practice*, first ed., p. 69.
31 Romberg, *School*, p. 132.
32 In interpreting eighteenth- and nineteenth-century comments on sound production, it must be remembered that, while use of larger violoncellos gradually became less common among accompanists, violoncellists continued to use heavier stringing for chamber music and orchestral playing than for solo performances.

importance, and whether it is too close to, or too far from, the bridge. If, for example, in a large ensemble he carries delicacy too far, and plays so softly that he seems to be touching the strings with a featherduster rather than a bow, he will earn little praise.[33]

In orchestral situations, the violoncellist would often be called upon to lead the group through strongly articulated and sonorous playing. For instance, J. P. Duport was praised by Gerber at the Berlin Kapelle for "his strong, full sound, his powerful bow and his confidence, with which he always gives his full weight to the bass, thereby improving the accents and those notes which stand out."[34] He continued his summation of Duport's orchestral skills:

Truly! There is more to a violoncellist than merely conquering all the notes in thumb position with ease. His ear must at the same time grasp the whole, and grasp the meaning of the composer with lightning speed. This is certainly the duty of every instrumentalist; but of the entire orchestra none can accomplish this with such power as a violoncellist who knows how to use his bow with power.[35]

In playing chamber music, the violoncellist was generally expected to blend with the ensemble, subordinating his sound to the melody. This was true even of those who played Beethoven quartets, such as Joseph Lincke. "Linke treats his instrument as well as anyone in a quartet can ever manage it," wrote the violinist Michael Frey, "he is the only one that never allows his tone to be loud and overwhelming."[36]

The professors of the Conservatoire encouraged careful voicing, participation in sonatas, trios, quartets, and quintets requiring "that taste must serve as the guide and proper sentiments be formulated by the limits of expression."[37] In practical terms, the player had to determine which notes were strictly those of accompaniment, such as the bass of a continuo sonata or solo song, and which required greater equality of the violoncello with the other parts. To execute a bass line correctly, the professors instructed that

notes of accompaniment should be in general *détaché*, pulled quickly and separated from one another as in the following example, and neither dragged nor played feebly, in order to contrast with the melody which should always be connected and sustained.

---

33 Quantz, *On Playing the Flute*, pp. 241–242.
34 Gerber, *Lexikon*, vol. II, col. 955.
35 Ibid.
36 Schmidt-Görg, "Tagebuch Frey," p. 139.
37 Baillot, *Méthode*, p. 140.

Example taken from a quartet of Mozart[38]

Violoncello parts that interacted motivically with the melodic line required different bowing skills. According to the professors, to execute this type of writing tastefully, the violoncellist had to blend with the upper part in order to form a perfect ensemble. Melodic phrases were to imitate or otherwise enhance the sustained bowings of the upper voice;

they chose a legato phrase from a Boccherini work to further illustrate

their point.[39]

The addition of any special effects, such as vibrato or natural harmonics, to an accompaniment was not mentioned by any eighteenth- or early nineteenth-century violoncellist. However, as discussed in Chapter 6 (p. 209), *sul ponticello* was a unique effect considered by French teachers to be applicable only to the accompanying voice. The Conservatoire's demonstration of how this technique was juxtaposed against a melody is shown in Ex. 8.2.

Ex. 8.2 Baillot, *Méthode*, p. 135

38 Ibid., pp. 140–141.
39 Ibid.

Numerous writers considered attention to dynamic nuances to be of the greatest importance. As Quantz explained, "since the violoncello has the sharpest tone of all the basses, and can state its part the most distinctly, its player is in an advantageous position to help the other parts in the expression of light and shadow."[40] Baumgartner similarly asserted that as an accompanist, *piano, forte, crescendo, diminuendo*, etc. must be carefully observed.[41] Audiences were appreciative of accompanists who were sensitive to dynamic contrast. Lamare was especially well regarded for his finesse, accomplished through absolute control of the bow stroke. A contemporary reviewer remarked:

Lamare is therefore a greater accompanist than a solo player; he accompanied quartets (in which he really appeared to be accomplished) with expression and passion, having completely within his power the ability to produce from each and every note the necessary charm…each note is calculated from piano to fortissimo, and he always continues to take such care about his shading, a rare virtue that I have noticed in few artists."[42]

Dotzauer specified that dynamic markings were interpreted in the context of the musical genre, those in accompaniments being played with less volume than the same markings in solo music. In general, he recommended that dynamics notated in accompaniments be played one degree less than written, "so that one executes the <u>forte</u> as <u>mezzoforte</u>, this last as <u>piano</u> and the <u>piano</u> as <u>pianissimo</u>."[43]

ORNAMENTATION?

Ornamentation within violoncello accompaniments is an area in which it seems that practice varied occasionally from doctrine. The scarcity of instruction in ornamentation from early eighteenth-century players (see Chapter 7) leaves performance practice for the first half of the century open to question. Mid-century teachers dictated that ornamentation of the bass line was inappropriate, but then followed this observation with exceptions to their rubric. According to Quantz, players from the earlier part of the century had added ornaments to the bass line. He firmly stated that this was currently improper in orchestral playing, but went on to specify occasions in the accompaniment of solos in which the violoncellist might enhance the ornamentation presented by the melodic voice, particularly identifying continuo sonatas as a genre in which the bass line might judiciously copy the soloist's embellishments:

40 Quantz, *On Playing the Flute*, p. 244.
41 Baumgartner, *Instructions*, p. 30.
42 "Etwas über Lamare," 102.
43 Dotzauer, *Violonzell-Schule*, p. 56.

The violoncellist must take care not to garnish the bass with graces, as some great violoncellists were formerly in the habit of doing; he must not try to show his skill at an inappropriate time. If, without understanding composition, the violoncellist introduces extempore graces into the bass, in a ripieno part he will do even more harm than a violinist, especially if he has a bass part before him above which the principal part is constantly embellishing the plain air with other additions. It is impossible for one player always to divine the thoughts of the other, even if both have equal insight. Besides, it is absurd to make an upper part of the bass, which should support the embellishments of the other parts and make them harmonious; by robbing the bass of its serious movement, the necessary embellishments of the upper part are obstructed or obscured. It is undeniable that some melodic and concertante bass parts in solos [continuo sonatas] allow something in the way of additions, if the performer of the bass has sufficient insight, and knows where it may be done; it is likewise true that the piece becomes more perfect if on such occasions a few embellishments are added in a skilful manner. But if the violoncellist cannot rely sufficiently upon his knowledge, he is advised to play the bass as the composer has written it, rather than run the risk of ignorantly adding many absurd and discordant notes. Only in a solo is a skilful addition of embellishments permissible. Even there, whenever it is essential that the principal part add something to the plain notes, the notes of the bass must be executed entirely without extempore ornaments. If, however, the bass imitates some phrases of the principal part, the violoncellist may repeat the same graces used in the principal part. And if the principal part has rests or held notes, he may likewise vary the bass in an agreeable manner, provided that his principal notes are not obscured, and that the variations are so made that they express no other passion than that which the piece demands. Thus the violoncellist must seek constantly to imitate the execution of the player of the principal part, with respect both to loudness and softness of tone and to the expression of the notes. In a large ensemble, however, the violoncellist must abstain entirely from extempore additions, not only because the fundamental part must be played seriously and distinctly, but also because considerable confusion and obscurity would be caused if all the other bass players were to take similar liberties.[44]

Crome, writing thirteen years after Quantz, allowed one exception to the rule of no ornamentation of the accompaniment: "The Notes in Basses shou'd be always play'd plain, Tune, and Time are all that is requir'd; the only and principal Grace we should make use of is the Shake [trill], which borrows the sound from the Note above it."[45] Baumgartner gave the impression that he found even trills distasteful, forthrightly stating that "it is absolutely forbidden to play ornaments, runs, or anything else in the accompaniment: if you do so you will be taken for one who is ignorant."[46] Notwithstanding the inappropriateness of improvisation and ornamentation in the bass line, reviews of Lindley make clear that, at least in England,

44 Quantz, *On Playing the Flute*, pp. 242–243.
45 Crome, *Compleat Tutor*, p. 16.
46 Baumgartner, *Instructions*, p. 31.

ornamentation from the principal violoncellist was routine well past the period of which Quantz spoke. Apparently Lindley enjoyed playing to the crowd, becoming so enamored with his improvisation that he overstepped accepted boundaries of taste. One review describes Lindley's treatment of a Handel overture, the work preceding Marcello's Psalm VII:

The duet and chorus of Marcello which followed the overture *Otho* in the second act, is of a superior order to the pieces we have of late heard of that composer; but Mr. Lindley's flourishing Cadenza to the Symphony was, in every point of view, objectionable, not to say offensive; but it shows, alas! the all-prevailing power of vanity over men of the highest talent. It is quite impossible that Mr. Lindley's soberer judgement could have suggested a *cappricio* as a precursor to very sacred words; but the opportunity of challenging that applause which he well knew he should receive from a certain part of his audience was not to be resisted.[47]

Similar condemnation was made after a performance of Horsley's cantata *Alexis*, which included an obbligato violoncello accompaniment:

Alexis – which as generally performed, is an instrumental piece, accompanied by a tenor voice, – pleased every body, because what is intrinsically good, and full of melody, always gratifies an audience. But Lindley, in one of his eternal, though surprising, cadences, actually introduced "Over the hills and far away," and by this *mauvaise plaisanterie* excited the risible muscles of the company in no slight degree. There are times when we must either laugh or scold: it was well for the excellent violoncellist that the thing took a favourable turn.[48]

Such chastisement apparently had little effect upon England's beloved violoncellist. In accompanying "a very sweet quartet, of Marcello," performed in a concert directed by the Archbishop of York for the Duke of Cambridge, Lindley "was rather too *flighty* on his violoncello; and we wish this inimitable performer to consider, oftener than he does, the times and seasons when to flourish, and when not."[49]

RULES RELATED TO HARMONY

If the violoncellist understands composition, or at least something of harmony, he will find it easy to help the soloist to bring out and make apparent the different passions expressed in a piece by its composer.[50]

The Violoncellist should have some acquaintance with harmony, otherwise he cannot properly accompany a Quartett. The Bass may be considered the foundation of the construction of music. Distinctness and promptitude are not sufficient,

47 *The Harmonicon*, 2 (May 1824), 99–100.
48 Ibid., 3, no. 34 (October 1825), 178.
49 Ibid., 5, no. 4 (April 1827), 74.
50 Quantz, *On Playing the Flute*, p. 244.

as the expression contained in the Harmony is especially confided to the Bass. A knowledge of Harmony is therefore indispensable to the Violoncellist.[51]

The study of harmony was considered essential to the education of a violoncello accompanist and basic instruction detailing chords and pitch intervals was a common element to the tutors of Baumgartner, Kauer (Fig. 8.1), Baudiot, Romberg, Crouch, and Merrick. Students of the Conservatoire were additionally expected to learn such skills through specialized instruction, Charles Catel's *Traité d'Harmonie* (1802) being cited as the text for this purpose. Other recommended treatises were those on composition by Rameau and Rousseau; Baumgartner was especially adamant that well-trained players should move beyond the simple rules which he outlined.[52]

There were several reasons why such knowledge was considered important. Although Quantz and Romberg wrote at opposite ends of a hundred-year span, both were in absolute agreement that the violoncello accompanist could markedly improve the quality of a performance by knowing how to stress harmonically important notes, especially at cadences.[53] According to both writers, dissonances, in particular, required special attention. Such dissonances included the intervals of the second, diminished fifth, augmented sixth, and seventh. Notes marked with an accidental through the addition of a flat, natural, or sharp also fell into this category, as did leading tones and suspensions. Quantz amplified his explanation as follows:

The same rule applies when the upper part makes a cadence, and the bass, which ordinarily must leap up a fourth or down a fifth in order to move to an octave with the upper part, by a deception or so-called *inganno* moves up or down only a step, as, for example, when the upper part cadences to C, and the bass, instead of the octave below C, has the lower third, A or A flat, or the diminished fifth, F sharp, as the key requires (Fig. 55).

FIG. 55

Here it is very effective if the notes mentioned, A, A flat, and F sharp, are stressed by the violoncello, and expressed a little more forcefully than the preceding notes. If, however, a piece, especially an Adagio, moves to its final cadence, the violoncellist may treat the preceding two, three, or four notes in the same fashion, in order to direct the attention of the listeners to the cadence (Fig. 56).[54]

FIG. 56

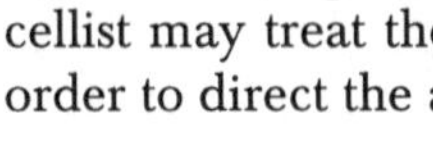

f   *p*

51 Romberg, *School*, pp. 132–133.
52 Baumgartner, *Instructions*, p. 23.
53 Quantz, *On Playing the Flute*, pp. 244–255; Romberg, *School*, p. 134.
54 Quantz, *On Playing the Flute*, p. 245.

Tabella Intervallorum.

	Secunda			tertia		quarta	
unisono	minor	major	superflua	minor	major	vera	falsa

quinta		sexta			septima		
vera	falsa	minor	major	superflua	minor	major	octav

Fig. 8.1 Table of intervals by Kauer

The necessary nuance, according to Romberg, was accomplished by an accent, "but the accent must not be too marked: It must be especially remembered that it is of consequence that this accent should be very slight."[55]

Quantz not only gave instructions for correct expression but also described improper treatment of harmonic elements. The vehemence of his opposition to any improvisation by an orchestral accompanist suggests that not all violoncellists adhered to playing bass lines as written:

All notes must be played in the register in which they are written; some must not be taken an octave higher at one time, an octave lower at another, especially those with which the other parts move in unison. Progressions of this kind constitute a formal bass melody that cannot and must not be varied in any way. Were such notes played on the violoncello an octave lower than they are written, the distance from the violins would be too great, and the notes would at the same time lose the sharpness and animation that the composer had in mind. Other bass notes which do not move in unison with the other parts may be played an octave lower now and then if no double bass is present;[56] but they must be harmonic rather than melodic passages, that is, passages that do not form a truly independent melody, but serve only as the foundation for the upper melodies. Leaps of a third, fourth, fifth, sixth, seventh, and octave upwards or downwards must not be inverted, since these leaps often serve to form a distinct melody, and are rarely written without a special purpose on the part of the composer (Fig. 53).

The same is true if a passage of a whole or a half bar is often repeated in such a way that the same notes are set each time an octave lower or higher (Fig. 54).

---

55 Romberg, *School*, p. 134.
56 Baumgartner, likewise, stated that in orchestral music, the violoncello may play harmonic notes down an octave if there is no contrabass. In chamber music, however, he affirmed that the notes must be played exactly as written. Baumgartner, *Instructions*, p. 31.

FIG. 54

A bass like this must be played as it is written. If the leaps are inverted, the effect will be entirely different.[57]

The rewriting of a bass line was not limited to violoncellists of Quantz's era. As discussed in Chapter 9 (p. 288), Lamare was taken to task by one reviewer for transposing some of the violoncello part of Mozart's third Prussian quartet (K590) up an octave because he was uncomfortable in the lower range of his instrument.[58]

The study of harmony was required of violoncellists for practical reasons additional to enhancing a performance by sensitive phrasing. Like keyboard players, they were expected to be skilled at understanding modulation and realizing a figured bass. For the latter, the player had to understand both how to read the intervals and how to adapt them to suit idiomatic fingerings upon the instrument. According to Baumgartner, who covered the issue in detail, this ability was fundamental to accompanying recitatives, but it could also be useful in orchestras: adding chords to the bass line of symphonies or other large-scale works was sometimes a nice effect.[59] This did not give interpretive license to the player, but merely allowed him to supplement the written part with other harmonically correct notes.

Evidence from printed music implies that chord filling was not limited to those who played recitatives or in large groups, but was also added to accompaniments of continuo sonatas, as a keyboard instrument was not always required or available for this type of composition. The accompaniment to Corelli's op. 5 sonatas, for instance, is designated "Violone o Cembalo."[60] Another example is the two collections entitled *Sonates à Deux Violonchelles* (1736) by the French violoncellist J. B. Masse. Both sets of Masse's sonatas additionally specify performance by other duos of like instruments – bassoons, viols, or violins – but keyboard accompaniment is not presented as an option. Nevertheless, the lower part contains figured bass numerals, presumably for realization by the second violoncellist.

In the 150 years which preceded the accompanied piano sonata genre, violoncellists routinely provided the accompaniment for a continuo so-

57 Quantz, *On Playing the Flute*, pp. 243–244.
58 "Etwas über Lamare," 103.
59 Baumgartner, *Instructions*, p. 25.
60 For evidence of improvised accompaniments and figured bass realization see David Watkin, "Corelli's Op. 5 Sonatas: 'Violino e Violone o Cimbalo'?" *Early Music*, 24, no. 4 (November 1996), 645–663.

nata. As his father had done for him on their family tours, so Boccherini likewise accompanied his subsequent touring partner, the violinist F. Manfredi. J. L. Duport made his debut at the Concert Spirituel in 1768, accompanied by his brother, J. P. Duport. He was also accompanied by Bréval at this venue in 1780 and provided the same service for James Cervetto at the Hanover Square series in 1783.[61] Well schooled in harmony and improvisational skills, player-composers such as Boccherini, Duport, and Bréval would not have refrained from filling out the bass line had they considered it musically advantageous; the presence of figured basses in published collections and the emphasis placed on harmonic training in tutors suggests that violoncellists were, in fact, encouraged to practice this skill.

Baumgartner, unfortunately, did not provide excerpts from specific works where such chords might be tastefully complementary, but rather gave general instruction as to how the violoncellist should adapt chords to suit harmonic movement. The most common addition was that of the third, which could be applied to all bass notes except in the chords $\frac{6}{4}$, $\frac{5}{4}$, and $\frac{6}{4}$. One only had to determine whether the third need be major or minor. More complex additions were expected to be accomplished within the rules which governed harmony. For instance:

If the Bass jumps a third higher, or a sixth lower, one gives the sixth (Fig. 3).

effet

As the same jumps by a fourth higher, or by a fifth lower, & as it makes the preparation for the cadence, one gives 5 & 6 (Fig. 4).

effet

If the bass makes a jump of a fourth higher, or of a fifth lower on the first or the third beat of the bar, this is a cadence, (Fig. 5)

effet

61 Pierre, *Histoire du Concert Spirituel*, pp. 293, 313; *The Public Advertiser*, February 24, 1783.
62 Baumgartner, *Instructions*, p. 26.

Baudiot's tutor replicated the system taught at the Conservatoire by Catel, and discussed harmony and figured bass as a requisite skill for performing the accompaniments to recitatives.[63] Romberg directed his study of the subject towards the improvement of chamber music skills, the understanding of modulation being fundamental to "that light and shade so necessary in Quartett-playing." Writing that "it requires great practice to accompany a Quartett with taste and accuracy," he provided an etude demonstrating the realization of figured bass (Ex. 8.3) "in order to furnish the Pupil with a sort of modulating study for this Art."[64]

Ex. 8.3 Romberg, *School*, p. 135

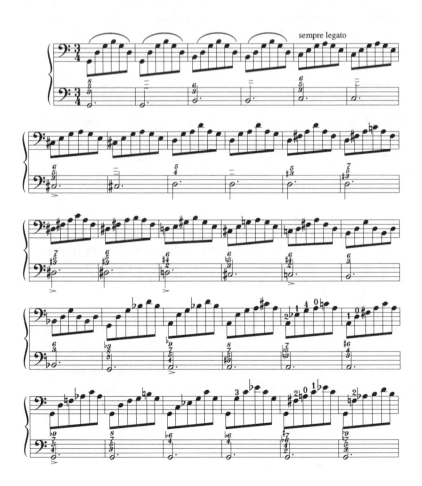

63 Baudiot, *Méthode*, vol. II, pp. 190–192.
64 Romberg, *School*, p. 134.

THE ACCOMPANIMENT OF RECITATIVE

One of the most secure forms of employment for an eighteenth- or nineteenth-century musician was to be a member of an opera orchestra. For the principal violoncellist and contrabassist, such employment required them not only to be competent tutti players, but also to execute recitatives. As was the case with Lindley and Dragonetti, proficiency in this form of accompaniment could engender considerable local prominence. Of the former, described as "second to none" as an accompanist, contemporary gossip related that "when there was a quarrel between the proprietors [of the opera] and the instrumentalists, so necessary was Lindley's accompaniment to the singers, that they absolutely refused to perform unless he was retained."[65] Lindley very possibly learned his craft from his teacher, James Cervetto, of whom it was stated "that for the Accompaniment of the Recitative, no Violoncello could be more perfectly excellent than Cervetto's."[66]

The nuances of this craft were undoubtedly passed on through the master/student relationship, but most of the violoncello methods from Corrette to Romberg also give some form of instruction. All who wrote on the subject were in agreement that a thorough knowledge of harmony was absolutely indispensable to the performer. As the professors of the Conservatoire explained:

To accompany a recitative well, one must have a perfect knowledge of harmony and the violoncello, be familiar with figured chords and able to execute them without difficulty. This art is the perfection of talent, because this presupposes the requisite knowledge, and moreover the experience necessary to its application.

If the accompanist is uncertain of how to resolve his dissonances, or accurately indicate to the singer whether he has to make a full cadence or an interrupted cadence, if he does not know how to avoid consecutive fifths and octaves in his chords he risks misleading the singer and cannot fail to produce a most disagreeable effect.[67]

Kauer provided little written instruction, but furnished a comprehensive table of "chords that one needs to know for the Accompaniment of Recitative [Ex. 8.4]."

65 "Rise and Progress of the Violoncello," 480.
66 *The Public Advertiser*, October 24, 1782.
67 Baillot, *Méthode*, p. 137. This excerpt was also quoted by Dotzauer and Merrick.

Ex. 8.4 Kauer, *Kurzgefasste Anweisung*, p. 12

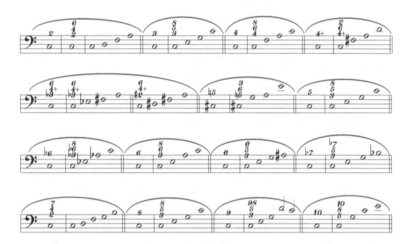

Various writers made specific points of clarification on the accompaniment
of recitative. Baudiot remarked that in discussing recitative, he was referring to the style of performance used in Italian opera. Ascribing his authority to the fact that he had accompanied all the recitatives performed at the
court of Napoleon, he nevertheless failed to mention how the performance
of Italian recitative differed from French practice.[68]

Baumgartner carefully differentiated between accompanied recitative
and ordinary recitative (later called *recitativo secco*). He was the only violoncellist to provide instruction for the execution of accompanied recitative,
writing:

> The *accompanied recitative* is the one to which, besides the continuo bass, one adds
> an accompaniment of violins and other instruments. This accompaniment is ordi-
> narily formed with long sustained notes over the whole bar, & for that reason one
> writes the word *sostenuto* on all the parts, but principally in the bass, who, without
> this, would articulate the strokes short & detached at each note change as in the
> *ordinary recitative...*
>
> It should be observed in the *accompanied recitative* that the sounds should be
> sustained according to the full value of the notes, & if you wish add a [figured bass]
> numeral with the note of the bass; but this is not necessary in this sort of *recitative*,
> because the chord is already complete & full with the other instruments; pay at-
> tention only to the words & to the first violin, so that you move together.[69]

Other sources indicate that instrumentation was sometimes dictated by
availability, the limited resources of some institutions no doubt influencing

---

68 Baudiot, *Méthode*, vol. II, p. 190.
69 Baumgartner, *Instructions*, p. 19.

performance practice. A review of a performance of Haydn's *The Seasons*, presented by Ritter on the occasion of the King of Sweden's 1803 visit, speaks to such necessity at Mannheim during the war years. The writer first made the comment that the only violoncellist in Mannheim capable of playing the recitative was Ritter, the other members of the section being amateurs drawn from the wider community. However, at least for this performance, Ritter did not play with the orchestra, but – probably trying to keep an insecure ensemble together – stood in front of the fortepiano beating time, even during the recitatives.[70] He was described as using the instrument to give the singers their pitch, with occasional chords. It was therefore left to the contrabass player to sound the bass note, the full chord normally articulated by the violoncellist being completely absent; in the reviewer's opinion the violoncello part should have been covered by a violinist or violist, the absence of the arpeggiated chord being unsuitable.[71] The reviewer was critical of both Ritter's keyboard skills and the quality of the instrument from which he was conducting: Ritter's fortepiano chords were apparently not audible to the audience. In the writer's opinion, Ritter, as Kapellmeister, ought to have been "a very skilled keyboard player (*Klavierspieler*)" able to execute the necessary *arpeggios*. This was apparently not the case. He concluded by noting that in the absence of other stringed instruments to substitute for the missing violoncello, "a good fortepiano" (presumably with a proficient player) was always preferable to completely leaving out the important intervals.[72]

The review of this performance also brings attention to the role which the keyboard could take in recitative. In the eighteenth century, the composer or other responsible party, such as the Kapellmeister, commonly directed large vocal productions from the keyboard. Handel conducted both operas and oratorios from the keyboard, until blindness made this an impossibility after 1752.[73] Haydn similarly conducted the opera at Esterháza and continued to direct Viennese productions of his works even after his retirement, one example being the benefit concert of *The Creation* given on January 16, 1801.[74] Cherubini toured various European capitals directing his operas from the keyboard. His appearance in London in 1785 was used for promotional purposes, advertisements for the opera *Demetrio* announcing the fact that he would direct from the harpsichord.[75] However, eighteenth-century accounts remark that the harpsichord's sound was not

---

70 Ritter normally directed operas from his position at the violoncello. *AMZ* (November 1803), col. 84.
71 *AMZ* (January 1804), cols. 221–222.
72 Ibid.
73 Christopher Hogwood, *Handel* (London: Thames and Hudson, 1984), pp. 224–225.
74 "The Diaries of Joseph Carl Rosenbaum 1770–1829," ed. Else Radent, *The Haydn Yearbook*, 5 (Bryn Mawr, Pennsylvania: Theodore Presser Co., 1968), p. 88.
75 *The Public Advertiser*, January 10, 1785.

sufficiently sustained to give singers their pitch in recitative, making the use of a bowed instrument necessary. Corrette was a vocal advocate for the violoncello at a time when the viola da gamba also served this function:

Those jealous of the violoncello will always lose their arguments against the progress it makes every day; to the rest it satisfies ears sensitive to the harmony, and voices too are charmed to be accompanied by it, realizing that nothing makes them shine like the accompaniment of this sonorous instrument which articulates its tones well, speaks cleanly and distinctly; so different from those instruments which are cymbal-like and nasal, of which it is necessary to ask each minute the name of the note which they have just played, the ear having heard only a confused noise which forbids hearing all the beauty of the harmony, of which the bass is the principal object.[76]

The inclusion of instructions for the execution of recitative in nineteenth-century violoncello methods suggests that such skills remained important well into the nineteenth century, the sound from keyboard instruments remaining too transparent to obviate the need for the violoncello. Audiences responded to the resonance of the contrabass and violoncello and Ritter's desertion of his instrument at the Mannheim performance truly distressed his reviewer, who exclaimed: "who doesn't know the wonderful effect in such recitatives with only figured bass, where the key note is struck on the *violon*, and the prescribed intervals in double-stops are added to it on the violoncello!"[77]

Nineteenth-century inclusion of the fortepiano in recitatives probably varied from place to place. Writing in the 1820s, Stiastny described the accompaniment of *recitativo secco* with the implication that, at least in Prague, the *clavier* was commonly included; the violoncellist had to strike his chords precisely and in tune with that instrument.[78] On the other hand, Baudiot made no reference to the inclusion of a keyboard instrument and neither do descriptions of Lindley's performances. What is clear is that at least through the 1840s, the contrabass and violoncello were the instruments that commonly executed the accompaniments to simple recitatives. Speaking of the violoncello in 1842, Freinach Blanchard wrote that "it is already over fifty years that this instrument has been valued as the reciting voice in the musical drama, that one plays in France, Italy, Germany, and so forth."[79]

Explicit instruction for the execution of simple recitative was provided by Baumgartner, Kauer, Raoul, the professors of the Conservatoire, Schetky, Baudiot, Crouch, Stiastny, and Merrick, with Dotzauer quoting

76 Corrette, *Méthode*, p. B.
77 *AMZ* (January 1804), cols. 221–222.
78 Stiastny, *Violoncell-Schule*, vol. II, p. 21.
79 Freinach H. Blanchard, "Die Violoncellisten," *Allgemeine Wiener Musik-Zeitung*, 2, no. 138 (November 17, 1842), 554.

abbreviated instructions from the tutor of the Conservatoire. To play the recitative in its most basic form, the note printed in the part was executed by the contrabass, with the violoncello outlining the harmonically correct chord as a brief *arpeggio*. The most precise example of how the contrabass and violoncello executed their individual parts comes from the method of B. Stiastny (Ex. 8.5). While the *arpeggios* in bars 1 and 6 are placed before the singer's entrance, the small notes are executed in the rests of the third beat.

Ex. 8.5 B. Stiastny, *Violoncell-Schule*, vol. II, p. 21

Placement of the violoncello *arpeggio* was addressed by Baumgartner and Schetky. Both indicated that short chords were struck immediately after the singer had enunciated their text, although this practice was not visibly perceptible in their musical examples. According to Baumgartner:

It is against the rules to sustain the sound in this type of recitative. It is necessary to wait until the note of the bass changes: while waiting, you will look for the note which follows, and you wait for the last word, then you will give the note of the bass with a dry stroke, and at the same time the principal harmony note of the melody part...[80]

---

80 Baumgartner, *Instructions*, p. 20; see also Schetky, *Practical and Progressive Lessons*, p. 38.

While the *arpeggio* was the violoncellist's most common mode of execution, the chords did not have to be arpeggiated in every instance. Two
notes of the chord could be played as a solid double-stop (Ex. 8.6).

Ex. 8.6 Baillot, *Méthode*, p. 138

Baumgartner's illustration of ordinary recitative demonstrates the integration of two-, three-, and four-string chords (Ex. 8.7).

Ex. 8.7 Baumgartner, *Instructions*, supplement p. 12 (the discrepancy between voice and bass line at
bar 6 is present in the original: there appears to be an 'extra' bar in both parts here)

Recitatif.

The order in which the notes of the chord were executed was necessarily determined by the position of the left hand on the fingerboard. Although adamant that the pitch of the key note could not be altered, Baumgartner stated that if the notes of the bass were set too high to easily facilitate an *arpeggio*, the figure could be taken down an octave.[81] Baudiot added that the chords were not necessarily struck in the position in which they were written, but that the third was frequently placed above the sixth, with no detrimental effects to the listeners.[82] In contrast with other authors, Stiastny was less dogmatic about beginning the *arpeggio* with the bass note. He refingered his chords with inversions when it suited the hand position, the presence of a keyboard instrument at the Prague theater perhaps making it unnecessary for him to reiterate the bass notes.

Preparation for the singer's note was of concern to Schetky and Kauer, who preferred to arrange their *arpeggios* so that the highest note was the singer's next pitch. However, the examples of other players often placed the singer's pitch in a lower position in accordance with the layout of the notes on the fingerboard. In Baumgartner's example (Ex. 8.7), the singer's ensuing pitch is not always duplicated within the violoncellist's chord, the assumption being that the singer was capable of finding the correct pitch from the bass note.

Although there was general agreement as to the fundamental rules governing the accompaniment of *recitativo secco*, there is no question that players varied in their approach. This appears to be due more to individual personalities than to the style of a particular time or place. A key issue was the subject of improvisation within the recitative. In print, improvisation was discouraged. According to the teachers at the Conservatoire, the duty of the accompanist was to support the singing, not to spoil and cover it, and to keep the accompaniment simple "without embellishments, without runs."[83]

In practice, violoncellists certainly added ornamental flourishes within the correct harmony at points where the singer's words stopped. Lindley, noted for his love of improvisation at any given opportunity, is known to have also embellished his recitatives.[84] Baudiot gave a valid explanation as to why improvisation was sometimes necessary to the continuity of the performance:

It happens sometimes that the actors stay on the stage, without speaking, either because of forgetting the words, or for some other reason, and sometimes they also take a long time to come on stage; when this is the case the accompanist may

---

81 Baumgartner, *Instructions*, p. 20.
82 Baudiot, *Méthode*, vol. II, p. 193.
83 Baillot, *Méthode*, pp. 137–138.
84 Nicholas Gatty, "Recitative," *Grove's Dictionary of Music and Musicians*, ed. Blom.

play short preludes and embellishments of his own fancy; but he should be re-strained in his ornaments and know their proper place; and play always with taste.[85]

Unfortunately, Baudiot gave no examples of his improvisatory skills as applied to the recitative. In his method, he included two preparatory exer-cises for the accompaniment of Italian recitative and an arpeggiated ex-tract from Mozart's *Don Giovanni.* Excerpts from the exercises are illustrated in Ex. 8.8. The performance guide to *Don Giovanni,* which ab-breviates the recitatives from the second and third scenes of act II, is shown in Ex. 8.9. The inaccuracies of the libretto are Baudiot's.

Ex. 8.8 Baudiot, *Méthode,* vol. II
(a) p. 193

EXERCICE PRÉPARATOIRE A L'ACCOMPAGNEMENT DU RÉCITATIF ITALIEN.

(b) p. 195

2d Exercice préparatoire.

85 Baudiot, *Méthode,* vol. II, p. 193.

(b) p. 195 (*cont.*)

Ex. 8.9: pp. 196–197

Récitatif extrait de l'opera de Don=Juan.

Ex. 8.9 pp. 196–197 (*cont.*) (* extra note in Baudiot's version)

9

Elements of aesthetics and style

What constitutes "good" music? This is a subject on which there is no shortage of eighteenth- and nineteenth-century opinion. The aristocracy had their viewpoint, as did the varied members of the professions and the merchant class, and musicians themselves expressed strongly held convictions. Intimately concerned with the issues of taste and style, the French Enlightenment saw a vast promulgation of aesthetic concepts, shared through edicts, pamphlets, journals, letters, and treatises.

For French violoncellists at least, conflicts of taste began early in the eighteenth century, when it was unclear whether the violoncello was even an acceptable instrument in polite society. Pitted against the viola da gamba, whose popularity among the French nobility kept that instrument fashionable throughout Europe for the better half of the eighteenth century, the violoncello became an unwitting pawn in the war of French taste against Italian. Although contentions diminished to an undercurrent towards the end of the century, distinctions in sound production remained a central issue between those who favored the French style against that of Italy, Austria, and Germany.

Quality of sound was but one facet of "good" music. Assessments included the suitability or merit of the composition, the manner in which musical phrases were shaped, and whether or not the "correct" character of a work was conveyed. Playing the violoncello idiomatically was also considered a requisite factor. In addition to conveying the aesthetic qualities of music, the performer, upon whom was placed the ultimate responsibility of creating "good" music, was continually challenged with changing perceptions as to what constituted "good" performance. This was especially recognizable in the aftermath of the French Revolution, as the shifting rules of engagement were wedded to the growing importance of the public concert hall as a venue for soloists. While audiences naturally varied in their evaluation of individual violoncellists, regional favorites almost always being preferred to their foreign counterparts, concert reviews increasingly contained appraisal of a player's "entertainment" value. A very small number of charismatic players became adept at amalgamating "good" music, "good" performance, and "good" entertainment, and, in achieving this expedient balance, devised the etiquette of performance which remains largely unchanged to the present.

THE PURPOSE OF "GOOD" MUSIC

Music as a moral influence was intrinsic to Reformation theology and re-mained a tenet long after the sixteenth century. Ingrained into the aesthetic doctrines of the eighteenth century, the difference between "serious" mu-sic – i.e. that which engendered cultivated respect – and "entertaining" or "popular" music was the ability of "serious" music to convey expressions which uplifted the moral character of the listener. When Romberg wrote that "the great object of music…is, not merely to serve as a pastime, but to cultivate the affections and to mould the human heart to a quick percep-tion of the Good and the Beautiful," he was reiterating the thoughts of such writers as Johann Mattheson (*Der vollkommene Capellmeister*) and J. G. Sulzer (*Allgemeine Theorie der schönen Künste*).[1]

While German theoreticians were especially vociferous on the subject, this perception of music's purpose was echoed among many other writers. The professors of the Conservatoire believed that violoncello performance could be particularly effective in the transmission of elevated "passions." Merrick's nineteenth-century English translation of the Conservatoire method effectively conveys the essence of both French and English thought, stating that "when the Violoncello performs a solo, its tone be-comes touching and sublime, not such as paints and excites the passions, but moderates them, by raising the mind into a higher region."[2]

Conventional wisdom prescribed that music's higher purpose was car-ried out through performing a composition of suitable character. The sub-stance of this character was, of course, subject to controversy, especially when virtuoso display became a means of success. The heat of this discus-sion becomes apparent through the writings of the professors of the Paris Conservatoire and Romberg, all of whom were well acquainted on a per-sonal basis. Of particular importance was the question of what musical genres were appropriate to the violoncello's size and intrinsic nature.

Conservatoire opinion, most probably reflecting the heavy hand of Baillot and possibly Levasseur, imposed strict limitations.[3] These state-

---

1 Romberg, *School*, p. 131.
2 A. Merrick, *Method for the Violoncello by Baillot, Levasseur, Catel & Baudiot, Adopted by the Paris Conservatory of Music* (second edition, London: R. Cocks & Co., [before 1855]), p. 10.
3 Baillot apparently maintained good relationships with his violoncellists, Lamare, Baudiot, and Norblin, but it must be noted that these gentlemen were musically subservient to the violinist.

ments contain a degree of underlying resentment towards virtuoso display, implying condemnation of the technical advances that Romberg introduced to Parisians just at the time this tutor was being written. The constraints are at variance with the earlier strides in technical proficiency made by the violoncello school of Berteau, but years of political turmoil had inflicted career reversals and other misfortunes upon French violoncellists. One indication of this fact is the limited number of violoncello concertos of French authorship performed and published during the nineteenth century: the works of Romberg, in fact, were used with greater frequency than those of French-trained composers, as can be seen from the listing of the *Morceaux de Concours* for the Conservatoire from 1818 to 1900 (Fig. 9.1)[4]

According to the professors of the Conservatoire, "the violoncello possesses by the nature of its tone, the length of its strings and the range of its diapason, a grave, sensitive and spiritual character"[5] which did not allow it to accomplish the virtuoso effects available to the violin. It was not that these effects were not possible on the larger instrument; rather, Conservatoire opinion considered virtuoso display, like copious ornamentation (see Chapter 7, p. 215), to be debasing to the violoncello:

If one wants to make a virtue of difficulty, it [the violoncello] lends itself to all the advantages of modulation, double-stops, arpeggios and harmonics. But there are limits which may not be exceeded; the gravity of its progress does not permit it all the intemperate movements taken on the violin, which is more flexible, more delicate and more varied. Mixing the different genres is a snare which should be avoided in the arts; before limits have been more or less established and a style of composition has been more or less set, every man of talent adds to the discovery; has one found [even] the qualities which are acceptable to taste and reason, let alone perfection, which is unknown to us? The desire to innovate will sometimes intrude to spoil everything, making useless additions, encroaching on the domain of others, tormenting art for the sake of art, causing its degeneration while trying to improve it...

One could not arm the students too much against this danger, to which their pursuit of a great facility of execution and the desire to distinguish themselves with some novelty [may lead]. The violoncello is, one might say, a new instrument, as it has very little solo music.[6]

Such professed limitations were reiterated by later French writers, who paraphrased Conservatoire dogma. Writing of the violoncello for the 1818 edition of *Encyclopédie Methodique Musique,* J. J. de Momigny quoted the

Baillot's son-in-law, Eugène Sauzay, remarked that Baillot disliked performance material, such as the late quartets of Beethoven, in which the instrumental voices were equal, rather than dominated by the first violin. See François-Sappey, "Mémoires d'Eugéne Sauzay," 195.

4 Pierre, *Conservatoire,* p. 615.
5 Baillot, *Méthode,* p. 1.
6 Ibid., pp. 1–2.

MORCEAUX DE CONCOURS.

1818.	1er concerto	Romberg.
	1er concerto	Platel.
1824.	2e concerto	Baudiot.
1832.	Concerto	Romberg.
1833.	Concerto	Romberg.
1835.	Concerto	Romberg.
1836.	1er concertino	Baudiot.
1837.	2e concerto	Romberg.
1838.	4e concerto (frag.)	Romberg.
1839.	8e concerto	Romberg.
1840.	Cantilena	Romberg.
1841.	Concertino	Meinhard.
1842.	2e concerto, *la* mineur	Baudiot.
1843.	2e concerto	Romberg.
1844.	Solo	Franchomme.
1845.	4e concerto	Romberg.
1846.	9e concerto	Romberg.
1847.	Concerto	Delamarre.
1848.	5e concerto	Romberg.
1849.	2e cto *la* min. (1er morc.)	Baudiot.
1850.	2e conc. *ré* maj. (allo)	Romberg.
1851.	4e concerto, *mi* mineur	Romberg.
1852.	9e concerto	Romberg.
1853.	Concerto (fragment)	Franchomme.
1854.	Concerto	Romberg.
1855.	9e concerto	Romberg.
1856.	8e concerto (fragment)	Romberg.
1857.	1er cto (1er solo.)(op.33)	Franchomme.
1858.	9e concerto (1er morc.)	Romberg.
1859.	8e concerto (1er morc.)	Romberg.
1860.	15e concerto (1er morc.)	Romberg.
1861.	Concerto (1re pie) *la* min.	Lamare.
1862.	2e conc. (2e pie) *ré* min.	Romberg.
1863.	4e concerto (1er morc.)	Romberg.
1864.	9e concerto	Romberg.
1865.	8e concerto (1er morc.)	Platel.
1866.	Concerto	Lamare.
1867.	5e concerto	Romberg.
1868.	2e concerto (1er morc.)	Romberg.
1869.	1er concerto	Platel.
1870.	Divertissement *la* min.	Sziastny.
1872.	9e concerto	Romberg.
1873.	8e concerto	Romberg.
1874.	1re concerto *mi* min	Platel.
1875.	6e concerto	Romberg.
1876.	Concertino *mi* mineur	Striastny.
1877.	1er concertino	Baudiot.
1878.	8e concerto	Romberg.
1879.	9e concerto *si* mineur	Romberg.
1880.	Morc. de conc. (op. 14)	Servais.
1881.	4e concerto	Romberg.
1882.	3e concerto *si* mineur	Goltermann.
1883.	Concerto *ut* mineur	Franchomme.
1884.	8e concerto	Romberg.
1885.	Morc. de conc. (op. 14)	Servais.
1886.	5e concerto	Romberg.
1887.	Concerto *si* mineur	Servais.
1888.	9e concerto	Romberg.
1889.	Concerto *ut* mineur	Franchomme.
1890.	8e concerto	Romberg.
1891.	2e concerto	Goltermann.
1892.	4e concerto	Romberg.
1893.	Morc. de conc. (op. 14)	Servais.
1894.	5e concerto *fa* # mineur	Romberg.
1895.	1er concerto	Davidoff.
1896.	9e concerto *si* mineur	Romberg.
1897.	Concerto *ut* mineur	Franchomme.
1898.	1er concerto	Popper.
1899.	2e concerto *ré* mineur	Goltermann.
1900.	Concerto	Romberg.

Fig. 9.1 *Morceaux de Concours*, 1818–1900

professors' statement that the violoncello was not an old instrument and that it was, "by its nature, noble, majestic, and sensitive." However, while the instrument "takes without doubt different characters according to the skill and the kind of talent of those who play it," it was not allowed to become playful or trivial: "One should not want to play the violin on the 'bass,' nor play the 'bass' on the violin," he wrote, for "it has limits which one rarely passes with enough pleasure to make its audacity or its impudence forgivable."[7]

Romberg agreed with his French colleagues as to the dearth of suitable violoncello music, but his point of view was colored by his ability to vanquish any technical challenge. Seeking to eradicate restrictions on violoncello performance, he was a vocal advocate of "modern" music, this notwithstanding the fact that he used works in the "old" style when teaching Dotzauer. Dissatisfied with the bowing style, sound production, technical requirements, and melodic and harmonic contrasts of his predecessors (in other words, everything about eighteenth-century violoncello writing), he believed that older music did not possess the necessary "character" to convey elevated sentiments to the audience:

In the composition of the old Concerto, so little attention was paid to Harmony and so little ingenuity displayed in construction, that it could not be said to possess any fixed character. In the present improved state of the Art, it cannot be expected that such a composition can any longer please. The modern epoch of Concerto-Music dates from Mozart's Concertos. The compositions of Sebastian Bach and other great Musicians who lived before the time of Mozart, have had little influence on the modern Style of Concerto writing.

There is, unfortunately, not a sufficient number of compositions for the Violoncello, of such intrinsic worth, and solid merit as to reward the young Artist for his trouble in practising them, or by the study of which he may succeed in acquiring a good style and a fine execution. Some, however, of the old compositions possess much merit, but are not sufficiently imaginative to suit a modern taste (my own Compositions in this kind I leave to the judgment of the present and future generation.)[8]

Romberg ranked genres of compositions into a precise order, based on "seriousness" of character and complexity of construction. Heading the list was the concerto, his preferred form emulating the French violin concertos of Viotti and his disciples. For Romberg, virtuoso display was the chief merit of this species:

The great object in view, in the invention of this species of composition, was to give the Artist an opportunity of displaying his talent both in quick and in slow

---

7 *Encyclopédie Méthodique Musique*, compiled by Nicolas Etienne Framéry, Pierre Louis Ginguené, and Jérôme Joseph de Momigny, 2 vols. (New York: Da Capo Press, 1971), vol. II, p. 553.
8 Romberg, *School*, p. 130.

movements. The solos in a concerto therefore consist partly of sustained melodies, and partly of quick phrases, and difficult of execution. These latter give rise to those divisions in music termed *passages*.[9]

According to Romberg, harmony, rather than the nature of the violoncello, determined the spirit of a performance. "When a Concerto is written in a major-key," he remarked, "it should be executed with brilliancy and animation: when composed in a minor-key, an expression of melancholy should prevail throughout."[10]

Romberg's ability to duplicate the fast passage work of violin concertos on his instrument was not appreciated by the professors of the Conservatoire. They considered that the violoncello was best suited to performing slow movements and, unlike the violin, should not attempt to play music marked at a *presto* tempo with force and audacity. If playing an *allegro*, the professors argued, the player should "take a tempo more suited to its timbre"; moreover, "actually if [the instrument] is allowed rapid movements or solo passages, it should only be done with reserve, with dignity, and always with gentleness; these are the attributes of its majesty."[11]

Baillot and his compatriots ended their discussion by remarking that, while students should study the few concertos composed for the instrument, the study of chamber music by Haydn and Boccherini yielded greater rewards. Boccherini's quintets, favored by Baillot, were cited as the premier genre. The quintets required the violoncello to play accompaniment as well as melody, thus demonstrating the instrument's true character as perceived at the Conservatoire.

Romberg completed his list of respectable genres by citing species used by soloists, namely concertinos, fantasias, variations, and music of a playful style, such as airs and caprices. He also explained that chamber music was categorized differently from that played by the public soloist. Solos written in a chamber-music style "are not of the same length, and require less accompaniment than Concertos," he instructed, "these are generally played in Soirées and private music parties."[12] Unlike eighteenth-century performers, Romberg considered that continuo sonatas and duets were inappropriate for public performance and that chamber music should consist of works for three to nine players.[13]

According to Dotzauer, character could also be inferred from the tessitura used by the composer. Like the Conservatoire writers, Dotzauer prefaced his remarks by stating that violoncellists could not accomplish all of the virtuoso feats performed on the violin, owing to the violoncello's

9 Ibid.
10 Ibid.
11 Baillot, *Méthode*, p. 3.
12 Romberg, *School*, p. 131.
13 Ibid.

strings being thicker and placed further apart. However, contradicting Conservatoire opinion, Dotzauer came to the positive conclusion that such limitations did not prevent players from executing a multiplicity of techniques and expressions:

The special range of the violoncello allows for a great variety of characters. Grave and thoughtful phrases, which the composer gives to the lower strings, are effective when performed with power.

The sounds from the A and D string have much that is pleasing and in that tenor range the sensitive player is able to speak from the heart. The upper and highest sounds of the soprano appear to exact a more lively mood and gaiety. In addition arpeggios, double-stops, harmonics, and ponticello offer a great wealth of nuances to the violoncellist, when he uses his instrument for solos.[14]

Concerned in his later years by what he regarded as frivolous virtuosity, Romberg mentioned two customs which did not meet with his concept of the higher order of music. The first addressed the practice, common during this era, of performers writing a composition by joint effort. (Presumably Romberg's criticism did not extend to the works he composed with his cousin, Andreas.) Discussing the technique as it affected chamber music, Romberg wrote:

It is by no means an easy matter to write classical and pleasing Chamber-Music. This difficulty has given rise to a custom replete with evil, and one which cannot be too strongly reprobated. Two Professors meet, and, each furnishing his part for his respective Instrument, will thus produce a work by their joint efforts. These insignificant compositions must necessarily be deficient in that unity of feeling and purpose which is so indispensable to the just expression of art, and consequently they can never affect the feelings of the hearers.[15]

The second was the use of the instrument by "popular" musicians to amuse audiences with musical "tricks": in playful music "there are bounds which should never be transgressed, even where the nature of the Instrument will admit it."[16] He used as an example the well-known violinist Jakob Scheller (1759–1803), whom Spohr also held in abhorrence:

Among other things, an attempt has been made to introduce, on the Violin, an imitation of the sounds of various animals. An old Violinist of some fame named Scheller, was one of those who employed this trick to gratify his auditors. This might be done with the same ease on the Violoncello, but it would indeed be shameful to prostitute so fine an Instrument to so base a purpose.[17]

14 Dotzauer, *Violonzell-Schule*, p. 1.
15 Romberg, *School*, pp. 131–132.
16 Ibid.
17 Ibid., pp. 131–132. Louis Spohr's condemnation of this style of playing was yet stronger. Spohr, who compared Paganini's style of virtuosity with that of Scheller, wrote, "But that by which he [Paganini] captivates the Italian public and which has acquired for him the name of the 'Inimitable,' which is even placed under his portraits, consists, on a nearer enquiry, in a succession of feats

HOW TO ACHIEVE "GOOD" MUSIC

Once suitable species of compositions were determined, correct execution became the issue, questions of style rising above the basics of fingering and bowing technique. Kummer summarized the pre-eminent rule for instrumentalists of the period when he wrote that violoncellists "preferably should mold themselves after a good singer."[18] This stricture dominates instructions for correct sound and phrasing among writers of all nationalities during both centuries. Leopold Mozart expressed the sentiment when he asked "and who is not aware that singing is at all times the aim of every instrumentalist[?]"[19] The professors of the Conservatoire considered that "the principal merit of the violoncello is in its quality of sound, in its timbre which greatly resembles the human voice."[20] Dotzauer followed suit: instead of striving always to play difficult passages, one's priority should be to play with a beautiful sound and to sing on the instrument, "since approaching the most noble of all instruments, the human voice, must remain the example and ideal of every musician."[21]

The importance of the vocal medium for these musicians cannot be overemphasized. Even with the increasing popularity and recognized value of instrumental music as conceived by the Romantic movement, vocal music, and particularly opera, remained the favored genre of most audiences. The influence upon instrumental writing was noted by Romberg, who considered himself an opera composer who wrote instrumental music only from the necessity of providing works for his own performance. In recommending himself to Friedrich Wilhelm III for the position of Kapellmeister at the Berlin Court in 1815, Romberg remarked that it was by composing for the theater that he had come to perfect his instrumental music.[22]

How to achieve this goal in practical terms had already been described by Quantz, oratorical declamation being the expedient comparison:

which, in the dark times of good taste, the one so famous *Scheller* performed in the small towns and some capitals of Germany, and which at that time equally excited the admiration of our countrymen, viz., in the flageolet tones; in variations upon one string, in which for the purpose of imposing more upon the audience, he takes off the other three strings of the violin; in a peculiar kind of *pizzicato*, produced with the left hand without the help of the right or of the bow; and in many tones quite unnatural to the violin, such as the bassoon tone, the voice of an old woman, etc. etc. – As I never heard the wonderful *Scheller*, whose saying was; '*One God! One Scheller!*' I should much like to hear *Paganini* play in his peculiar manner, and the more so, because I presume that so admired an artist must possess some more real merits than those adverted to." *Spohr's Autobiography*, vol. I, p. 280.

18 Kummer, *Violoncell-Schule*, p. 45.
19 *Mozart's Treatise on Violin Playing*, pp. 101–102.
20 Baillot, *Méthode*, p. 133.
21 Dotzauer, *Violonzell-Schule*, p. 56.
22 Letter of Romberg to Friedrich Wilhelm III, December 30, 1815 in Schäfer, *Romberg*, appendix.

Musical execution may be compared with the delivery of an orator. The orator and the musician have, at the bottom, the same aim in regard to both the preparation and the final execution of their productions, namely to make themselves masters of the hearts of their listeners, to arouse or still their passions, and to transport them now to this sentiment, now to that.[23]

Romberg, nearly eighty years later, made the same comparison but in more specific terms, giving a lengthy illustration of his manner of phrasing. He first identified melodically important notes which he termed suspensions (*Vorhalte*). Describing how these pitches are "held out," Romberg noted that this term should not be confused with harmonic suspension. According to his directions:

Music may be considered in the light of declamatory language. The spirit and signification of a speech depends, on the importance of the information it conveys, on the variety of tone used in the pronunciation of the words it contains, on the rising and falling inflexions, and on the strength or weakness of the voice. If a speech be pronounced monotonously, it must utterly fail in its desired effect, and can produce no other feelings in the hearers but those of languor and ennui. It is precisely the same case with Music, whenever it is played without a due admixture of light and shade, and a proper regard to feeling and expression. There is also a close analogy between the Rythm [*sic*] of Music, and the Rythm of Verse, for in the former, the long and short syllables are regulated in the same manner as in the latter; for instance, the words "*I love thee*" would be executed in Music thus:

Here the D is a suspension to C. If an appoggiatura were introduced, both the Rythm and expression would be entirely altered; and it would then be expressed thus: The Appoggiatura, which is marked with a small note, would require no more accent than the note which it precedes; on the contrary, the suspension whenever it falls upon a large note, when marked either *Forte*, or *Piano*, (of course in proportion) requires a slight accent. This adaptation of the strength of emphasis in proportion to the pitch of the voice must also be carefully attended to in discourse. When however the Composer wishes to produce a peculiar effect, his intention must be expressly notified. Suspensions, which occupy a prominent position in Melody, are of various kinds: some commence from above, others from below, Sometimes they consist of long, sometimes of short notes. To those who have not studied Thorough Bass, the following remarks may serve as a more certain guide, and as a rule to be applied in execution. The suspension together with the following note, is not always accompanied by a rest, but the melody is frequently continued. Sometimes several suspensions will occur in succession, thus:

23 Quantz, *On Playing the Flute*, p. 119.

In such cases, the accent must be marked with great precision. In passages like the following, the proper accent is easily perceived. In passages such as or the accent should be scarcely audible; it will not fail to be properly expressed if the semiquaver be played very short. The quicker the time of the movement, the less time should be given to the last note of the suspension, in order that the music may not produce a heavy, protracted effect. At the end of a phrase, the finishing note of the suspension may be made so short as to be scarcely audible. Care should be taken to distinguish between the cadence itself, and the concluding note of a suspension.[24]

The idea of notes emulating words is reiterated by Romberg in his instructions for determining the precise character of a work. "When some story or poem is the subject of the composition," he wrote, "the player should make it his business to acquaint himself perfectly with the spirit and feeling of the subject on which the composition is founded, in order that the notes should have almost the effect of words."[25]

Romberg then described the manner in which he phrased the opening bars of music of varying characters and tempos. Characteristic of his approach is the emphasis on a broad style of playing, and his remarks on the character of notation are also of special interest:

The *Auftackt*, or Preparatory-Bar, requires particular attention in its execution. In the Adagio, and in all slow movements, the Preparatory Bar, when it consists of only one note, should be played with even more time than strictly belongs to it, in order that it may be more perfectly blended, as it were, with the full Bar. In the Allegro, on the other hand, it should be played shorter than it is noted, to give more force to the notes of the full Bar (it must be here understood, that this is the case when the Preparatory Bar introduces a fresh movement or a new phrase of the movement): Even in playing the first note of the full Bar, it will make some difference whether the time be Allegro or Adagio. The first note of a full Bar in an Allegro movement marked *Forte*, requires the strongest possible force; whereas in the Adagio it is not necessary to mark it so strongly, in order to give more scope for an increase or diminution of power as the movement proceeds. The Adagio will thus acquire softness and fluency, and the Allegro, power and spirit. In the same manner, the first note of a full Bar in the Allegro, when marked *Piano*, is always played soft; in the Adagio, on the other hand, the same note is always executed with a slight emphasis. As a general rule, the player should endeavour to give more attention to expression in the Adagio, and other slow movements, than

24 Romberg, *School*, pp. 127–128.
25 Ibid., p. 131.

in any of those pieces marked to be executed in a quick time; for if any one were to attempt to introduce the same variety of light and shade in the Allegro movement of a Concerto, as in an Adagio, he would find it entirely destructive of a fine broad style of playing. In fine, it must all depend upon whether the music be noted in long or short notes. When written in short notes, the expression is never so marked, as when written in long notes, both in quick and in slow movements.[26]

The expressive performance of slow movements was a quality emphasized not only by the duration of these movements in Austro-German compositions, but also by German reviews of performers. For instance, one of the first writers to describe Romberg's style of playing was Karl Ludwig Junker, who, hearing Romberg in a private performance given by the Bonn Kapelle at Mergentheim, wrote:

the connoisseur has yet another standard by which he measures the greatness of artists, namely the manner of playing, the perfection of expression or the spiritual interpretation. Once on this point, the connoisseur will pronounce in favour of the expressive "Adagio". It is impossible more deeply to penetrate into the more delicate hues of feeling – impossible to colour them with more variety – to enhance them, moreover by greater light and shade – impossible to hit more exactly the very tones through which this feeling has utterance, tones which appeal more directly to the heart, than Romberg succeeds in doing in his "Adagio."[27]

Performers from other regions, while all agreeing that an expressive slow movement was a commendable quality, differed in their assessment as to how such expression was best attained. Austro-Germans emphasized variation of dynamic levels (light and shade); English audiences favored simplicity to the exclusion of excessive ornamentation;[28] while many French writers stressed elegance and taste, achieved through a controlled bowing style. As one French reviewer stated in an excoriation of Max Bohrer, "French players like to be ornamental, witty, declamatory, accentuating: yet they never deteriorate into weak, soft, passive emotionalism."[29] This critic considered Bohrer's "German" playing to be overly sweet (*süsslich*) and trifling (*tändelnd*), lacking in strength and nobility. He remarked that other German virtuosos also indulged in this sweet and effeminate (*verweichlicht*) style; while at first hearing these players would cause a sensation, audiences would soon become indifferent. This, according to the writer, was the case with Bohrer. While he had thrilled audiences at his initial concerts, given eighteen months earlier, his playing was now judged to be monotonous, cold, and disappointing. French connoisseurs had the

---

26 Ibid., p. 128.
27 Written for *Musikalische Korrespondenz der Teutschen Filarmonischen Gesellschaft*, quoted in *Beethoven: Impressions of Contemporaries*, p. 12.
28 McVeigh, *Concert Life in London*, p. 145.
29 *AMZ* (May 1818), cols. 345–346.

tendency to judge harshly instrumentalists who did not meet their concept of elegance. Lindley, for instance, failed to impress Fétis, who opined that "when he *sings* upon his instrument, he produces a fine tone, and possesses much tact in the management of difficulties; but his style is vulgar."[30]

The natural inflections inherent in the shape of a musical line were an avenue of discussion on which there was greater consent. The tutors of the Conservatoire and Romberg discuss this aspect of phrase shaping in similar terms. The French teachers considered that dynamic change contributed to the direction of a musical phrase: when a phrase rose in pitch, the volume of sound should increase, and decrease when it fell. Notes of a similar pitch level could be executed *forte* or *piano* (Ex. 9.1).

Ex. 9.1 Baillot, *Méthode*, p. 135

Romberg explained the same concept in greater detail, including exceptions to the basic rule caused by varying harmonic structures, the phrasing of works in minor keys being the more complex. In this regard, he also noted that intonation could be judiciously shaded for additional emphasis:

The swelling and diminution of the tone is invariably regulated by the rising or falling of the scale. The ascending scale is more prominently marked than the descending. But if, in the descending scale, a note should occur at the end which does not belong to the key in which the music is there written, this note will require a stronger accent, and there are very few cases in which it will not be made a prominent feature of the passage. The following figure will perhaps more clearly illustrate the accent with which this melody should be

played:

Here it may be perceived, that the expression of passion increases in proportion as the notes rise in the scale, and that the accent becomes less strong as the scale descends. The last note but one is a suspension [a melodically important note], and therefore requires a stronger accent than the note which precedes it, although the latter stands higher in the scale. Every phrase of a melody may be illustrated in the same manner as the above, and when the principle I have just explained is well understood, the player will seldom fail in giving every passage its just expression. There is but one exception to the rule here laid down, which is in pieces

---

30 "M. Fétis on the State of Music in London," *The Harmonicon*, 7, no. 9 (September 1829), 219.

written in counterpoint, where a Theme is introduced for several parts, and where the melody of the Theme must be made rather more prominent. This will seldom happen in Solo-pieces, though some few expressions to that effect are sometimes found. Very rapid passages however, do not require the same marks for expression, since in these cases it is only requisite to make a few notes here and there, prominent, in order to deprive the passage of its otherwise monotonous effect.

The following passage will serve as an example of the ease in which a single note is introduced, which does not belong to the key, and which although in the descending scale must be played with a marked accent.

This B flat, A: must however be considered a suspension. The Orator, when delivering a speech, lowers his voice in those parts where he wishes to make a serious impression upon his auditors, and raises it when endeavouring to excite their spirits. The minor keys, in a descending motion, are used in music in the same manner, whenever deep feeling is intended to be expressed. The cause of this is, that in the major keys, the notes, both of the ascending and descending scales, remain unaltered, whilst in the ascending scale of the minor keys, one, and sometimes two notes must be raised, in order to get a leading-note to the octave, without which, the scale cannot be concluded. Whenever this occurs as the last note, whether in the ascending or descending scale, it must, for the sake of expression, be played with rather more accent than the other notes. Also, if in a minor key, a note should occur, which is not marked in the signature (i.e. an accidental sharp or flat) it will require a particular accent. The melancholy expression, which is peculiar to minor keys, is found in these accents. Hence, in order to elevate the character of this mode, the major seventh (the leading note) is made rather sharper, and the minor seventh somewhat flatter than in the major scale. We must take care however, not to carry this rule to extremes, or it will produce a most disagreeable effect. I must here again repeat that it is impossible for me to lay down rules for all the cases in which a note may require a particular accent. A few cases illustrative of the above remarks are here subjoined.

In No. 1. C♯ is the leading-note, although the lowest in the scale; it must therefore have the strongest accent.

In No. 2. E♭ is the expressive note, and requires to be played with emphasis.

No. 3. is a common passage, and subject to the same rules as the major key.

In No. 4. the accent must fall upon the C sharp, although it occurs in a descending scale, because it is an accidental, and does not properly belong to the key.

No. 5. the C♯ must not be considered as an appoggiatura, and must therefore have a stronger accent than the following note.

The remarks upon suspensions in major scales are equally applicable to minor scales.[31]

It is difficult to assess to what degree other players applied these rules to their own compositions. As shown by Dotzauer's ascending *decrescendos* in Ex. 9.2, contradictory examples may be found. However, the Conservatoire's and Romberg's instructions form a useful guide to the general concepts held by contemporaries for the correct phrasing of melodic figures.

Ex. 9.2 Dotzauer, Concerto op. 27, *Andantino*, bars 27–30

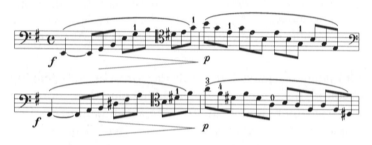

"GOOD" SOUND

More contentious statements exist on the issue of sound production than on any other aspect of violoncello playing, for "good" sound was the foundation of all pleasing performance. From a comparison of the numerous testaments and reports, it is clear that most violoncellists indeed sounded very different from each other. This is not surprising when it is taken into account that players were using instruments and bows of greatly varying construction. Differences in pitch standard were also a factor to some degree, as were right and left hand techniques and the general regard for individuality of expression. There is also no question that there were regional preferences, with most players striving to conform to the expectations of their local audiences.

Conflicting preferences are first encountered at about the time Corrette's method was published, the question being whether or not the violoncello even had a "good" sound. Corrette was positive in his assessment, but for devotees of the viola da gamba the answer was clearly negative. The Frenchman Hubert Le Blanc was the most vociferous denigrator of the violoncello, but preference for the sound of the viola da gamba was not limited to France. Leopold Mozart also held that the violoncello was an inferior instrument. He remarked that the viola da gamba "has a more

31 Romberg, *School,* pp. 128–130.

pleasant tone, and serves mostly for playing an upper part," the violoncello being relegated to the bass line.[32] Although he is renowned for his love of the violoncello, Friedrich Wilhelm II of Prussia also cultivated the viola da gamba, having studied with Hesse until the teacher's death in 1770.[33] One of the century's most respected gambists was Dresden-born Carl Friedrich Abel, who emigrated to London and performed in England until 1787, the year of his death.[34] His talents were so valued that he spent the summer months with a French patron, according to one London daily:

Abel also is gone to Paris, according to his annual Custom, for a Couple of Months. His Patron there is one of the *Fermieres Generales*, who is passionately fond of the Viol di Gamba, and who allows Abel for his two Months Performance on it *Two Hundred Guineas* a Month, a Gratification equal to that which Abel receives from our *Queen*![35]

The violoncello ultimately superseded the viola da gamba because, having greater volume of sound, flexibility of pitch, and matching the sonority of the violin, it was an instrument better suited to the accompaniment of recitative and participation in the "Classical" orchestra (see Chapter 8, pp. 242–243). However, many auditors retained the preference for the lighter, unforced sound of the viola da gamba. Indeed, French regard for this instrument extended into the nineteenth century, as witnessed by Raoul's attempt to repopularize the viola da gamba even after he had published his violoncello method.[36]

Sonority and volume of sound were issues addressed by violoncellists in varying manners. French performers placed much emphasis on the resonance yielded by natural overtones, with precision of tuning and intonation the key to success. Interest in overtones was manifested in the eighteenth century through the use of natural harmonics, Tricklir's *nouveaux* concertos exemplifying such fascination. J. L. Duport drew further attention to the inherent benefits that overtones could add to the violoncello's quality of sound. His recommendations extended first to tuning. Adamant that the instrument had to be precisely pitched so that octaves and unisons were exact (Ex. 9.3), he nevertheless counseled against continually moving the pegs. He remarked that the violoncello could never settle into exact pitch if the string balance was chronically altered, the requisite tension against the bridge being disturbed when the pegs were turned; small discrepancies in the pitch of open strings should be compen-

32 *Mozart's Treatise on Violin Playing*, pp. 11–12.
33 Eitner, *Quellen–Lexikon*, vol. IV, pp. 354–355.
34 McVeigh, *Concert Life in London*, p. 89.
35 *The Public Advertiser*, May 18, 1782.
36 Raoul owned the Tieffenbrucker viola da gamba made for Francis I of France; see Fétis, *Biographie universelle*, vol. VII, p. 182.

sated for through altered bow pressure, more pressure, for instance, pushing the pitch higher.[37]

Ex. 9.3 Duport, *Essai*, p. 130

Duport considered one of his great strengths as a musician to be his understanding and exploitation of the violoncello's natural overtones, writing
that knowledge of this subject "is necessary to play in tune and draw out a
pure sound."[38] Explaining the overtone system and the physical properties
of string vibrations, Duport demonstrated how such information could be
applied to creating string vibrations that were "very clean and very equal."
In addition to those pitches naturally enhanced through overtones available from open strings and their partials, Duport explained that artificial
overtones could be created by fingering octaves and playing the higher of

the two notes, i.e. ♩ . He considered this to be especially effective with

the "wolf" notes of E and F.[39]

Purity of sound and precision of the tuning fifths was a like concern for
Raoul. He drew attention to the fact that accuracy was dependent on the
quality of the strings used. He was not satisfied unless perfect fifths could
also be fingered, each finger lying flat across the four strings, as in Ex. 9.4.
Describing gut strings, he recommended choosing an equally pure A and
D string, without knots. To evenly balance the top strings, he added a G
string with a gut core of the same diameter as that of the A string, the C
string having a core equal to the D string.[40]

Ex. 9.4 Raoul, *Méthode*, p. 3

Although they regarded accurate intonation as requisite to fine playing,
German players did not link intonation to sound production as their
French compatriots did. While Dotzauer touched on Duport's analysis of
string vibrations in an extremely abbreviated form, he viewed such discussion as having little meaning to students, the subject being more appropriate to professional dialogue.[41] Violoncellists of Romberg's school were

37 Duport, *Essai*, pp. 130–133. 38 Ibid., p. 134. 39 Ibid., p. 142.
40 Raoul, *Méthode*, p. 3. 41 Dotzauer, *Violonzell-Schule*, preface.

considerably more interested in instrument construction, amplified sonority being achieved through physically refitting the instrument. By contrast with Duport's many pages about the overtone series, Romberg wrote extensively about how the violoncello should be built in order to produce "a fine powerful tone."[42] His instructions for tuning the instrument were designed to assist beginners who were without the immediate assistance of a teacher and carry no import of improved sonority. Romberg recommended tuning the violoncello A string to a tuning fork and using harmonics to find matching pitches between the strings, e.g. tuning the A harmonic of the A string to the A harmonic of the D string.[43]

Regional biases regarding sound production are also documented through concert reports. Comparisons between performers are always somewhat subjective, and descriptions of sound production, particularly in the absence of sound recordings, can never be completely divorced from those of other performance traits. However, there is a plethora of written opinions favoring one performer's sound, or style, over that of another – further evidence that differences did exist. These reports also lend a delicious sense of eighteenth- and nineteenth-century gossip to a modern study. To the degree that there is some consistency in the assessment of individuals, certain definable traits may be ascertained: French sound was referred to as the "lightest," while that of Romberg was the most forceful; English and Viennese violoncellists generally adopted a style of playing somewhat between the two extremes.

Preference for one performance school over another was prompted by fashion. In most instances, specific comparisons were generated by a performer's adoption of the latest trends in style or technique, i.e. perceptions of "new" or "better" received comment. French violoncellists were a dominating force just before the turn of the nineteenth century, a fact which coincides with the expatriation of prominent performers and their introduction of the "French" bow to audiences outside of Paris. The technical proficiency and polished style of the Duports gained much attention, Gerber being especially impressed. In comparing the brothers, however, he made the interesting observation that an "old" and a "new" French school existed, albeit without providing explicit details:

Those who have heard both brothers side by side are easily convinced that the older brother is a perfect virtuoso out of the old French school, which above all sought the greatest expression, and the younger is an equal virtuoso of the new French school. The elder is evenly accomplished in dexterity and precision, in a large full sound and power and expression in performance.[44]

---

42 Romberg, *School*, p. 5.
43 Ibid., p. 18.
44 Gerber, *Lexikon*, vol. IV, p. 44.

J. L. Duport elicited praise for combining "the greatest taste and execution with the purest and most beautiful tone"[45] and for "his easy command of the bow, clear intonation, and most expressive sound."[46] Despite his use of a Tourte-design bow, German commentators remarked upon the "lightness" of Duport's sound. Writing of Duport's performance in a solo aria in 1797, Gerber stated: "it was enough to hear his delicate and thoroughly pure tone and to notice the light, unforced use of his bow."[47] Romberg made a similar comment in a letter to his friend Kunst, ascribing the reason to the fact that Duport did not use Romberg's oblique left hand position: "in Duport's manner one plays lightly, but the sound gets lost, because the fingers have no strength."[48]

According to contemporary assessments, the only other French violoncellist comparable to J. L. Duport was his own student, Lamare. Lamare was in Vienna in 1805, reportedly seeking a Stradivari violoncello to replace his French instrument – an activity attesting to the increasing necessity for soloists to have such equipment.[49] Stemming from this episode is a remarkable report and interview of the violoncellist in the *BMZ*, which, although undoubtedly tinged with a degree of bias against a foreign performer, nevertheless presents considerable detail about Lamare's style of playing, and, because of the inevitable comparison, that of Romberg.

Although somewhat mystified as to why Lamare held the instrument on his left foot (see Chapter 3, p. 99), the reviewer was complimentary of his playing and stressed the sensitivity of his phrasing. It was noted that his strings were very high off the fingerboard, causing some difficulty in the execution of trills in his solo works. This feature is in keeping with his role of Baillot's quartet partner in Russia, and it may be that Lamare was not using an instrument strung for solo performance.

This report remarked on a facet of French playing which is reiterated among many differing sources and is also discernible from French solo works composed before 1815, but for which it is presently difficult to ascribe a cause: it appears that French violoncellists simply did not like to use the C string (see Chapter 4, p. 129 and Chapter 5, p. 159). This peculiarity received much comment from German reviewers, and elicited comparisons with Anton Kraft and Romberg, players who exploited the sonority of the C string. In Lamare's case avoidance of the lowest string reflected his instrument hold and resulted in his rewriting passages of works that did not fit his style. His instrument hold also induced a preference for using the tip of the bow, apparently in imitation of the violinist Rode.

45 Romberg, *School*, p. 73.
46 Blanchard, "Die Violoncellisten," 554.
47 Gerber, *Lexikon*, vol. II, col. 957.
48 Letter of Romberg to Friedrich Kunst, June 13, 1807 in Schäfer, *Romberg*, appendix.
49 "Etwas über Lamare," 102. Baudiot, Boccherini, Crosdill, J. L. Duport, Franchomme, Kummer, Romberg, and Vaslin owned Stradivaris.

As an example of how Lamare's style affected his manner of performance, the author of the *BMZ* report discussed the violoncellist's execution
of Mozart's third Prussian Quartet (K590). Of the opinion that Lamare's
"French playing" did not have the power of Kraft or Romberg, the reviewer related that instead of playing this passage as written –

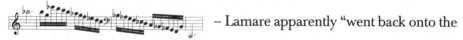 – Lamare apparently "went back onto the

A string; I still cannot forget even today how weak this passage sounded
to me."[50]

This observation was followed by the recounting of a direct interview
with Lamare. Doubtless cognizant of the comparisons made between himself and Romberg, Lamare observed in a most gentlemanly manner that
Romberg "was the most accomplished violoncellist, that he had ever
heard, that he had a hand as if especially made for the violoncello, and
because of this he could elicit from the instrument a truly round sound."[51]
The *BMZ* report continued:

[Lamare] still remembered that Romberg had played his B♭ major concerto like an
angel, and praised his compositions as excellent pieces of music. He could not at
that time be induced to play them, excusing himself on the grounds that the C
string of his instrument was not sufficiently responsive and that he really did not
like to play from the music, and so [the compositions] seemed strange to him.
From the little that he played for me between ourselves, I concluded well enough
that Romberg's compositions did not appear as strange to him as he had pre-
tended, only that this is not his style of playing, in that he never can execute such
solid bass passages with the extreme tip of the bow brilliantly and with sufficient
power to be rewarding; therefore, he appears to avoid all violoncello compositions that contain bass passages up the string, and where these passages came up,
limited himself to playing in the French style.[52]

This reporter was not the only writer to compare French and German use
of the C string. Earlier comment from a *BMZ* review by Reichardt makes
the same points:

With most [violoncellists] I found that they didn't know how to bring out a clear,
comfortably ringing sound from the overspun G and C strings. Generally they
swipe their bow across the so-called wire, as comes from Sul Ponticello or [alla]
Gamba, where the bass whistles indistinctly, not singing, and therefore becomes
inharmonious. But I didn't find this with our Romberg; each sound, the lower as
well as the upper, was clear as a bell, his violoncello sang equally fully and beautifully in the lowest passages as in the highest, and this same fullness of sound is in
my opinion the most difficult for a violoncellist, because I found it more or less

50 "Etwas über Lamare," 102.
51 Ibid.
52 Ibid., 103.

lacking in almost everyone that I heard before and after him. Exactly because of this, I think, he stands out as particular and unique, and leaves all others far behind. Yes, I even believe that Duport, who, as Beethoven said, had given him the greatest pleasure of any instrumentalist, and also Lamarre, who is said to imitate Rode's method to perfection, and whose playing many in Berlin believe to equal that of Duport, do not have these two strings under their control.

Although I have not heard Lamarre, his three published concertos obviously demonstrate that he did not use the lowest tones of the violoncello, in which Romberg knows so much spirit, dignity and expression, as one would expect from a fully accomplished artist, but then most violinists play his [Lamare's] concertos...[53]

In light of Germany's somewhat chauvinistic regard for Romberg's abilities, such comparisons might be considered overblown, except that similar thoughts about J. L. Duport's use of the lower strings were voiced by earlier British reviewers. When playing in London in 1783, Duport was compared with John Crosdill and James Cervetto. A review of a Hanover Square concert commented:

Duport is, to our Sense, equal to Cervetto and Crosdill in the upper and middle Parts of the Instrument. It is in the lower Tones, if any where, that he is deficient.[54]

French reviewers, not surprisingly, held differing opinions about Romberg's sound, Crosdill's receiving greater approbation. According to one report, Romberg placed his bow close to the bridge in the execution of fast passage work, thereby sounding harsh:

After Madame Branchu, we heard Mr. Romberg perform one of his concertos on the bass [cello]. The superiority of his talent is already too well known for us to need say very much about it. It has been noticed that, in the difficult passages and arpeggios, his instrument would lose some of the beauty of its sounds. This is the result of his playing the string very close to the bridge, where he has often come upon beautiful sounds; but these sounds escape him through the fast tempo of the playing. We have had the opportunity of hearing a very gifted man playing this instrument, Mr. Krossdell, and he seemed to us to have, in great measure, avoided the unpleasant effect which the bass [cello] produces when, in difficult passages, the string is not held down by the fingers or struck by the bow with the exact amount of pressure required to obtain a beautiful quality of sound. These defects which we deplore in Mr. Romberg and which we have had occasion to remark upon on other occasions were absent in the adagio and in the rondeau of his concerto, which is, moreover, very well written.[55]

Following his tenure in Paris, Romberg became a dominating force against whom all other violoncellists were measured. Other reviews compare him with Merk: unusually, the latter was hailed as an equal, owing to his com-

53 *BMZ,* no. 45 (1805), 178.
54 *The Public Advertiser,* March 13, 1783.
55 *Correspondance des Amateurs Musiciens,* no. 8 (January 15, 1803), 3.

pletely differing style. While Romberg was known for power and seriousness of expression, reviews of Merk emphasize "mischievous joviality,"
grace, and "extraordinary" beauty of sound.[56] For instance, from an 1826
report from Prague, it was written of Merk:

A charming sound, the greatest clarity and precision and a very characteristic
delivery have caused critics hungry for comparison to place this artist – excellent
in every respect – next to the great Romberg, whose unique expression is, however, so different from that of his young artistic compatriot that, on the contrary,
it has been very surprising to us to see two musical geniuses treat one and the
same instrument in such a completely different manner and yet both so superbly.
Let him therefore be called not the second Romberg, but rather the first Merk...[57]

Further information is supplied by comparisons of Merk with Lincke and
Lindley. Reviews of Lincke praise his abilities as an accompanist but re-
peatedly draw attention to the "smallness" of his sound, probably reflecting the state of his instrument, bow, and bow grip. Contemporaries did not
uniformly view this as a defect: Mannheim violinist Michael Frey considered Lincke's less obtrusive sound to be an attribute in quartet performances.[58]

Among Beethoven's friends, Merk was clearly considered a stronger,
more forceful player than the crippled Lincke. Two separate statements
expressing this opinion were made to Beethoven by his nephew between
March 15 and 23, 1825. Discussing a possible performance of the op. 127
string quartet by Mayseder and Merk, Carl von Beethoven remarked, "Of
Mayseder it is known that he plays your quartets very beautifully"; he subsequently wrote, probably in response to a comment regarding the fact that
Lincke did not play with Mayseder, "He [Merk] is stronger than Linke."[59]
In a later conversation on this same subject, Carl stated that "*Merk* is a
concerto performer stronger than Linke."[60]

Comments made by the English traveler Edward Holmes portray a
slightly different view of Merk's sound, and reiterate the frequently expressed English prejudice against lengthy passage work:

The Germans possess many violoncello players of much execution, and Bernhard
Romberg is the one generally cited as being at the head of them; the fact is, that
although talent is more extensively diffused in Germany, and that country produces many artists, it is less concentrated than among us. The taste of Robert
Lindley is more nearly approached in Vienna than his firm hand and brilliant
tone; hence the execution of Merk on the violoncello was weaker in point of articulation than might have been wished, as his feeling was good, his intonation

---

56 *AMZ*, no. 10 (March 1826), col. 164; *AMZ*, no. 15 (April 1836).
57 Ibid., col. 167.
58 Schmidt-Görg, "Tagebuch Frey," pp. 138–139.
59 Beethoven, *Konversationshefte*, vol. VII, p. 175.
60 Ibid., p. 179.

exact, and the passages were distinct, but they were without force. I was much gratified by the performance of Merk, and should rate him higher than any of our players except Lindley; but the want of strength and pressure of the finger is his principal defect. Merk's proficiency was chiefly shown in bowing across the strings, in the delicacy of his taste, and in accurate stopping on the thumb parts of the instrument. There is perhaps too great a love of scrambling over difficulties among the artists in Vienna, who suffer that ambition to swallow up some of those energies which should be devoted to the art abstractedly.[61]

Lindley accommodated his audiences' taste by extensively incorporating "popular airs" into both his accompaniments and his solo works. This was an idiom popularized by Romberg, who gathered regional folktunes during his widespread European travels and integrated them into concertos and variations. Unlike Romberg, who amplified his folk melodies with "the most extraordinary difficulties,"[62] Lindley kept his melodic presentations uncomplicated, despite possessing technical expertise on a par with his Austro-German contemporaries. Another description of the English violoncellist's style and sound production relates:

As a violoncellist, Lindley perhaps can overcome greater difficulties than any performer that ever lived…His tone is rich, powerful, and sweet, and his upper notes are most beautiful. His concertos are peculiar, and are suited to every species of audience. He introduces, amid most extraordinary difficulties, with a quaint yet elegant humour, popular old airs, and plays them in a style of characteristic simplicity.[63]

And what of French contemporaries of Lindley and Merk? Detailed reports about the generation of French violoncellists who followed J. L. Duport and Lamare are sparse and, with the exception of Norblin and Franchomme, generally uncomplimentary. The most exacting are those provided by Fétis, who presumably had ample opportunity to compare his countrymen's talents against those of Romberg, Bohrer, and Lindley, foreigners whom he had personally heard in concert. Of Hus-Desforges, who was perhaps handicapped by a missing finger on his right hand, he wrote:

Hus-Desforges had the reputation of a violoncellist of some talent, although he has always lacked a brilliant execution and he drew little sound from his instrument; however, he phrased with taste.[64]

The obligatory mention of taste was also taken up by German reviewers, who stated that Hus-Desforges played tastefully in the French manner, but had neither a large nor a beautiful sound.[65]

---

61 Edward Holmes, *A Ramble Among the Musicians of Germany* (New York: Da Capo Press, 1969), pp. 122–123.
62 "Rise and Progress of the Violoncello," 478.
63 Ibid., 480.
64 Fétis, *Biographie universelle*, vol. IV, p. 391.
65 *AMZ* (September 1812), col. 602.

Baudiot received harsh criticism from several sources. Chopin considered his playing to be extremely boring,[66] as did Fétis, whose incipit reads:

The nature of the talent of this artist was a pure sound, but not a powerful one, precise intonation and clean performance in the passage work; but his bow lacked variety: his playing was cold and lifeless.[67]

Descriptions of Vaslin are almost nonexistent, owing to his limited participation in Parisian concert life. A concert in which he played with de Beriot and Liszt produced one short comment: "this artist draws a large sound from his instrument, and sings well."[68] Further laudatory reports are reserved for Norblin and Franchomme, none of which give many specific details as to how the two artists sounded. Fétis' description of Norblin's playing brings to mind statements made of J. L. Duport: "Norblin was an extremely remarkable virtuoso, who was praised always for his taste, style and beautiful sonority as well."[69]

Franchomme's playing gained an enthusiastic response from Fétis, who wrote numerous reviews of the artist for the *Revue Musicale*. One of the most detailed is from an early performance at the Société des Concerts du Conservatoire:

A young man, a child, Franchomme, has come, unknown, playing without pretension a solo for violoncello, in a manner which places him suddenly in line with the greatest artists. He played a theme, without any ornament, and all of the audience was transported with pleasure. The talent showed itself through a few notes; it was enough. A good technique, perfect intonation, beautiful sound, good bowing and dexterity of the fingers are something, are indeed a great deal. Franchomme has all that; but the spirit, the sentiment! Here is talent: Franchomme has this too. Three, four, five rounds of applause were barely enough to express the pleasure the assembly had felt.[70]

"GOOD" PERFORMANCE, "GOOD" ENTERTAINMENT

In the review of Franchomme just quoted, his solo performance received spirited approbation: conclusive evidence of a "good" performance. The ability of a soloist to captivate the public imagination became requisite to a successful performance career, vitality of expression or startling technique being frequently cited as the means of appeal to nineteenth-century audiences. Lack of such qualities was also frequently remarked upon, as in this

---

66 *Correspondence of Chopin*, pp. 327–328.
67 Fétis, *Biographie universelle*, vol. I, p. 274.
68 *Revue Musicale*, 3, no. 12 (April 1828), 277.
69 Fétis, *Biographie universelle*, vol. II supplement, p. 278.
70 *Revue Musicale*, 5, no. 10 (April 1829), 237.

Dresden review of Nicolaus Kraft: "he appeared not to make all too great an impression on our public, for which the selection of the pieces may be blamed, for the lively, varying, and impressive was missing, which an educated ear demands."[71]

Such concepts of "good" differ significantly from the expectations placed on earlier generations of violoncellists. In the more intimate climate of the eighteenth-century court or public salon, beauty and taste were the virtues extolled, as in this 1755 review of Janson:

Mr. Janson, musician to the Prince de Conti, who had been absent because of a large number of traveling engagements, played a sonata for violoncello. This artist, already famous, has reappeared with new qualities. A more positive touch, an execution still more precise and more finished, a mellowed and beautiful sound, all combine to prove how fruitfully Mr. Janson has worked to attain this perfection.[72]

Likewise, in 1789, Anton Kraft in Dresden was greeted with enthusiastic applause owing to his "ability in the Adagio, his sweet sound, and the sentiment which he is able to reach through the most simple notes."[73] While also admired for the expressiveness of his slow movements, the young Romberg was already setting a standard against which all other violoncellists were soon to be judged. Speed and a penetrating sound, attributed to him as early as 1792, were qualities appreciated in a new era. According to Junker's description:

Romberg the younger, combines in his violoncello playing extraordinary rapidity with charming rendering; this rendering is the more marked and decided when he is heard in connection with the greater number of violoncellists. The tone which he produces from his instrument is, moreover – especially in the expressive parts – extremely clear, firm, and penetrating.[74]

Changing notions of "good" performance were intertwined with other vicissitudes experienced by professional musicians as Europe's social structure and cultural life transformed themselves between 1789 and 1840. Few musical careers testify to the shift in perceptions of virtuoso stature, with its attendant dependence on public audiences, as succinctly as does that of Romberg. As junior employees of the Bonn court in 1792, he and Beethoven, not atypically for eighteenth-century Kapelle members, had performed kitchen duties as well as chamber music.[75] Twenty years later, as a renowned public virtuoso, Romberg was able to defy a Prussian court

71 *AMZ* (April 1819), col. 255.
72 *Mercure de France* (April 1755), quoted in Barry S. Brook, *La symphonie française dans la seconde moitié du XVIIIe siècle*, 3 vols. (Paris: Publications de l'Institut de Musicologie de l'Université de Paris, 1962), vol. II, p. 387.
73 *Musikalische Real-Zeitung* (January 24, 1789), col. 198.
74 *Beethoven: Impressions of Contemporaries*, p. 12.
75 Wegeler and Ries, *Beethoven Remembered*, p. 22.

summons to return to work in Berlin, remaining instead on a lucrative tour of Russia.[76] Anton Kraft had attempted this same tactic in 1781 and was consequently fined one month's salary at the Esterháza Kapelle.[77] By comparison, Friedrich Wilhelm III of Prussia was reduced to offering Romberg a raise in an attempt to lure him back to Berlin, a ploy which was not successful until 1816.

The transformation of instrumentalist from court lackey to public celebrity, beginning towards the end of the eighteenth century, is perhaps best witnessed by the travels of W. A. Mozart, or Hus-Desforges' grandfather, the violinist Giornovichi. Despite the numerous public performances given by both, however, the focus for this generation of musicians was not in the main to conquer the public concert hall, but to exact money and advancement from the aristocracy. Twenty-five years of war shattered such dreams for those who followed, financial exigencies destroying the stability of aristocratic and monarchial support upon which most eighteenth-century musicians solely depended. Virtuosos turned to the public in desperation – in 1807 Romberg, at that time still a member of the Berlin Kapelle, wrote to his friend Kunst: "I am going to Leipzig for a few days in order to make some money because the times are too difficult here."[78]

This is not to say that aristocratic patrons were not influential in nineteenth-century music making – they certainly were – but the financial success made possible by the public concert hall no longer required nineteenth-century virtuosos to remain subservient to the proprieties of court. The change in attitude may be demonstrated by two descriptions from the Dresden court, one by W. A. Mozart, who visited it in 1789, and a second from Ignaz Moscheles, recorded in 1813. Mozart's description, from a letter to his wife relating an extemporaneous performance arranged by himself and Anton Kraft, was enthusiastic:

While we were at table a message came that I was to play at court the following day, Tuesday, April 14th, at half past five in the evening. That is something quite out of the ordinary for Dresden, for it is usually very difficult to get a hearing, and you know that I never thought of performing at court here. We had arranged a quartet among ourselves at the Hôtel de Pologne. So we performed it in the Chapel with Anton Teiber ... and with Herr Kraft ...[79]

Moscheles recalled:

The Court actually dined (this barbarous custom still prevails), and the Royal household listened in the galleries, while I and the Court band made music to

---

76 See letter of Iffland to Romberg, July 14, 1811 and letter of Iffland to Friedrich Wilhelm III, July 28, 1812 in Schäfer, *Romberg*, appendix.
77 Harich, "Das Haydn-Orchester im Jahr 1780," pp. 61–62.
78 Letter of Romberg to Friedrich Kunst, April 25, 1807 in Schäfer, *Romberg*, appendix.
79 *Letters of Mozart*, vol. III, p. 1373.

them, and barbarous it really was, but in regard to truth, I must add that Royalty, and also the lackeys, kept as quiet as possible, and the former actually so far condescended as to admit me to friendly conversation.[80]

During this period of slowly changing mores, musical performance was often only part of an evening's recreation. However, the transition from instrumentalist as background entertainment to instrumentalist as focal point allowed virtuosos to be increasingly dissatisfied with anything less than complete attention from their audiences. Louis Spohr went far beyond Moscheles' privately voiced discontent while visiting Stuttgart in 1807. He successfully demanded that the King cease his card game while he and his wife presented their concert:

Quite horrified at so bold a request the Court-Chamberlain made one step backward, and exclaimed: "What? You would prescribe conditions to my gracious Master? Never should I dare make such a proposal to him!" "Then must I renounce the honour of playing at Court," was my simple reply.[81]

Ambition to please a more inclusive public exacted new obligations for artists, however, as listeners increasingly required personality and charisma in addition to proficiency and pleasant delivery. Of all violoncellists, no one met this challenge with greater efficacy than Romberg. While the tools of his success included all the skills of virtuosity, a vibrant sound aided by the most up-to-date instrument fittings and bow, and compositions considered brilliantly effective by critics, he also devised a stage persona which engendered intimacy between himself and his audience. Carl von Beethoven and Carl Holz described to Beethoven the novelty by which Romberg enthralled his public: the nephew related that "Romberg always plays without the music," to which Holz added, "and therefore cuts a splendid appearance."[82]

Reviews of Romberg's playing attest to the redefinition of "good" performance in the nineteenth century. In keeping with the Romantic perception of instrumental music, J. F. Rochlitz delighted in Romberg's ability to compose and perform "such very diverse compositions" which the listener "could more intimately acquire according to his own individuality." His execution, of "the greatest perfection, without the smallest appearance of exertion," was especially effective owing to the

overall captivatingness of his own appearance, when he plays, without any music, just as if that which his eyes proclaim and his instrument expresses was at that very minute welling up from his soul – all this unites, transporting every listener...[83]

80 Moscheles, *Diaries of Moscheles*, p. 22.
81 *Spohr's Autobiography*, vol. I, pp. 106–107.
82 Beethoven, *Konversationshefte*, vol. VIII, p. 28.
83 *AMZ* (May 1818), col. 352.

E. T. A. Hoffmann also wrote of Romberg's playing, publishing a concert review as part of a lengthier description of the state of music in Berlin following the end of the war. He spoke to several issues reflective of the changing state of solo performance at this time: the perception of the increased excellence of instrumentalists; his own interest in listening to an instrumentalist as the main focus of a concert; his reaction to Romberg's compositions and programming; the impact of Romberg's performance style. Hoffmann was strongly moved by Romberg's mode of presentation:

Who else could come to mind, as I speak of the high degree of perfection with which instrumental music is now practised, but a splendid composer whom to my greatest joy I encountered again here after his long absence?...He [Romberg] has played in many other concerts, with a liberality befitting the true artist,[84] but I wanted to see and hear him only in his own, where he himself was the focus of attention. I say *see* and *hear* advisedly. The general desire not only to hear in a concert, but also to see, the pushing for seats in the hall, where this is possible, certainly does not arise merely from idle curiosity. One hears better when one sees. The secret relationship between light and sound is clearly demonstrated; both light and sound assume an individual form, and thus the soloist or singer himself becomes the sounding melody! That sounds strange, I admit; but see and hear our splendid Bernhard, then you will fully understand what I mean, and surely not accuse me of eccentric obscurantism...He is in complete control of his instrument; or rather, with all its strength and grace and its rare abundance of sounds, it has become so much an extension of the artist that it seems by itself to vibrate with all the sensations of the spirit, seemingly with no expenditure of mechanical effort whatsoever.

It is not insignificant in this regard that Romberg never has music in front of him, but plays everything from memory, sitting clearly visible before the audience. You cannot imagine what a singular impression this made upon me. The sol[o] passages of his concerto seemed like free fantasies, conceived at the moment of highest inspiration. All the wonderful figures, often flashing upward from the darkest depths to the most brilliant heights, seemed to burst forth from his elated spirit, and the notes seemed to be produced purely by the strength of his imagination, matching and following it in every nuance, before resounding from the orchestra.

That is why I say that one must not only hear this splendid musician playing, but also *see* him playing. Then one will be able even better to appreciate how high this artist stands, and how his playing bears witness to the greatest facility and absolute mastery of the means of expression...

Also in the concert, as was right and proper, a symphony composed by this artist was performed; it proved to me once again how the spirit of his playing also permeates his compositions. Both, his playing and his compositions, possess a quite distinctive clarity, grace, and elegance, and the symphony too, with its many melodious phrases and smooth modulations, had the most pleasurable effect...

---

84 Romberg frequently played in other performers' concerts when chamber music was programmed.

Romberg had called the concerto he performed a *military* concerto [op. 31]...
The opening Allegro of this concerto was especially pleasing. I could not help
thinking of Fouqué's tale *Die beiden Hauptleute*, and in the burning brilliance of the
southern sun I saw Spanish regiments moving past with flying colours and jubilant
hurrahs. You know that such images cannot appear to me unless I am genuinely
aroused. So the military concerto, which I had in fact viewed with some misgiv-
ing, made such an agreeable impression on me that I was unable to enjoy to the
same extent the *Rondoletto* which the artist went on to play. Although bright and
attractive, it deviated into all sorts of intriguing byways. But my head was still full
of the Spaniards, and their banners still fluttered before my eyes. The artist finally
paid his tribute to lovers of musical curiosities by bringing forth even a pretty little
bagpipe.[85]

There was also singing in the concert, and very good it was, although the pieces
did not seem to me particularly well chosen.[86]

Success with the public gradually led to changes in program structure, the
virtuoso being expected to give an audience its money's worth. As is
evident from the numerous concertos and concert pieces in Romberg's
programs, an hour or more of such virtuoso music demanded a level of
physical stamina never expected of his predecessors. Public concerts of the
eighteenth century usually required the violoncellist to participate with the
orchestra, perhaps accompany a piece of chamber music, and occasionally
perform one solo, either a continuo sonata or a concerto. Such was the case
at the Concert Spirituel on August 15, 1778. The program included a symphony by Mozart, a trio in which J. L. Duport played the violoncello part,
a sonata written and performed by Bréval, at least three different vocalists,
and a violin concerto.[87] English programing was of a similar nature, as
shown by Abel's subscription concert of January 27, 1785. The concert
opened with an overture by Abel, concertos were played by Salomon and
Fischer, Crosdill performed a sonata, Salomon, Fischer, and Crosdill executed a "new" symphonie concertante for violin, oboe, and violoncello,
and vocal numbers were performed by Signor Bartolini and Madame
Mara.[88]

Concerts composed of a melange of items remained popular well into
the nineteenth century, but performers in such programs were judged by
much the same standards as those imposed upon touring virtuosos. The
pressure of such comparisons, as well as the burden of pleasing increasingly large and demanding audiences, led to a phenomenon absent from
eighteenth-century discourse – that of stage fright. Jan Stiastny, for example, was never heard in concert because of his "sensitive" nature, this de-

---

85 The third solo piece on the program was *Capriccio sur des airs suédois.* Hoffmann's analogy to bag-
   pipes most likely refers to Romberg's inclusion of harmonics.
86 *AMZ* (January 1815), cols. 19–21, trans. in *E. T. A. Hoffmann's Musical Writings,* p. 390.
87 Pierre, *Histoire du Concert Spirituel,* p. 309.
88 *The Public Advertiser,* January 27, 1785.

spite the popularity of his violoncello compositions. Although Robert Lindley's son, William, frequently performed as a young man with his father, he also withdrew from public performance because of nerves. Baudiot, likewise, suffered from stage fright; this may be the foundation for a malicious story related by Fétis in his biography of the violoncellist.[89] Baudiot was concerned enough about this affliction – a subject rarely mentioned by other successful performers – to provide a practical solution:

One problem, which one cannot guard against early enough, is timidity or too lively an emotion when one has a public performance or just in a gathering. The remedy for this problem, which is very harmful for an artist, is to play as frequently as possible before an audience; one should create opportunities for this if they do not present themselves.[90]

Discomfort before the public also reflects the fact that, while negatively worded reviews of violoncellists are a rarity before 1815, they became increasingly pointed in the aftermath of the war years. While it is tempting to infer that more detailed criticism reflected the greater visibility of soloists and growing discernment on the part of audiences and writers, much negativity can be attributed to the influence of higher ticket prices and increasing nationalism. Nationalism, always a factor to some degree in the evaluation of a performer, now became a pretext for intensely parochial remarks. Max Bohrer, in particular, received harsh comment in this vein. While his technique seems to have been always irreproachable, his style was criticized for being "too German"[91] by at least one French writer, "too French" by a German reviewer,[92] and completely unsuitable for English audiences: compositions by him and his brother were "thought unworthy of the performers."[93]

One kind of performance which remained exempt from harsh comment was that given by an artist together with his children. Numerous players passed their own legacy on to their offspring, violoncello being the family trade for Cervetto, Danzi, J. L. Duport, Levasseur, Crouch, Lindley, Romberg, Dotzauer, Kummer, and three generations of Krafts. Reviewers were kind on these occasions, respectful of family pride. Karl Romberg was described as a "splendid blossoming branch of this artistic family."[94] William

---

89 Fétis, *Biographie universelle*, vol. I, p. 274. According to Fétis, at a concert given by Mme. Catalani, Baudiot unknowingly followed the performance of a Haydn symphony with a solo fantasy for violoncello and orchestra written on a theme from that same symphony. Beginning his performance, Baudiot is said to have been laughed off the stage. The reason for Fétis' antipathy towards Baudiot is unknown, but his incipit has few kind words for the violoncellist.
90 Baudiot, *Méthode*, vol. II, p. 4.
91 *AMZ* (May 1818), col. 345.
92 *AMZ*, no. 20 (May 1820), cols. 340–341.
93 *The Harmonicon*, 6, no. 5 (May 1828), 110.
94 *AMZ* (February 1822), col. 146.

Lindley "seems to tread in his father's steps, promising to become – many years hence, we hope – a worthy successor of his parent."[95]

Notwithstanding varied responses to individual players, the increasing enthusiasm expressed by audiences for the violoncello was a just reward for the men who made playing and teaching this instrument their life's work. Although skilled accompaniments have always remained a respected avenue of violoncello performance, by 1840, violoncellists were no longer solely regarded as useful appendages to singers and instrumental soloists. In 1762, J. P. Duport had elicited astonished praise in the *Mercure de France* for his solo performance: "this instrument is not recognizable in his hands; it speaks, expresses, it renders all of the charm that was heretofore believed to be exclusively reserved for the violin."[96] Later commentators were equally enthusiastic, if less astonished by the violoncellists' skill. In Vienna it was noted that "since Romberg, this instrument is great, popular, and since frail ladies and effusive men took it under their protection, has spread widely, and therefore more and more artists appear."[97] But as an English writer remarked, the development of violoncello performance was not due solely to the merits of a few distinguished soloists such as Romberg, but resulted from the contributions of many players. As to the rise and progress of the violoncello, it may be reiterated:

The Violoncello has been rising gradually since the beginning of the last century into estimation, and may now be said to enjoy an almost equal reputation with the violin as a concerto instrument, and as an accompaniment its merits as well as its character are far higher. The Cervetto[s], Crosdill, and Lindley, in this country – the Duports, Janson, Baudiot, and Muntzberger, in France, and many other eminent artists, have given by their extraordinary performance (particularly as it regards their wonderful execution) this magnificent instrument a new nature.[98]

95 *The Harmonicon*, 4, no. 6 (June 1826), 106.
96 Quoted in Pierre, *Histoire du Concert Spirituel*, p. 127.
97 *Allgemeine Wiener Musik-Zeitung*, no. 29 (March 8, 1842), 114.
98 "Rise and Progress of the Violoncello," 351.

Select bibliography

Chronological list of violoncello methods

Corrette, Michel, *Méthode théorique et pratique pour apprendre en peu de temps le violoncelle dans sa perfection. Ensemble de principes de musique avec des leçons*, op. 24, Paris: 1741/ R 1972.

Tillière, J. B., *Méthode pour le violoncelle contenant tous les principes nécessaires pour bien jouer de cet instrument*, Paris: Imbault, [1764].

Crome, Robert, *The Compleat Tutor for the Violoncello*, London: [1765].

Lanzetti, Salvatore, *Principes ou l'application de violoncelle, par tous les tons de la maniére la plus facile*, Amsterdam: J. J. Hummel, [c. 1756–67].

Cupis, François, *Méthode nouvelle et raisonnée pour apprendre à jouer du violoncello* [1772], facsimile edition Arnaldo Forni, Civico Museo Bibliografico Musicale di Bologna.

Baumgartner, Jean, *Instructions de musique, theorique et pratique, a l'usage du violoncello*, The Hague: Daniel Monnier, [1774].

Schetky, Johann, *Twelve Duetts for Two Violoncellos, with some Observations & Rules for playing that Instrument*, op. 7, London: Preston & Son, [c. 1780].

Kauer, F., *Kurzgefasste Anweisung das Violoncell zu Spielen*, Vienna: Johann Cappi, [1788].

Gunn, John, *The Theory and Practice of Fingering the Violoncello*, London: [1793].

Reinagle, Joseph, *A Concise Introduction to the Art of Playing the Violoncello*, London: Goulding, Phipps & D'Almaine, [1800].

Alexander, Joseph, *Jos. Alexanders Anleitung zum Violoncellspiel*, Leipzig: Breitkopf und Härtel, [c. 1801].

Aubert, P. F. O., *Méthode ou nouvelles etudes pour le violoncelle*, op. 9, Paris: [1802].

Bideau, Dominique, *Grande et nouvelle méthode raisonnée pour le violoncelle*, Paris: Nadermann, [1802].

Raoul, J. M., *Méthode de violoncelle*, Paris: Pleyel, [c. 1802]/R 1972.

Bréval, J. B., *Traité du violoncelle*, op. 42, Paris: Imbault, [1804].

Baillot, P., J. H. Levasseur, C. -S. Catel, and C. -N. Baudiot, *Méthode de violoncelle et de basse d'accompagnement*, Paris: A l'Imprimerie du Conservatoire, [1805].

Duport, Jean-Louis, *Essai sur le doigté du violoncelle, et sur la conduite de l'archet*, Paris: Janet et Cotelle, [1806].

New and Complete Instructions for the Violoncello, London: Clementi, Banger, Hyde, Collard & Davis, [before 1810].

Schetky, Johann, *Practical and Progressive Lessons for the Violoncello*, London: R. Birchall, 1811.

Crouch, Frederick W., *A Compleat Treatise on the Violoncello*, London: Latour [1827].

Baudiot, Charles, *Méthode pour le violoncelle*, op. 25, 2 vols, Paris: Pleyel, [1826, 1828].

300

Hus-Desforges, Pierre-Louis, *Méthode de violoncelle*, Paris: [1829].

Stiastny, Bernard, *Violoncell-Schule*, 2 vols., Mainz: Georges Zulehner, [1829].

Dotzauer, J. J. F., *Violonzell-Schule*, Mainz: B. Schott, [1832].

Kummer, F. A., *Violoncell-Schule*, op. 60 [1839], ed. Hugo Becker, Leipzig: Peters.

Romberg, Bernhard, *A Complete Theoretical and Practical School for the Violoncello*, London: Boosey & Sons Foreign Musical Library, [1839].

Violoncell Schule von Bernhard Romberg, Berlin: Buch u. Musikalische Handlung, [1840].

Lindley, Robert, *Lindley's Handbook for the Violoncello*, London: The Musical Bouquet Office, [before 1855].

Merrick, A., *Method for the Violoncello by Baillot, Levasseur, Catel & Baudiot, Adopted by the Paris Conservatory of Music*, London: R. Cocks & Co., second edition, [before 1855].

Vaslin, Olive, *L'art du violoncelle: conseils aux jeunes violoncellistes sur la conduite de l'archet*, Paris: Richault, [1884].

Periodicals

Allgemeine Musikalische Zeitung, Leipzig, 1798/9–1848.

Allgemeine Wiener Musik-Zeitung, ed. August Schmidt, Vienna, 1841–48.

Berlinische Musikalische Zeitung, ed. J. F. Reichardt, Berlin, 1805–06.

Correspondance des Amateurs Musiciens, ed. Cocatrix, Paris, 1802–05.

Harmonicon: a Journal of Music, The, ed. W. Ayrton, London, 1823–33.

Journal de Paris, Paris, 1799–1801.

London Times, The, London, 1814.

Morning Chronicle and Public Advertiser, The, London, 1774–92.

Musikalische Real-Zeitung, ed. H. P. C. Bossler and J. F. Christmann, Speyer, 1788–90.

Musical Times, The, 30, no. 559 (September 1, 1889), p. 548.

Quarterly Musical Magazine and Review, The, ed. R. M. Bacon, London, 1818–28.

Revue et Gazette Musicale de Paris, September 30, 1849.

Revue Musicale, ed. F. J. Fétis, Paris, 1827–35.

Wiener Allgemeine Musikalische Zeitung, ed. I. von Schönholz, Vienna, 1813.

Books, dissertations and journal articles

Adas, Jane, "Le célèbre Berteau," *Early Music*, 17, no. 3 (August 1989), 368–380.

Anderson, Emily, (ed. and trans.), *The Letters of Beethoven*, 3 vols., London: Macmillan, 1961.

The Letters of Mozart to His Family, 3 vols., London: Macmillan, 1938.

Baines, Anthony, *European and American Musical Instruments*, London: B. T. Batsford Ltd., 1966.

Barnett, Dene, "Non-uniform Slurring in 18th Century Music: Accident or Design?" *The Haydn Yearbook*, 10 (1978), 179–199.

Beethoven, Ludwig van, *Konversationshefte*, ed. Karl-Heinz Köhler and Gita Herre, 9 vols., Leipzig: VEB Deutscher Verlag für Musik, 1972–88.

Beethoven: Impressions of Contemporaries, New York: G. Schirmer, Inc., 1927.

Blees, Gisela, *Das Cello-Konzert um 1800: Eine Untersuchung der Cello-Konzerte zwischen Haydns op. 101 und Schumanns op. 129*, Regensburg: Gustav Bosse Verlag, 1973.

Bonta, Stephen, "From Violone to Violoncello: A Question of Strings?" *Journal of the American Musical Instrument Society*, 3 (1977), 64–99.

"Terminology for the Bass Violin in Seventeenth- Century Italy," *Journal of the American Musical Instrument Society*, 4 (1978), 5–42.

Boomkamp, C. Van Leeuwen and J. H. Van Der Meer, *The Carel Van Leeuwen Boomkamp Collection of Musical Instruments*, Amsterdam: Frits Knuf, 1971.

Boyce, Mary Frances, "The French School of Violin Playing in the Sphere of Viotti: Technique and Style," Ph.D. thesis, University of North Carolina, 1973.

Boyden, David D. et al., *The New Grove Violin Family*, London: Macmillan, 1989.

Brook, Barry S., *La symphonie française dans la seconde moitié du XVIIIe siècle*, 3 vols. Paris: Publications de l'Institut de Musicologie de l'Université de Paris, 1962.

Brook, Barry S. (ed.), *The Breitkopf Thematic Catalogue: the Six Parts and Sixteen Supplements, 1762–1787*, New York: Dover Publications, 1966.

Brown, James D. and Stephen S. Stratton, *British Musical Biography*, London: William Reeves, 1897.

Burnett, Henry, "The Bowed String Instruments of the Baroque Basso-Continuo (ca. 1680–ca. 1752) in Italy and France: The Various Meanings of the Term 'Violone,'" *Journal of the Viola da Gamba Society of America*, 8 (1971), 29–63.

Burney, Charles, *An Eighteenth-Century Musical Tour in Central Europe and the Netherlands (1789)*, 2 vols., ed. Percy A. Scholes, Oxford University Press, 1959,

Cairns, David (ed. and trans.), *The Memoirs of Hector Berlioz*, New York: Alfred A. Knopf, 1969.

Charlton, David (ed.), *E. T. A. Hoffmann's Musical Writings*, trans. Martyn Clarke, Cambridge University Press, 1989.

Childs, Paul, "The Bows of Etienne Pajeot," *The Strad*, 104, no. 1236 (April 1993), 372–375.

Chorley, Henry F., *Musical Recollections*, New York: Alfred A. Knopf, 1926.

Cowling, Elizabeth, *The Cello*, London: B. T. Batsford Ltd., 1975.

Cox, H. Bertram and C. L. E. Cox (eds.), *Leaves from the Journals of Sir George Smart*, London: Longmans & Co., 1907/R 1971.

Cucuel, Georges, *La Pouplinière et la musique de chambre au XVIIIe siècle*, Paris: Librairie Fischbacher, 1918.

Curry, Pat Bryan, "The François Tourte Violin Bow: Its Development and Its Effect on Selected Solo Violin Literature of the Late Eighteenth and Early Nineteenth Centuries," Ph.D. thesis, Brigham Young University, 1968.

Cyr, Mary, "*Basses* and *basse continue* in the Orchestra of the Paris Opéra 1700–1764," *Early Music*, 10, no. 2 (April 1982), 155–170.

Decourcelle, Maurice, *La Société Académique des Enfants d'Apollon 1741–1880*, Paris, 1881.

Deutsch, Otto Eric, *Schubert: a Documentary Biography*, trans. Eric Blom, London: J. M. Dent & Sons, Ltd., 1946.

Deutsch, Otto Eric (ed.), *Schubert: Memoirs by His Friends*, trans. Rosamund Ley and John Nowell, London: Adam & Charles Black, 1958.

Dilworth, John, "Mr Baker the Fidell Maker," *The Strad*, 106, no. 1261 (May 1995), 475–481.

Donington, Robert, "James Talbot's Manuscript," *The Galpin Society Journal*, 3 (March 1950), 27–45.

Ducancel, C. P., *Mémoire pour J. F. Lesueur*, Paris: Goujon Fils, 1802.

Eckhardt, Joseph, *Die Violoncellschulen von J. J. F. Dotzauer, F. A. Kummer und B. Romberg*, Regensburg: Gustav Bosse Verlag, 1968.

Eitner, Robert, *Biographisch-bibliographisches Quellen-Lexikon der Musiker und Musikgelehrten*, 10 vols., New York: Musurgia, 1898.

Elsen, Josephine, "The Instrumental Works of Peter Ritter," Ph.D. thesis, Northwestern University, 1967.

Fauquet, Joël-Marie, *Les sociétés de musique de chambre à Paris de la restauration à 1870*, Paris: Aux Amateurs de Livres, 1986.

Fétis, F. J., *Antony Stradivari*, trans. John Bishop, London: William Reeves, 1864/R 1964.

Biographie universelle des musiciens et bibliographie générale de la musique, second edition, 8 vols. and supplement, Paris: Librarie de Firmin-Didot et Cie, 1887–88.

Framéry, Nicolas Etienne et al. (compilers), *Encyclopédie Methodique Musique*, 2 vols., New York: Da Capo Press, 1971.

François-Sappey, Brigitte, "La vie musicale à Paris à travers les mémoires d'Eugène Sauzay," *Revue de Musicologie*, 60, nos. 1–2 (1974), 159–210.

"Pierre Marie François de Sales Baillot (1771–1842) par lui-même," *Recherches sur la Musique Française Classique*, 18 (1978), 127–211.

Gallay, Jules (ed.), *Un inventaire sous la terreur. Etat des instruments relevés chez les émigrés et condamnés par Bruni*, Paris: Georges Chamerot, 1890.

Geiringer, Karl, *Haydn: A Creative Life in Music*, third edition, Berkeley: University of California Press, 1982.

Geminiani, Francesco, *A Treatise of Good Taste in the Art of Musick*, New York: Da Capo Press, 1969.

Gerber, Ernst Ludwig, *Historisch-Biographisches Lexikon der Tonkünstler und Neues Historisch-Biographisches Lexikon der Tonkünstler*, 4 vols., Graz: Akademische Druck- u. Verlagsanstalt, 1977.

Ginsburg, Lev, *History of the Violoncello*, ed. Dr. Herbert Axelrod, trans. Tanya Tchistyakova, Neptune City, New Jersey: Paganiniana Publications, 1983.

Istoriya violonchel'nogo iskusstva, kniga vtoraya, Russkoe violonchel'noe iskusstvo do 60'kh godov XIX veka [History of the Art of the Cello, Bk 2, Russian Cello Art up to the 60s of the 19th Century], Moscow: Muzgiz, 1957.

Grout, Donald Jay, *A Short History of Opera*, New York: Columbia University Press, second edition, 1965.

Grove, George (ed.), *A Dictionary of Music and Musicians*, 4 vols., London: Macmillan, 1879–89.

Harich, János, "Das Haydn-Orchester im Jahr 1780," trans. Eugene Hartzell, *The Haydn Yearbook*, 8, Bryn Mawr, Pennsylvania: Theodore Presser Co., 1971, 5–69.

Hartzell, Eugene (trans.), 'The Diaries of Joseph Carl Rosenbaum', ed. Else Radant in *The Haydn Yearbook*, 5, Bryn Mawr, Pennsylvania: Theodore Presser Co., 1968, 7–158.

Hedley, Arthur (ed. and trans.), *Selected Correspondence of Fryderyk Chopin*, collected and annotated by Bronislaw Sydow, London: Heinemann, 1962.

Heron-Allen, Edward, *Violin-Making as It Was and Is*, London: Ward Lock & Co., Ltd., 1885.

Hill, W. Henry, Arthur Hill and Alfred Hill, *Antonio Stradivari: His Life and Work*, R/New York: Dover Publications, 1963.

Ho, Allen and Dmitry Feofanov, *Biographical Dictionary of Russian/Soviet Composers*, New York: Greenwood Press, 1989.

Holmes, Edward, *A Ramble Among the Musicians of Germany*, New York: Da Capo Press, 1969.

Holmes, Henry (ed.), *Spohr's Violin School*, trans. Florence A. Marshall, London: Boosey & Co., n.d.

Iffland, Aug. Guil., *Collection des mémoires sur l'art dramatique*, Paris: Chez Etienne Ledoux, 1823.

Johann Anton Fils (1733–1760): Ein Eichstätter Komponist der Mannheimer Klassik, Tutzing: Hans Schneider, 1983.

Kelly, Michael, *Reminiscences*, ed. Roger Fiske, Oxford University Press, 1975.

Knocker, Editha (ed.), *Leopold Mozart's Treatise on the Fundamentals of Violin Playing*, second edition, Oxford University Press, 1951.

Kohlmorgen, Fritz, "Die Brüder Duport und die Entwicklung der Violoncelltechnik von ihren Anfängen bis zur Zeit Bernhard Rombergs", Ph.D. thesis, Friedrich-Wilhelms Universität, 1922.

La Borde, J. B. de, *Essai sur la musique ancienne et moderne*, 4 vols., Paris: Ph. D. Pierres, 1780.

Landon, H. C. Robbins, *Haydn Chronicle and Works*, 4 vols., Bloomington: Indiana University Press, 1977.

Lassabathie, T., *Histoire du Conservatoire Impérial de Musique et de Déclamation*, Paris: Michel Lévy Frères, 1860.

Le Blanc, Hubert, *Défense de la basse de viole contre les entreprises du violon et les prétensions du violoncelle*, Amsterdam: Pierre Mortier, 1740/R 1975.

Lenneberg, Hans (trans.), *Breitkopf und Härtel in Paris: the Letters of their Agent Heinrich Probst between 1833 and 1840*, Stuyvesant, New York: Pendragon Press, 1990.

Leur, Irmgard, "Christian Gottlob Neefe und Andreas Romberg," *Zeitschrift für Musikwissenschaft*, 7, no. 137 (1925), 655–658.

Lindeman, Fred, "Dutch Violin Making down the Centuries," *The Strad*, 106, no. 1264 (August 1995), 782–791.

Lonsdale, Roger, *Dr. Charles Burney, a Literary Biography*, Oxford: Clarendon Press, 1965.

Markevitch, Dimitry, "A Lost Art? The Use of the Thumb in 18th- and Early 19th-Century Cello Works," *Strings*, 7, no. 1 (July/August 1992), 16–18.

  "A New Sound for Familiar Music: The Cello as an Accompanying Instrument in the 18th-Century," *Strings*, 6, no. 3 (November/December 1991), pp. 18–21.

McVeigh, Simon, *Concert Life in London from Mozart to Haydn*, Cambridge University Press, 1993.

Mendel, Arthur, "Pitch in Western Music since 1500, a Re-examination," *Acta Musicologica*, 50 (1978), 1–93.

Millant, Roger, *J. B. Vuillaume: sa vie et son œuvre*, trans. Andrew Hill, London: W. E. Hill & Sons, 1972.

Milliot, Sylvette, *Le violoncelle en France au XVIIIe siècle*, Paris: Champion-Slatkine, 1985.

Moore, Lillian, "The Duport Mystery," *Dance Perspectives*, 7 (1960), 12–17.

Moran, John, "Fingering in Beethoven's Cello Music: An Evaluation of the Historical Sources," Diplomarbeit, Schola Cantorum Basiliensis, 1994.

Morrow, Mary Sue, *Concert Life in Haydn's Vienna: Aspects of a Developing Musical and Social Institution*, Stuyvesant, New York: Pendragon Press, 1989.

Moscheles, Charlotte (ed.), *Recent Music and Musicians as Described in the Diaries and Correspondence of Ignatz Moscheles*, trans. A. D. Coleridge, New York: Henry Holt and Co., 1889.

Muffat, Georg, "Florilegium secundum für streichinstrumente," ed. Heinrich Rietsch in *Denkmäler der Tonkunst in Österreich*, vol. IV, Graz: Akademische Druck- u. Verlagsanstalt, 1959.

Niecks, Frederick, "Recollections of Violoncellists," *Monthly Musical Record*, 49, no. 582 (June 2, 1919), 122–123; 49, no. 583 (July 1, 1919), 145–147.

Otto, Irmgard, *Katalog für Streichinstrumente*, Berlin, 1975.

Otto, J. A., *Ueber den Bau und die Erhaltung der Geige und aller Bogen-Instrumente*, Halle, 1817.

Pierre, Constant, *Conservatoire National de Musique et de Déclamation*, Paris: Imprimerie Nationale, 1900.

  Histoire du Concert Spirituel 1725–1790, Paris: Société Française de Musicologie, 1975.

Pohl, C. F., *Mozart und Haydn in London*, 2 vols., Vienna: Carl Gerold's Sohn, 1867.

Quantz, Johann Joachim, *On Playing the Flute*, trans. Edward R. Reilly, London: Faber & Faber, 1966.

Raguenet, François, "A Comparison between the French and Italian Music," trans. Oliver Strunk, *The Musical Quarterly*, 32, no. 3 (July 1946), 411–436.

Reindorf, Mark, "Authentic Authorship," *The Strad*, 101, no. 1203 (July 1990), 546–550.

Rothschild, Germain de, *Luigi Boccherini: His Life and Work*, trans. Norbert Dufourcq, Oxford University Press, 1965.

Rousseau, Jean-Jacques, *Dictionnaire de musique*, Paris: Duchesne, 1768/R 1969.

Confessions of Jean Jacques Rousseau, The, New York: Random House, n.d.

Russell, Tilden A., "The Development of the Cello Endpin," *Imago Musicae*, 4 (1987), 335–356.

"New Light on the Historical Manner of Holding the Cello," *Historical Performance*, 6, no. 2 (Fall 1993), 73–78.

Sainsbury, John, (ed.), *A Dictionary of Musicians from the Earliest Times*, 2 vols., London: Salisbury and Co., 1825/R 1966.

Schäfer, Herbert, *Bernhard Romberg: sein Leben und Wirken*, Münster: Aschendorffsche Verlagsbuchhandlung, 1931.

Schmidt-Görg, Joseph, "Das Wiener Tagebuch des Mannheimer Hofkapellmeisters Michael Frey," *Beethoven Jahrbuch*, 6, Bonn: Beethovenhaus, 1969, 129–204.

Skeaping, Kenneth, "Some Speculations on a Crisis in the History of the Violin," *The Galpin Society Journal*, 8 (March 1955), 3–12.

Spohr, Louis, *Louis Spohr's Autobiography*, 2 vols., London: Longman, Green, Longman, Robert, and Green, 1865/R 1969.

Stowell, Robin, *Violin Technique and Performance Practice in the Late Eighteenth and Early Nineteenth Centuries*, Cambridge University Press, 1985.

Terry, C. S., "Baron Bach," *Music and Letters*, 12, no. 2 (April 1931), 130–139.

Trevelyan, Peter, "A Quartet of String Instruments by William Baker of Oxford (*circa* 1645–1685)," *The Galpin Society Journal*, 49 (March 1996), 65–76.

Van der Straeten, Edmund S. J., *History of the Violoncello, the Viola da Gamba, their Precursors and Collateral Instruments*, London: William Reeves, 1914.

Vidal, Antoine, *Les instruments à archet, les faiseurs, les joueurs d'instruments, leur histoire*, 3 vols., Paris: J. Claye, 1877/R 1961.

Viéville, Le Cerf de La, "From the Comparaison de la musique italienne et de la musique française," ed. Oliver Strunk in *Source Readings in Music History: The Baroque Era*, New York: W. W. Norton & Co., 1965.

Walden, Valerie, "An Investigation and Comparison of the French and Austro-German Schools of Violoncello Bowing Technique," Ph.D. thesis, University of Auckland, 1993.

Wasielewski, Wilhelm Joseph von, *The Violoncello and Its History*, trans. Isobella S. E. Stigend, London: Novello, Ewer, & Co., 1894/R 1968.

Watchorn, Ian, "Baroque Renaissance," *The Strad*, 95, no. 1139 (March 1985), 822–827.

Weber, Carl Maria von, *Writings on Music*, ed. John Warrack, trans. Martin Cooper, Cambridge University Press, 1981.

Wegeler, Franz and Ferdinand Ries, *Beethoven Remembered*, trans. Frederick Noonan, Arlington, Virginia: Great Ocean Publishers, 1987.

White, Chappel, "Giovanni Baptista Viotti," Ph.D. thesis, Princeton University, 1957.

Wild, Nicole, *Dictionnaire des théâtres parisiens au XIXe siècle*, Paris: Aux Amateurs de Livres, 1989.

Wolf, Eugene K., *The Symphonies of Johann Stamitz: A Study in the Formation of the Classic Style*, Utrecht: Bohn, Scheltema & Holkema, 1981.

Index

Hesse, Ludwig Christian, 10, 284
Hill family, 50, 56, 73
Hiller, Ferdinand, 26
Hoffmann, Ernst Theodor Amadeus, 38–39,
    296–297
Holz, Carl, 46, 64, 295
Holzbauer, Ignaz, 50
Hummel, Johann Nepomuk, 45
Hus-Desforges, Pierre-Louis, 13, 22–23, 190,
    214, 291, 294
  Concerto op. 23, 61, 174
  Méthode de violoncelle, 13, 22, 102–103

improvisation, 238–240, 258, 266–267
Italian violoncello school, 3, 7–12, 13, 26, 60,
    80, 81, 147, 170, 183, 243

Jacchini, Giuseppe, 7
Jansa, Leopold, 46
Janson, Jean-Baptiste-Aimé-Joseph, 4, 11, 17–18,
    22, 23, 30, 38, 74, 293, 299
  concertos op. 6, 61, 161, 163, 187–188
  concertos op. 15, 157, 180, 188
  left hand position, 100, 102, 221
  sonatas op. 4, 153

Kaiser, Martin, 56, 61
Kauer, Ferdinand, *Kurzgefasste Anweisung das
    Violoncell zu Spielen*, 34, 78, 89, 117, 222–
    224, 231, 234–235, 255, 256, 260–261,
    263, 266
Kelly, Michael, 32
Kraft, Anton, 43–44, 45, 131, 132, 178, 287, 288,
    293, 294
  Trois Grands Duos Concertans op. 3, 156, 209
Kraft, Nicolaus, 39, 42, 44–45, 47, 143, 293
  Concerto op. 4, 145
Kreutzer, Rodolphe, 4, 38, 72, 90
Kummer, Friedrich August, 34, 42–43, 143, 150,
    298
  Concertino op. 16, 144, 168
  Violoncell-Schule, 34, 43, 97, 103, 148, 206,
    212, 213, 277
Kunst, Friedrich, 77, 91, 287, 294

La Borde, Jean Benjamin de, *Essai sur la musique
    ancienne et moderne*, 2, 3, 50, 54
Lamare, Jacques-Michel Hurel de, 4, 20–22, 74,
    88, 287–288, 291
  accompanying skills, 99, 252, 257
  concertos (composed by Auber), 22, 125, 155,
    167, 178, 181, 191, 273, 289
  violoncello hold, 99, 287
Lancetti, Vincetto, 62
Lanzetti, Salvatore, 9, 61, 170, 183
  Principes ou l'application de violoncelle, 7–8, 78,
    110–111, 112, 127, 128, 129
  Six Solos After an Easy and Elegant Taste, 177
  sonatas op. 1, 76, 148, 153, 176, 180, 184
La Pouplinière, Alexandre-Jean-Joseph Le
    Riche de, 10
Le Blanc, Hubert, 194, 283

Le Cerf de La Viéville, Seigneur de Fréneuse,
    Jean Laurent, 182–183
Legrenzi, Giovanni, 242
Lesueur, Jean-François, 18
Levasseur, Jean-Henri, 20, 38, 122, 271, 298
  Conservatoire violoncello method, *see* Baillot
Lichnowsky, Prince Karl, 44, 64
Lindley, Robert, 26, 30, 32–33, 48, 123, 143,
    281, 290–291, 298, 299
  accompanying skills, 244, 253–254, 260, 263
  Handbook for the Violoncello, 26, 33, 87, 88–89,
    97, 103
Lindley, William, 298–299
Lincke, Joseph, 45–46, 47, 64, 66, 97, 250, 290
Liszt, Franz, 26, 48, 292
Lobkowitz, Prince Franz Joseph von, 44, 45
London, 4, 26, 70, 76, 248n
  Bach–Abel concerts, 9, 30
  Concert of Ancient Music, 31, 33
  Hanover Square Concerts, 16, 29, 31, 258, 289
  Pantheon Concerts, 31
  Philharmonic Concerts, 33, 55
  Professional Concerts, 31, 32
Lully, Jean-Baptiste, 10, 243
Lupot family, 73

MacDonald, John, 27
Maelzel, Johann Nepomuk, 248
Manfredi, Filippo, 11, 258
Mannheim
  court, 4, 34, 36, 70, 128, 163, 178, 185, 186,
    206, 243, 262
  violoncello school, 35, 128
Mara, Gertrude (née Schmähling), 29, 31, 297
Mara, Johann, 31, 31n
Marie Antoinette, Queen of France, 30
martelé, see bowings
Masse, Jean Baptiste, 257
Mattheson, Johann, 271
Mayseder, Joseph, 47, 290
Mendel, Arthur, 54, 55
Mendelssohn, Felix, 26, 39, 48
Merk, Joseph, 4, 39, 46–47, 143, 173, 289–291
  *Introduction et Variations sur une Valse Favorite
    de François Schubert*, 158
Merrick, A., *Method for the Violoncello*, 26, 255,
    260n, 263, 271
Mersenne, Marin, 242
Momigny, Jérôme Joseph de, 272, 274
Mondonville, Jean-Joseph Cassanéa de, 194n
Monn, Matthias Georg, 34
Montagnana, Domenico, 2
Monteverdi, Claudio, 242
mordent, see ornaments
Moscheles, Ignaz, 26, 39, 42, 294–295
Mozart, Leopold, 50, 52, 54, 277, 283
Mozart, Wolfgang Amadeus, 4, 9, 10, 15, 21, 36,
    44, 206, 248n, 251, 257, 267–269, 274,
    288, 294, 297
Muffat, Georg, 79, 80
Munich, 4, 34
multiple-string chords, *see* bowings